Leading Academic Change

Leading Academic Change

Essential Roles for Department Chairs

Ann F. Lucas and Associates

Foreword by R. Eugene Rice

Jossey-Bass Publishers • San Francisco

Jossey-Bass books and products are available through most bookstores. To contact Jossey-Bass directly, call (888) 378-2537, fax to (800) 605-2665, or visit our website at www.josseybass.com.

Substantial discounts on bulk quantities of Jossey-Bass books are available to corporations, professional associations, and other organizations. For details and discount information, contact the special sales department at Jossey-Bass.

Manufactured in the United States of America on Lyons Falls Turin Book. This paper is acid-free and 100 percent totally chlorine-free.

Library of Congress Cataloging-in-Publication Data
Lucas, Ann F.
  Leading academic change : essential roles for department chairs / Ann F. Lucas and associates.—1st ed.
    p. cm. — (The Jossey-Bass higher education series)
Includes bibliographical references and index.
  ISBN 0-7879-4682-6 (alk. paper)
  1. Departmental chairmen (Universities)   2. Educational change.
I. Title. II. Series.
  LB2341 .L82 2000
  378.1'11—dc21   99-006977

Credits are on p. 311

FIRST EDITION
HB Printing 10 9 8 7 6 5 4 3 2

The Jossey-Bass
Higher and Adult Education Series

Contents

Foreword

What makes this book especially useful is its grounding in a coherent strategy for institutional change and a clear understanding of the role of leadership in organizations. *Leading Academic Change* is the book for which many of us interested in the faculty role in a rapidly changing higher education have been waiting.

In 1994, Ann Lucas published *Strengthening Departmental Leadership.* This important book is her personal statement about the key role that department chairs must play in shaping the future of higher education. It is a powerful, comprehensive presentation of what department leaders need to know about their special role and changing responsibilities. In that book, Lucas draws on the rich knowledge she has garnered over the years from the fields of clinical psychology and organizational behavior and integrates it with her extensive practical experience as a faculty member, department chair, leader in faculty development, and major consultant to colleges and universities across the country.

This book, *Leading Academic Change,* builds on, complements, and advances Lucas's earlier work on the role of the department chair in a changing academy—in fact, the two books ought to be seen as companion volumes. In this new book, Lucas draws together the best work of those who have emerged as national leaders of the most significant change initiatives challenging higher education today: for example, Peter Senge, on the learning organization; Thomas Angelo, on the learning community; Edward Zlotkowski, on service learning; and Tony Bates, on technology. In each case, the academic department is the focus and the department chair is treated as the pivotal leader in advancing the particular change agenda.

Of the many changes we have seen in higher education over the last couple of decades, none is more important than the shift from the focus on faculty—who we are and what we know—to the concentration on learning. In the very recent past it was the scholarly preparation of faculty and their publication record—their research—that not only mattered most but in some settings was the only measure that counted. Research and publications are still highly valued, but the center of gravity is beginning to shift. The quality of student learning and evidence that it is being attended to—particularly at the undergraduate level—are being called for. Contributions of colleges and universities to the learning needs of local communities and the larger society are also being required. The critical changes highlighted in this book focus on strategies for taking learning seriously. Ann Lucas is right in her perception of which change initiatives hold the greatest promise, and she has mapped the terrain most deserving of exploration.

With this shift from the focus on faculty to learning has come a major change in the role of the department chair. Chairs are no longer there primarily to process the paperwork and protect the autonomy of faculty members to pursue their own professional interests, free from institutional imperatives. Rather, chairs are now expected to facilitate the collaboration of faculty in the achievement of institutional goals. Ann Lucas is more effective than anyone I know in assisting department chairs in making this transition, in enabling chairs to take seriously their functions as team leaders. The "guiding principles" Lucas sets forth in Chapter One will prove to be particularly valuable to faculty and academic administrators alike.

Leading Academic Change is an exquisite example of the kind of interdependent work Ann Lucas is advocating for the department chair. Each part of this book complements the others, and the individual contributions come together to form a whole that has its own significance. Each chapter, standing alone, is an important contribution to the work of department chairs, but together they reframe the role itself, giving the work of the department chair new power and meaning.

At a time when higher education and faculty work itself are being fundamentally altered, this book introduces a new way of thinking about the critical leadership role of the department chair.

We stand on the verge of a major "changing of the guard" in the faculty ranks. Technology and what we are learning about learning promise to revolutionize how faculty go about their work as teachers and scholars. As our institutions and faculties change, so the role of the department chair is going to have to be rethought and function in radically different ways.

The inadequacy of the old image of the department chair as one who minds the store and shuffles papers is by now patently obvious. The authors of the chapters in this volume are just as disdainful of the call for the decisive leader—one who takes charge. As Peter Senge points out, the "leader must drive change" mindset is bankrupt. Ann Lucas and the authorities she has assembled here set forth a vision of leadership that is both more appropriate at the department level and more effective for colleges and universities committed to being learning centered.

Readers of *Leading Academic Change* will find that this volume brings together the best we have learned from the collegial culture cultivated by faculties over the years with the most sophisticated ideas emerging from contemporary organizational studies. Deans and department chairs will find the work here intellectually intriguing while being eminently practical—addressing the everyday needs and concerns of faculty. We are fortunate to have someone with Ann Lucas's experience, wisdom, and imagination addressing this important topic. She exemplifies the kind of collaborative leadership needed in academic institutions in the turbulent days ahead.

August 1999   R. EUGENE RICE
                     Scholar in Residence and Director
                     Forum on Faculty Roles and Rewards
                     American Association for Higher Education

To my family,
for their abiding love and support—
my husband, Rawley Dean Lucas;
our children,
Mark Douglas, Kathleen Ann, and Paul Kevin;
and our grandson, Peter Gregory

Preface

Major efforts are under way throughout the country today to make student learning the central focus in higher education, to provide lifelong learning for members of the community, to integrate technology into education, and to transform the curriculum so that it reflects changes in the discipline and more accurately reflects students' needs. Such a monumental shift from an emphasis on teaching to a concentration on learning has required colleges to open their boundaries so that departments can become part of the larger external community instead of remaining separate from and above the outside world. Although strong vestiges of this attitude of superiority remain, in the last two decades higher education has opened its borders to partner with industry, the community, and primary and secondary schools. In addition, the student-driven service learning movement has actively engaged more than six hundred colleges in reciprocal academy-community relationships in which students learn through reflection and service.

These are great beginnings. But additional pressure for particular changes in higher education can be anticipated during the next decade. In particular, colleges and universities must respond to the increasing trend toward performance-based funding, they must push forward with rigorous programs of assessment in response to demands for accountability, and they must reexamine and adapt existing programs to provide expanded opportunities for lifelong learning, through both campus-based instruction and distance education.

To increase their success in handling the significant changes that are already impinging on them, chairs and faculty members have to examine the ways in which they function together. Many department members are now operating not as teams but as independent entrepreneurs, and some departments are fragmented as they engage in turf battles to retain ownership of courses or resources. Data based on 4,800 questionnaires I have collected indicate that only 40 percent of chairs rate themselves as successful in handling conflict within their department. Faculty have not been socialized to be team players. Yet chairs can create a climate in which faculty members act together as a team.

The material in this book provides a golden opportunity for discussions about strengthening the academic department. It encourages chairs and faculty members to consider how they work together; how to become reflective about the ways in which they function; how they handle change, and resistance to change; and how they can continue to build their own learning community. Guidelines are provided for department members to examine the processes they use to select, hire, retain, and promote their own faculty. These processes are clarified so that new faculty do not have to guess what criteria are being used to evaluate them for tenure and promotion. Annual goal setting is discussed as a tool for encouraging professional development of faculty in the department. Chairs and promotion and tenure committees will learn how to be strong advocates for their faculty so that their recommendations are taken seriously by those above them in the administrative hierarchy. Such discussions can empower departments so that academic administrators will recognize that chairs and their faculty can be trusted to develop strategic plans aligned with the college and university mission and thus give chairs and faculty more authority and control over resources. Only when the department members have formed a cohesive group, when they have learned to listen to and value each other, and when they can argue and still reach consensus can they successfully tackle the issues of outcomes assessment, develop ownership in the integration of technology, open up their boundaries through service learning, and renew the curriculum. Chairs need to know how to make these things happen—and that is what this book is about.

Because team leadership is the foundation on which successful and enduring change is built, this book has been written to provide chairs with the knowledge, and to show them how to develop the skills needed, to become more effective leaders and change agents. But deans and provosts will also discover that team leadership in departments can be key to effective change in their colleges and universities. Academic administrators will develop new insights into how they can become catalysts for the process of transformation and create teams at chair meetings. Prospective chairs and informal faculty leaders will have an opportunity to consider the role they can play in helping department members examine the ways in which they function together. Faculty developers who direct and staff centers for teaching and learning will discover information and strategies they can use to assist chairs in exploring fully their leadership role. Finally, doctoral students in higher education can become familiar with some of the compelling issues with which colleges and universities are struggling, and with the pivotal role that chairs and departments play in changing higher education.

Overview of the Contents

Part One of *Leading Academic Change* lays the foundation for chairs who want to or are required to launch and implement innovation while managing the resistance and conflict that often accompany change efforts. Chapter One begins with a discussion of why academic change is needed. I make the case that team leadership is the platform on which change is built. I discuss the characteristics of effective teams along with recommendations and resources for chairs to develop themselves as team leaders. Chairs can accomplish what needs to be done whether they serve as permanent or rotating chairs, as long as they act as facilitators and team leaders. They will not be successful if they are viewed either as autocrats or paper pushers. Basic to aligning faculty so that all are committed to achieving the goals of the department and are moving in the same direction is the development of a shared mission statement as the basis for assessing and evaluating departmental outcomes.

In Chapter Two I recommend a model that provides a series of stages for bringing about successful change. I then deal with how chairs can effectively open up departmental boundaries to allow students and faculty to join external groups to tackle real problems. An example of a project initiated by faculty is presented and its success is tracked in terms of positive outcome data obtained through an eight-year follow-up study. I also discuss other success-ful and not-so-successful attempts by departments and why some of them were short-lived.

Chairs who attempt to be change agents also face resistance or lack of support from faculty and administration. Chapter Three deals with the basis of such resistance and how resistance needs to be respected, honored, listened to, and learned from. Author Sandra I. Cheldelin also recommends strategies for dealing with the roots of the conflict, and not just the surface indications of resistance to change. She also provides strategies for dealing with the long-enduring tensions in the department that become exacer-bated when faculty members are faced with change.

For the members of a department to work together effectively to develop the department's own transformative, learning-centered vision and goals, the department must begin by transforming itself. In Chapter Four, Thomas A. Angelo describes the steps necessary for departments to become productive, scholarly learning com-munities. Academic reform efforts must be based on what is known about effective learning, and this can change the way faculty mem-bers teach. True reform, Angelo writes, requires systems-level change in the organizational culture, and what we know about learning can change the way we teach. Angelo provides research-based guidelines for creating productive learning communities and gives examples of their application in a variety of departments.

To improve student learning, faculty must work together to ensure their own continuing professional development and cohe-siveness through feedback and rewards and by affirming the value of what they do. Part Two presents several strategies for achieving such goals.

Tracing the work of the chair from recruitment through final recommendations for promotion and tenure, Robert M. Diamond, in Chapter Five, presents a comprehensive approach to hiring and retaining good faculty members. Included are practical suggestions for recruiting and selecting individuals who fit with the institution, mentoring and developing faculty and sharing guidelines for pro-fessional development and tenure, and documenting a faculty member's accomplishments.

Next, in Chapter Six, Christine M. Licata examines post-tenure review, a process that has raised emotional debate on both sides of the issue. Licata discusses how quickly this concept has caught on, its popularity, and the opposition to the movement. She also writes about some practical considerations important to chairs when post-tenure review has been mandated, and how a sense of community can be maintained in the department along with a sense of accountability. New procedures and guidelines need to be developed, published, and disseminated in ways that are consonant with campus culture and practice, and individuals need to play new roles. Success is determined by how well key concerns and problems are anticipated and dealt with. Impediments to change and some strategies for dealing with specific problems and issues are discussed.

Once faculty begin to change to student-centered learning, they will want to be certain that their efforts are valued by college promotion and tenure committees and administrators. Because many chairs and departments see themselves primarily as faculty advocates, those higher up in the personnel decision-making process often do not take the recommendations of chairs and departments seriously. Yet faculty and the chairs in the discipline are in the best position to evaluate the work done by their colleagues. Howard B. Altman demonstrates in Chapter Seven how the work of faculty can be documented so that the recommendations of chairs and of department promotion and tenure committees are respected by others involved in personnel decision making.

Part Three of the book deals with innovative ways in which academic leaders have wrestled effectively with significant change. The use of outcomes assessment has been gathering momentum in higher education for more than a decade. In Chapter Eight, Lion F. Gardiner presents the rationale for assessment in the department and the role of the chair in ensuring the quality of the assessment process. He deals with the relationship between the department's mission statement and the definition of outcomes; the assessment of student inputs, outcomes, and educational processes; and the utilization of findings to improve the quality of student learning.

In Chapter Nine, Edward Zlotkowski writes about how service learning can engage the entire department, linking it not only to the scholarship of application and teaching but also to faculty professional service, undergraduate research, and other forms of active learning. His experience as senior associate of the American

Association for Higher Education's Service Learning Projects enables him to identify concrete steps that chairs can take to make service learning one of their most valuable departmental initiatives, and allows him to discuss the actual experiences of chairs from a variety of disciplines who have championed service learning as a vehicle of departmental renewal.

The role of technology in higher education is eagerly discussed by many chairs and faculty yet strongly resisted by others. In Chapter Ten, A. W. (Tony) Bates discusses integrating technology with the vision, mission, and strategic goals of a department, as well as including faculty in planning, choosing appropriate teaching models, managing projects, and evaluating outcomes in a teaching and learning environment that is fundamentally different. He considers such questions as whether the use of technology benefits the department, whether it disconnects people, how it challenges the structure of the department, and what the dilemmas and challenges are for chairs.

Good teaching and learning are directly connected to whether the curriculum supports the mission of the institution and is responsive to changing societal needs. Renewing the curriculum is basic to good teaching and learning. What a chair might do to facilitate an understanding of the curriculum, to test whether it meets contemporary student needs, to encourage curriculum transformation that reflects trends in the discipline, to support the integration of new knowledge, to build interdisciplinary bridges, and to link the curriculum with new pedagogies are the questions dealt with in Chapter Eleven. Ann S. Ferren and Kay Mussell discuss practical strategies built firmly on key questions in curriculum renewal.

Finally, in Chapter Twelve, Peter M. Senge translates the abstract ideas of systems theory into tools for better understanding of organizational change. A highly respected authority whose expertise extends well beyond higher education, Senge contributes a new perspective to the task of institutional change and improvement. He articulates a cornerstone position of human values in the workplace, challenges traditional thinking about higher education, and helps chairs understand the value of learning communities.

The ideas in this book provide invaluable assistance to chairs who are entrusted with moving their departments forward in the new century. The role of the chair in transforming departments has never been more important than it is today. I wish you great success in leading your department through the process of change.

Acknowledgments

My work with department chairs began in 1982 when, as founder and director of the Office of Professional and Organizational Development at Fairleigh Dickinson University, I invited R. Eugene Rice to conduct a formative evaluation of the program. One of his suggestions was that I work with and listen to department chairs because of the significant role they play in universities. As a result of his recommendation, my career took a significant turn in a highly productive direction. So, first, I am grateful to Rice for starting me on a profound and very satisfying shift in my scholarly endeavors.

I am also indebted to the more than 6,500 chairs and deans at 175 different campuses across the United States and abroad where I have consulted and conducted workshops. The insights and data that have been generated through research and discussion with these chairs and deans have formed the foundation for much of my work.

A very special thanks goes to the contributing authors of this volume. Each is an authority in the area on which they have written and I have been impressed with the depth of their wisdom. Their task, and mine, has been to shape their expert knowledge about these topics so that information and practical suggestions are offered to chairs, who have little time to keep themselves informed about the major thrusts of higher education beyond their own disciplines and campuses. The authors of these chapters have been very gracious throughout two revisions of the manuscript. They have responded positively to deadlines and maintained an upbeat attitude throughout the process. I have particularly enjoyed their sense of humor in the exchange of many e-mail messages and in phone conversations.

I am grateful to Gale Erlandson, senior editor of the Jossey-Bass Higher and Adult Education Series, whose recommendations about organization of the book have been extremely helpful. She has been generous with her time and encouraging at several significant points in the development of the manuscript. Gale not only is extremely knowledgeable about higher education but also has a special talent for knowing what works in a manuscript.

My appreciation goes to Margaret A. Miller for her positive reaction at the early stage of my writing this book. Her advice was to write about chairs as collaborative leaders, and all of the contributors to this volume have done just that.

I give thanks to Howard Altman, who made several valuable suggestions about the organization of my chapters, and to those who reviewed the manuscript. I appreciate their careful reading and their scholarly and practical advice, which were so helpful in the second stage of revision.

I also greatly value the help of my family, who provided both emotional and technical support. My husband, Rawley Dean Lucas, has been loving, supportive, and patient from our undergraduate days together through all the days of our lives. Our older son, Mark Douglas Lucas, an author of computer software for the Macintosh computer, persuaded me to buy a Macintosh in 1984 and has seen me through upgrades of hardware and software and been a troubleshooter when I have had technical problems. Ongoing conversations about the application of relevant topics in industrial organizations with our daughter, Kathleen Ann Lucas, president of an organization development firm, have been a source of constant stimulation. Our younger son, Paul Kevin Lucas, a producer and writer, has frequently given me helpful feedback on writing style on many manuscripts, including early versions of this one. I am constantly grateful for their celebration of the good times and their support during crises.

Finally, I thank the two gracious and dedicated librarians at Fairleigh Dickinson University Library—Judith Katz, head of reference and the Bibliographic Institute, and Laila Rogers, assistant to the head of reference, who constantly obtained materials essential to the writing of this book.

Englewood, New Jersey   ANN F. LUCAS
January 2000

The Authors

HOWARD B. ALTMAN is professor of modern languages and linguistics, director of the Linguistics Program, and special assistant to the provost for faculty development at the University of Louisville, where he has taught since 1973. He received his Ph.D. from Stanford University in 1972. Altman has published more than a hundred books and articles on such topics as foreign language teacher education, faculty development, and department chair training. He is a member of the national advisory board for Kansas State University's Academic Chairpersons Conference and has consulted widely in chairperson training and faculty development issues in general. He was the founder and executive director of the Kentucky Consortium for Faculty Development, the first statewide faculty development network in the United States to encompass all of the higher education institutions in an effort to promote faculty growth and student learning. He is a past member of the board of directors of the Professional and Organizational Development Network in Higher Education and serves on the advisory board for the *Journal of Staff, Program, and Organizational Development* and for the newsletter *Academic Leader*.

THOMAS A. ANGELO is associate professor and founding director of the School for New Learning's Assessment Center at DePaul University in Chicago. The School for New Learning is a competency-based liberal arts college for adults. Previously Angelo held appointments as faculty member, faculty developer, administrator, and researcher at the University of Miami, the American Association for Higher Education, Boston College, the University of California at Berkeley, and Harvard University. He earned his B.A. degree (1975) in government from California State University–Sacramento, his M.A. degree (1977) in political science from

Boston University, his Ed.M. degree (1981) in English as a Second Language from Boston University, and his Ed.D. (1987) from Harvard University. Angelo's work focuses on applying research to improve teaching and learning, academic assessment, and faculty development. He coauthored, with K. Patricia Cross, *Classroom Assessment Techniques: A Handbook for College Teachers* (1993); edited *Classroom Research: Early Lessons from Success* (1991) and *Classroom Assessment and Research: An Update* (1998); and has published more than a score of articles and chapters. Angelo has presented more than fifty keynote speeches and two hundred workshops in the United States and abroad. Named one of the Forty Young Leaders of the Academy in a 1998 *Change* magazine poll, he has served as a Fulbright scholar in Italy, a Gulbenkian Foundation Research Fellow in Portugal, and the 1998 Visiting Scholar of the Higher Education Research and Development Society of Australasia.

A. W. (TONY) BATES has been responsible since June 1995 for developing distance education programs and flexible delivery of credit and noncredit programs at the University of British Columbia (UBC), in conjunction with faculty and program directors, including the development of innovative off-campus programming using technology delivery. He is project leader for a national research study on cost-benefit analysis of telelearning. He is also project leader for a study of the impact of technology on adult learners for the Canadian Federal Office of Learning Technologies. Prior to moving to UBC, he was executive director of research, strategic planning, and information technology at the Open Learning Agency (OLA) of British Columbia, from 1990 to 1995. Prior to that, he was professor of educational media research at the United Kingdom's Open University (UKOU), where he was one of the founding members of the staff and worked for twenty years. His research groups at the UKOU and OLA published more than 350 papers on distance education and the use of technology for teaching. He is the author of five books, including his latest, *Technology, Open Learning and Distance Education* (Routledge, 1995). His next book, *Managing Technological Change: Strategies for Academic Leaders,* will be published by Jossey-Bass in 2000. Bates has worked as a consultant in more than thirty countries. In 1995 he was awarded the degree of Doctor Honoris Causa by the Open University of Portugal.

SANDRA I. CHELDELIN is director of the Institute for Conflict Analysis and Resolution at George Mason University, Fairfax, Virginia. She earned her B.S. degree (1969) in sociology at Oregon State University and both her M.Ed. (1971) and Ed.D. (1976) degrees in psychological foundations of education at the University of Florida. She has served on the faculty and as provost at the McGregor School of Antioch University, Yellow Springs, Ohio, and on the faculty and as academic dean at the California School of Professional Psychology in Berkeley. Prior to those positions, she was on the faculty and director of education, development, and research at the medical school at Ohio University, and instructor in the behavioral sciences department at Columbus State College. Throughout her career in the academy, Cheldelin has been an active practitioner. As a licensed psychologist and expert in organizational behavior she has applied her skills to support collaborative leadership, mediation, conflict resolution, strategic planning, and institution building to more than one hundred organizations, including colleges and universities, medical schools, associations, treatment facilities, religious organizations, and corporations. She has served as keynote speaker and invited lecturer on workplace issues, including conflict resolution and change. She is currently writing a book on organizational conflict and coauthoring a textbook on the structures, processes, and resolution of human conflict. She has also authored and coauthored a number of articles on effective teaching. She is a member of the American Association for Higher Education, the American Psychological Association, the Ohio Psychological Association, and the International Alliance for Invitational Education.

ROBERT M. DIAMOND is research professor and director of the Institute for Change in Higher Education at Syracuse University, where he was formerly assistant vice chancellor and director of the Center for Instructional Development. He received his Ph.D. degree in educational communications and his M.A. degree in health education from New York University and his B.A. degree in economics from Union College. Diamond has held administrative and faculty positions at the State University of New York, Fredonia; the University of Miami; and San Jose State University. He was a Senior Fulbright Lecturer in India and has been president of the Division for Instructional Development of the Association for Educational Communication and Technology, codirector of the Syracuse University Focus on Teaching Project, and director of the National Project on Institution Priorities and Faculty Rewards, funded by the Lilly Endowment with additional support from the Fund for the Improvement of Postsecondary Education, the Pew Charitable Trusts, and the Carnegie Foundation for the Advancement of Teaching. He is a consultant to colleges and universities throughout the United States and overseas. Diamond was also responsible for the design and implementation of Syracuse University's award-winning high school–college transition program, Project Advance. In 1989 he received the Award for Outstanding Practice in Instructional Development from the Division of Instructional Development of the Association for Educational Communication and Technology, and the Center for Instructional Development was the recipient of the 1996 Theodore M. Hesburgh Award for Faculty Development to Enhance Undergraduate Learning. Diamond has authored numerous articles and books, including *Designing and Assessing Courses and Curricula* (1991) and *Designing and Assessing Courses and Curricula: A Practical Guide* (1997), both published by Jossey-Bass; the chapter "Instructional Design: The Systems Approach" in the *International Encyclopedia of Education* (1986); *Serving on Promotion and Tenure Committees: A Faculty Guide* (1994); *Preparing for Promotion and Tenure Review: A Faculty Guide* (1995); and "What It Takes to Lead a Department," in the *Chronicle of Higher Education* (1996). He coedited an issue of New Directions in Higher Education, *Recognizing Faculty Work: Reward Systems for the Year 2000* (1993), and *The Disciplines Speak: Rewarding the Scholarly, Professional and Creative Work of Faculty* (1995); and he coauthored the 1987 *National Study of Teaching Assistants*, the 1992 *National Study of Research Universities on the Balance Between Research and Undergraduate Teaching*, and *Changing Priorities at Research Universities: 1991–1996*.

ANN S. FERREN is vice president for academic affairs and professor of education at Radford University. Previously she held positions as associate dean of the College of Arts and Sciences, associate dean of faculties, director of general education, vice provost for academic development, and interim provost at American University. She was honored for her work on undergraduate curriculum by the National Center for the Study of the First Year Experience. Her research on curriculum, instruction, and faculty development has been published in the *Journal of General Education, College Teaching, To Improve the Academy, Liberal Education,* and the *Handbook of the Undergraduate Curriculum,* edited by Jerry Gaff and James Ratcliff (Jossey-Bass, 1996). She received her A.B. degree (1961) in economics from Radcliffe College, her M.A.T. degree (1962) from the Harvard Graduate School of Education, and her Ed.D. degree (1971) from Boston University.

LION F. GARDINER is associate professor of zoology at the Newark campus of Rutgers University. He received his B.S. degree (1960) in zoology from Wheaton College, his M.S. degree (1964) in zoology from the University of Michigan, and his Ph.D. degree (1972) in biological science from the University of Rhode Island. He has served as a Faculty Fellow in the Office of Learning Assessment of the New Jersey Department of Higher Education, helping to develop a statewide outcomes assessment program. His books include *Planning for Assessment: Mission Statements, Goals and Objectives* (1989); *Redesigning Higher Education: Producing Dramatic Gains in Student Learning* (1996); and *Learning Through Assessment: A Resource Guide for Higher Education* (1997). Gardiner's professional interests in higher education include student development and college effects on students, faculty development, specification of outcomes and use of assessment to improve student learning, and leadership and reform in higher education. He has served on the governing board of the Professional and Organizational Development Network in Higher Education, and currently serves as a consultant to campuses and a presenter at conferences.

CHRISTINE M. LICATA is associate dean for academic affairs at Rochester Institute of Technology/National Technical Institute for the Deaf, and senior associate with the American Association for Higher Education's (AAHE) New Pathways II Project—Academic Careers for the Next Century: From Inquiry to Practice. She earned her B.S. degree (1963) in business administration and her M.S. degree (1972) in education at George Washington University. Before joining the staff at Rochester Institute of Technology, she held faculty and administrative posts within the Buffalo and Rochester city school systems; at Montgomery College, Maryland; and at Monroe Community College, New York. Licata's main research activities have focused on faculty evaluation. She has published articles on post-tenure faculty review, is author of *Post-Tenure Evaluation: Threat or Opportunity* (1986), and is coauthor of *Post-Tenure Review: Policies, Practices and Precautions* (1997) and *Post-Tenure Review: A Guidebook for Academic Administrators of Colleges and Schools of Business* (1997). She has served on the board of directors of the American Association of University Administrators. She works with organizations, institutions, and school system offices throughout the country on issues related to post-tenure review, and in her role with AAHE she provides leadership for a national project focusing on post-tenure review.

ANN F. LUCAS is a consultant and psychotherapist as well as professor emerita of organization development and former campus chair in the Department of Management and Marketing at Fairleigh Dickinson University (FDU). She is founder and former director of the Office of Professional and Organizational Development and has served as chair of the psychology department at FDU. In addition, she has had a part-time practice in clinical psychology for more than twenty-five years and has consulted with more than twenty-five Fortune 500 companies, with hospitals, and with the federal and city governments. Lucas has served on both the executive and core committees of the Professional and Organizational Development Network in Higher Education. Most recently she has been a member of the advisory committee on developing leadership programs for academic chairs for the American Assembly of Collegiate Schools of Business. She is currently a member of the advisory committee for the Kansas State National Conferences for Academic Chairs and serves on the advisory board for the publication *The Department Chair.* A consultant in leadership in higher education at the international level as well as in the United States, she has conducted workshops for more than 6,500 chairs and deans at more than 175 college and university campuses in the United States and abroad. A licensed psychologist with a diplomate from the American Board of Professional Psychology, Lucas received her B.S. degree in psychology from Seton Hall University and her M.A. and Ph.D. degrees in psychology from Fordham University, Rose Hill Campus. She is editor of *The Department Chairperson's Role in Enhancing College Teaching* (New Directions for Teaching and Learning, no. 37, 1989). Her latest book, *Strengthening Departmental Leadership: A Team-Building Guide for Academic Chairs* (1994) was also published by Jossey-Bass. Her more than fifty publications include chapters in books and journal articles on leadership in the academic department, leading academic change, creating quality departments, the chair's role in enhancing teaching effectiveness, increasing writing productivity, student motivation, performance evaluation, team building, conflict resolution, outplacement in a university setting, and faculty development. Nominated by her department chair and supported by faculty members in the department, Lucas was selected for the award Outstanding Educators of America. She has also been the recipient of the Zucker Memorial Award for outstanding teaching and dedication to higher education, given by the students in her college at FDU, and in 1999 she was awarded the William E. Cashin Distinguished Service Award for Outstanding Contributions to the Academic Chairpersons Conference and the Study of Academic Administration.

KAY MUSSELL is acting dean of the College of Arts and Sciences and professor of American studies and literature at American University. She has previously held positions as director of American studies, director of college writing, director of the university honors program, chair of the literature department, and associate dean for undergraduate affairs and for academic affairs in the College of Arts and Sciences. She received the university's faculty award for academic development in 1986. She has published books and articles on women's popular fiction as well as articles on faculty development. She received her B.A. degree (1965) in English and her M.A. (1970) and Ph.D. (1973) degrees in American civilization from the University of Iowa.

PETER M. SENGE is senior lecturer at the Massachusetts Institute of Technology (MIT), where he is part of the organizational learning and change group. He is also chairperson of the Society for Organizational Learning (SoL), a global community of corporations, researchers, and consultants dedicated to the interdependent development of people and their institutions. He is the author of the widely acclaimed *The Fifth Discipline: The Art and Practice of the Learning Organization* (1990), and with colleagues Charlotte Roberts, Rick Ross, Bryan Smith, and Art Kleiner, coauthor of *The Fifth Discipline Fieldbook: Strategies and Tools for Building a Learning Organization* (1994) and a new fieldbook, *The Dance of Change: The Challenges of Sustaining Momentum in Learning Organizations* (1999). *The Fifth Discipline* hit a nerve deep within the business and education community by introducing the theory of learning organizations. Since its publication, more than 650,000 copies have been sold. In 1997, *Harvard Business Review* identified it as one of the seminal management books of the past seventy-five years. There have been feature articles in *Business Week, Fortune,* and other leading business periodicals regarding the work of Senge and his colleagues at MIT and SoL. *The Fifth Discipline Fieldbook,* which has sold more than 250,000 copies, was developed in response to questions from readers of *The Fifth Discipline* who wanted to develop enhanced learning capabilities within their own companies. Senge has also authored many articles on systems thinking in management published in academic journals and the business press. He has lectured extensively throughout the world, translating the abstract ideas of systems theory into tools for better understanding of economic and organizational change. His area of special interest is decentralizing the role of leadership in organizations so as to enhance the capacity of all people to work productively toward common goals. His work articulates a cornerstone position of human values in the workplace—namely, that vision, purpose, reflectiveness, and systems thinking are essential if organizations are to realize their potential. He has worked with leaders in business, education, health care, and government. Senge received his B.S. degree (1970) in engineering from Stanford University, and his M.S. degree (1972) in social systems modeling and his Ph.D. degree (1978) in management from MIT. He lives with his wife and their two children in central Massachusetts.

EDWARD ZLOTKOWSKI is professor of English at Bentley College and senior associate at the American Association for Higher Education (AAHE). He received his B.A. degree (1966) in English and his Ph.D. degree (1978) in comparative literature from Yale. In 1990 he founded the Bentley Service-Learning Project, an institutionwide program that has pioneered ways to link enhanced learning with community engagement, especially in the business disciplines. In 1995 he was named a senior associate at AAHE and in that capacity has served as general editor of an eighteen–volume monograph series exploring the relationship between service learning and individual academic disciplines. Recently he was named Campus Compact's first national faculty fellow. Zlotkowski has designed and taught a variety of service-learning courses. He has written on topics ranging from issues in contemporary higher education to service-learning faculty development to diversity on and off campus. He has consulted to the Corporation on National Service, the Council of Independent Colleges, the Pew Charitable Trusts, and regional service-learning associations from Maine to Hawaii, as well as to dozens of individual colleges and universities. His latest book is *Successful Service-Learning Programs: New Models of Excellence in Higher Education* (1998).

Part One

Leading Change

The increasing emphasis on accountability in higher education, when introduced primarily by those not directly involved in academe, often reflects not only a lack of information but also a serious misunderstanding about academic life. The wrong issues are being raised when questions are asked about how faculty members use their time, when faculty workload is equated with hours spent directly in the classroom, and when recommendations are made that faculty teach more students or work more hours, or both. Although faculty members may decry the increasing public concern about accountability because they feel uncertain about whether what academics do can be adequately measured, such micromanagement by external critics illustrates that if the quality of higher education is to be measured accurately, it needs to be measured by those within the system. It is encouraging, therefore, that internal change agents, responding to external pressures, have made significant progress in advancing constructive conversation about measuring changing faculty roles.

Taking charge of our own accountability, one of the key themes of the American Association of Higher Education Forum on Faculty Roles and Rewards 1996 conference included defining our own futures, communicating effectively with legislators and trustees, rethinking faculty workload and productivity, defining faculty role in assessment, implementing post-tenure review, and developing new approaches to faculty compensation. Such initiatives demonstrate an agreement that we are accountable at the institutional and departmental levels, that we can measure the outcome of what we do in higher education, and that we can explain what we do in ways that make sense to others. And indeed there are problems.

Despite considerable effort from many quarters during the past three decades, students are still slipping between the cracks. As just one example, the National Center for Education Statistics reports that only 57 percent of the students who enrolled in U.S. colleges and universities in the academic year 1989–1990 had earned a bachelor's degree within the five-year period ending in 1994. Approximately 15 percent of the others were still enrolled after five years, but about a quarter of the total had dropped out (Rittenhouse, 1998).

Performance-based management, which has already been adopted by half the states for their public colleges and universities (Schmidt, 1998), allocates budgets on the basis of indices of success achieved by different institutions. A large percentage of graduates passing certifying exams, being accepted into graduate schools, and being happy with the jobs they get after graduation can never be the achievement of a single faculty member but is always the result of the combined efforts of faculty. The development of department goals based on consensus decision making and then the alignment of individual faculty goals with department goals cannot be accomplished successfully unless a process is developed for making these things happen. Discussion of such a process must be initiated and kept on track by the department chair, who functions as a team leader.

In Part One of this book, the authors argue that the department is the place from which change needs to be launched, and that the chair is the right person to lead such change. As Thomas A. Angelo writes in Chapter Four, "It may be time to rethink—and even to replace—our traditional ideas about academic change and improvement and the strategies that flow from them if we are to move from tinkering to transformation."

Frequently today departments function not as teams but as a group of independent entrepreneurs. Faculty have not been socialized to be team players. When such conditions exist, decisions made by individual entrepreneurs can fragment the department or, alternatively, generate the kinds of plans and projects that will crumble when stronger factions intervene.

Rather than changing in bits and pieces the ways in which they function, academic departments must undergo metamorphosis. Department chairs need to be given more authority and resources by academic administrators, yet they also need help in becoming more effective leaders and in learning to collaborate with members of their departments. My surveys of self-report data from 4,800 chairs indicate that about 25 percent use one of two strategies when there are problems in the department: mandate change if the climate is toxic (and they feel there will not be a major rebellion), or passively perform custodial chores until their years in the chair position are over. Although it is true that academics are very suspicious of power and have shied away from electing chairs who might bring about change, chairs need to examine the ways in which the department is structured, to develop facilitation skills, and to lead discussions that allow faculty to address head on where they want to go and whether the ways in which they are behaving toward each other will get them there. A first step for the chair is to affirm the value of every member of the department, build trust, and develop commitment to achieving shared department goals. In Chapter Four, Angelo provides a beginning exercise that a chair can use to do just that.

The process of making decisions about whether the road currently taken will create the desired results produces long-term approaches to which all department members are committed. Team discussions based on all available information demand an in-depth analysis of mission, goals, and implementation steps. Department chairs must learn to lead a departmental team that is cohesive, whose members are respectful of each other, and who believe that conflict is healthy when it is not a personal attack and when the good of the department is the desired outcome.

The department is where the rubber meets the road. It is where change is generated, where change initiatives from above are translated into what is good—and realistic—for the discipline, and where the way to implement such change is determined. Some of the changes that are needed will require commitment, hard work, and faculty ownership of ideas. If team leadership is used, changes will not come and go as new individuals become chairs. In all of this, it is the chair as team leader who moves the department in carefully considered directions to which faculty are committed.

Change Is a Team Effort

To be effective, chairs must obtain the knowledge and learn how to develop the skills required for team leadership, which is the foundation on which successful change projects are built. To maintain stability yet respond to change, chairs will need to consider their role as team leader. Such leadership skills are not innate. They are neither limited to charismatic individuals nor mysterious. They can be learned. In Chapter One, I discuss the characteristics of effective teams. For each of these characteristics, I integrate the specific strategies needed to be an effective team leader, providing examples for academic chairs. In Chapter Two, I present and illustrate how John P. Kotter's comprehensive eight-stage model for leading change has worked in academic departments. When steps are omitted, change efforts can fall apart. Although stages need not be implemented in a precise order, failure to include all of the stages is why some change efforts work and others do not.

The shift from "my work" to "our work," proposed by R. Eugene Rice (1996, p. 21) as a "major shift in the future of the academic workplace" requires leadership from a chair who knows how to be a team leader. Yet academics have not been trained to be either team leaders or team members. Work in the classroom has typically been a solitary activity, to the point where a number of faculty have strongly but erroneously expressed the point of view that peer classroom observation is a breach of their academic freedom. Moreover, research is often carried out in solitude as well. Although it is true that in medicine and science work must often be undertaken by large teams, in other disciplines promotion and tenure committees frequently undervalue research that is coauthored. The ideal has been solitary contributions to the literature made by a mature scholar who has spent years struggling to integrate the knowledge from his or her discipline with new insights based on research appropriate to the particular field.

Nonetheless, the shift from academics working in isolation to academics being part of a team that works together is the platform on which all other changes must be built. In the past, change in higher education has often been painfully slow, and although shared governance is a slow process, academics also have not learned the skills needed for collaboration and management of conflict. Higher education no longer has the luxury of changing slowly. If we do not direct and shape reform, we will be passive bystanders to change directed by someone else.

Whenever change is planned, resistance is predictable. Faculty are fearful that they will lose what power they have or that their resources will be reduced. Even when the status quo is painful, faculty at least know what they now have. Mandating change, using logic to try to persuade others to accept change, or ignoring resistance actually increases opposition. What chairs need to know in order to gain cooperation and minimize resistance is dealt with by Sandra I. Cheldelin in Chapter Three. In discussing the faces of resistance, Cheldelin demonstrates how chairs can recognize resistance when it is not overt. She shows how important it is to understand the basis for faculty resistance and what this means in terms of different strategies chairs can use when they are trying to deal with resistance. Long-standing simmering conflicts can manifest themselves and escalate once a change initiative is under way. Stages of conflict are predictable, Cheldelin writes, and she recommends several forms of face-saving interventions to prevent loss of faculty self-esteem.

Finally, in Chapter Four, Angelo states that in order for chairs to become effective as change agents, they must develop an entirely new perspective as they look at change. Angelo argues that despite a variety of efforts to promote change over the past three decades, there have been "surprisingly few well-documented examples of significant, lasting gains in student learning at the departmental or institutional level." As he identifies compelling reasons why these change efforts have not resulted in long-term improvement in student learning, he contends that faculty fear that these proposed changes will undermine scholarship and academic freedom.

Angelo shares seven transformative ideas that will completely reshape how student learning is designed in the department. He explains the implications of the social construction of knowledge for teaching and active student learning. He argues that chairs need to facilitate a conversation in which faculty examine their assumptions about teaching and learning, and he explores why unexamined assumptions can make it so difficult for faculty to change their approach to teaching. Based on these transformative ideas, Angelo provides a number of guidelines for transforming departments into scholarly learning communities. As faculty focus on their own ongoing professional development, they are better able to work on how and what students should learn.

Particularly useful as approaches to transforming departments into scholarly learning communities are several learning exercises that chairs can conduct at department meetings—exercises that begin to build trust through acknowledging and building on the strengths of each faculty member as a teacher instead of confronting or ignoring problems that poor teachers have. Angelo also recommends approaches to helping faculty identify common learning goals for themselves and for students, and he provides a series of practical steps for chairs in making transformational changes, including instructions on where to begin.

The chapters in Part One provide the foundation for chairs and faculty to become reflective about the ways in which they function and about the methods they can use to transform the department into a learning community.

References

Rice, R. E. *Making a Place for the New American Scholar.* American Association for Higher Education New Pathways: Faculty Careers and Employment for the 21st Century. Washington, D.C.: American Association for Higher Education, 1996.

Rittenhouse, G. (ed). *The Condition of Education 1998.* NCES 98–013. Washington, D.C.: U.S. Department of Education, Office of Educational Research and Improvement, 1998.

Schmidt, P. "States Increasingly Link Budgets to Performance." *Chronicle of Higher Education,* July 24, 1998, p. A26.

Chapter One

A Teamwork Approach to Change in the Academic Department

Ann F. Lucas

Change in higher education will be a compelling force in the next decade. This urgency for change is partly the result of budgetary constraints that force us to do more with less. But other factors are also making an impact. The rapidity with which information is expanding, the spiraling competition from corporate classrooms and virtual universities, the need to integrate technology in education, the changing expectations and demands of students and parents, the selection and management of a diverse faculty and student body, the increasing emphasis on accountability, and the decision by governors to allocate resources to public education based on performance—all of these challenges require that academic administrators develop a vision they cannot always precisely define and that department chairs lead thoughtful discussions and engage in creative problem solving at the disciplinary level, where real transformation occurs.

A discussion of the forces for change often creates a rather pessimistic picture of higher education as a system that is incapable of adapting. Jokes abound about the difficulty of changing higher education; for example, "It is easier to move a cemetery than to change a university," and "Being president of a university is like being the caretaker of a cemetery; there are lots of people under you, but nobody is listening."

A History of Successful Transformation

Despite this reputation, higher education can build on a history of successful adaptation to external forces. In the past 150 years, higher education has adjusted to change in ways that have required monumental efforts to transform itself. Two striking examples are the provision for land grant institutions in 1862 and the G.I. Bill of 1944.

The Morrill Act of 1862, which created America's unique system of land grant colleges and universities, forever changed the face of higher education. Prior to the passage of this act, higher education "prepared a small group of men for law, medicine, theology, and teaching but neglected the education of the vast majority of men who belonged to the industrial class. The primary purpose of education then was the preservation and transfer of acquired knowledge, and criticism and inquiry were discouraged" (Arnold, 1971, p. 318). Influenced by the German scientific model of higher education, as well as by economic forces in the United States, the land grant act democratized education so that it included scientific and practical education in agriculture and mechanical arts for large numbers of people who otherwise would not have attended college.

Often overlooked as part of the land grant movement is the impact it had on the education of women. "The land-grant objective took into account rapidly changing social patterns, and enabled increasing numbers of women to study at coeducational colleges. Women had previously been thought too weak to withstand the rigors of academic training, and it was feared that their presence on campus would lower the academic standards of the university" (Arnold, 1971, pp. 320–321). Although women were often limited to majoring in domestic arts and teacher preparation, the establishment of land grant colleges enabled large numbers of women to become college educated.

A second major force that required higher education to reshape the way it functioned was the G.I. Bill, officially the Serviceman's Readjustment Act of 1944. This bill, which existed until 1956, provided education and training benefits to nearly ten million veterans who served in World War II and in the Korean conflict—2.2 million of whom attended two- and four-year colleges

(Bennett, 1996, p. 242). The G.I. Bill "influenced a social change in America and its higher education system that could be compared to that caused by the Industrial Revolution. Making college a realistic expectation for many Americans, it also made future generations look upon a college education as an entitlement" (Kerr, 1994).

To accommodate the influx of students, new colleges were established and thousands of faculty members were hired. Veteran professors were confronted with serious students who were older than their nonveteran peers and eager to compare their life experiences with those of their professors. "Indeed they wanted to know whether what they had been told was worth dying for was worth living for" (Bennett, 1996, pp. 238–239).

The Morrill Act and the G.I. Bill required higher education to make sudden, rapid, and significant innovations in the basic ways in which it functioned. Although colleges made mistakes, particularly by offering no training to newly hired faculty—on the highly questionable assumption that if faculty knew the discipline they could teach it—colleges and universities handled these dramatic changes fairly well. From the perspective of the new millennium, problems that were solved—albeit not to everyone's satisfaction—in the last three decades of the twentieth century seem like less striking accomplishments. With the influx of thousands of international students and first-generation college students from immigrant families, English as a Second Language programs were initiated. Equal Opportunity programs helped attract and mentor a diverse student population. Learning centers and remediation courses assisted students in upgrading inadequate academic skills, which increased retention. Continuing education programs created lifelong learning possibilities for adults and seniors. Predictions of a decline in enrollment based on the decreased number of eighteen-year-olds who were available for college were moderated by marketing a college education to older students and to women who could return to school after raising families. These were major achievements, and they demonstrate the ability of higher education to adapt to changing conditions and react to crises.

The changes that institutions face in the next decade, however, can best be handled through an increase in proactive planning rather than through reactive crisis management. Colleges and universities must begin by giving more attention to their smallest though most important subsystem, the department, and by providing more support for the department chair as team leader and change agent, for it is the chair who can most effectively build commitment by problem solving with faculty about what policies and procedures will bring about the most fruitful implementation of significant change.

There is little doubt that change in higher education will be an ongoing process in the next decade. Change will not have a clear-cut beginning, a middle, and an end. Rather, it will be continuous. Chairs must accept that change is a constant, develop the flexibility to cope with change, and shape it rather than be shaped by it. A new leadership role is required of chairs, one that has not necessarily been entrusted to them in the past.

The Changing Role of the Chair

Colleges and universities are now beginning to take the position of department chair more seriously. As a result, the roles and responsibilities of the department chair have been expanding over the last decade (Arreola, 1997; Diamond, 1996; Giles-Gee and Lucas, 1994; Giles-Gee and McMahon, 1999). One recent survey of seventy-six institutions nationwide, reported by Helen Giles-Gee and M. J. McMahon (1997), showed a 79 percent increase in responsibilities for chairs, with greater emphasis on administration, accountability, productivity, and leadership functions than in the past decade.

Yet considerable variability exists in the position power—that is, responsibility and authority—and role of the academic chair, not only from one institution to another but frequently within the same institution. Differences in how the role is defined depend on whether a chair functions in a research university or comprehensive university, in a liberal arts college or a community college. Position power is usually highest in research universities. Professional schools, such as those for medicine, dentistry, engineering, and law, have traditionally invested chairs with more position power than have comprehensive universities.

Self-report data I have collected from 4,800 chairs at 175 campuses indicate great variability in a number of factors related to the role of the chair, some of which are discussed throughout this chapter. Because results have been examined separately for each institution rather than analyzed as a sample of 4,800, trends among colleges and universities will be reported. These findings indicate great variability from one institution to another. Even within the same institution, in some departments chairs are rotated every two, three, or four years, while chairs in other departments have continued in their positions for fifteen or twenty years. In state universities, chairs often feel a greater accountability to administration than to faculty; yet in unionized state institutions, chairs often feel greater accountability to faculty. In some comprehensive universities, untenured assistant professors become chairs because nobody else wants the job. In some community colleges, such as those in Wisconsin, a chair may be responsible for faculty in one discipline on as many as thirteen campuses. Some colleges have eliminated the role of department chair and created the position of division chair as a method of reducing costs, only to resurrect the role of department chair a few years later because the restructuring did not work. So although there is evidence that chair responsibilities are increasing, the rate of change from one institution to the next is far from uniform.

In describing the history of the chair leadership role, R. Eugene Rice (1994, p. xii) wrote:

> In the 1960s, in the democratizing spirit of the time, most academic departments instituted rotating chairs. Old curmudgeons who had ruled departments in authoritarian ways (or what passed for that) were summarily deposed, and the leadership—a word seldom used then because it smelled of power—of departments was passed around among colleagues in a comfortably egalitarian manner. In many cases, secretaries took over. What could have been seen as a leadership opportunity was systematically transformed into what we disparagingly talked about as a "paper-shuffling chore" or a "three-year sentence."

The policy of rotating chairs has created its own problems, however. Probably because rotating chairs viewed themselves and were viewed by administration and their own faculty as having little power, problems in departments were not addressed. Accepting the myths that they have neither carrot nor stick, are simply peers among equals, are taking a turn in the barrel, are neither fish nor fowl, or have no power, chairs often avoided taking actions that needed to be taken by a strong leader. (For a detailed discussion of these myths and rebuttal of them, see Lucas, 1994, pp. 6–19.)

What is changing is that many institutions that for decades used rotating chairs to perform perfunctory tasks are now viewing chairs as having important leadership roles—regardless of whether the chairs are rotating or serving on a more permanent basis. Whereas once a rotating chair might have handled primarily housekeeping functions, now the chair, whether rotating or more permanent, is being taken more seriously as a leader and change agent. This does not mean that the model of rotating chair is disappearing. Some faculty probably believe that, given the opportunity, the days of the autocratic chair might return. Moreover, in many institutions in which the level of trust in the organization is low, when chairs rotate every three or four years, faculty feel a greater sense of control over what happens in the department, and therefore in their own lives. Although great variability exists in the length of time that chairs serve and in the position power they hold, there are nonetheless some principles that are applicable to all chairs who want to, or are asked to, make a difference in the department.

Guiding Principles for Chairs as Effective Team Leaders

Because chairs are being given more leadership responsibility, they need to consider how their lives will be different. One good example of chairs who are trying to redefine their work in order to make the role of chair more attractive, powerful, and effective to their best faculty members has been reported by Richard P. McAdams (1997) at Lehigh University. Among other recommendations that chairs at Lehigh made to their provost, they requested that chair leadership dimensions rather than management tasks be emphasized, that they be given more autonomy in the day-to-day operations of their departments, and that they be provided with continuous leadership development, beginning with chair orientation, use of goal setting, and recognition of achievements. The following twelve principles of effective team leadership in the department have been derived from my work with chairs and deans on more than 175 college campuses, bolstered by a review of the literature:

1. Whether permanent or rotating, chairs can productively lead change.
2. Effective chairs function as team leaders, not as autocrats or peers.
3. Shared goals are developed.
4. All team members are motivated.
5. Excellence is the standard against which performance is evaluated.
6. A climate of trust is created.
7. Problem solving, rather than winning, is the basis for discussions.
8. Participative decision making is used whenever appropriate.
9. As team leader, the chair has good facilitation skills.
10. Conflict is managed effectively.
11. The team monitors its own functioning.
12. Chairs develop increased self-awareness.

PRINCIPLE 1. Whether permanent or rotating, chairs can productively lead change.

Chairs have the dual responsibility of representing faculty to administration and administration to faculty. Such role conflict is a major source of stress for most individuals. When chairs rotate, however, they are more likely to emphasize their role as faculty advocate and less able to function as representatives of administration. After all, they will be faculty again in a few years, subject to decisions made about them by their peers. Nonetheless, under certain circumstances chairs must be able to advance points of view that are necessary for the good of the college but that may not be perceived as equally good for the department or for individual faculty members. Finding the appropriate line between fighting for the faculty and persuading faculty to give up certain things to satisfy the needs of the institution is one of the major challenges for a chair.

Moreover, rotating chairs can lead change successfully if they themselves, the administration, and their faculty see them as team leaders who serve meaningful leadership roles. When chairs function as team leaders, they initiate the process for determining departmental direction. If chairs are courageous enough to introduce difficult conversations about matters of importance to the department and if they are good listeners who are respectful of the collective wisdom of their colleagues, continuity can be ensured despite the rotation of different people into the position of chair. Although individual chairs may have different styles of leadership, the department will move in a systematic direction and changes will occur only as a result of the department faculty revisiting the mission statement. There will not be the lurches and arbitrary shifts in direction that occur when rotating chairs try to implement their own agendas based on little or no consensus building or consultation with department members. The characteristics that define the new role of the chair are observable when the department functions as a team and when the chair as team leader maintains stability while initiating change that is carefully, but not obsessively, deliberated.

Rotating chairs are best able to act for the good of the institution when they participate in developing or revisiting a mission statement and goals for the college. The chair's responsibility in setting college goals is to bring the department's perspective to the goal-setting process. When this process occurs, chairs can work with faculty in the department to be creative in implementing the direction for the discipline.

PRINCIPLE 2. Effective chairs function as team leaders, not as autocrats or peers.

The benefits of being a leader of an effective team are great—people work well together and feel valued by other team members, they look forward to coming to work, they appreciate the synergy that comes from team discussion of issues, and they are motivated and feel a sense of accomplishment. Innovation in organizations is a team enterprise. Because most academics have worked in isolation throughout their careers, and because they know no other way of functioning, they need to learn the compelling reason for departments to function together as teams. That reason is that many tasks that now need to be accomplished in the department cannot be done alone, by the chair or by any single faculty member.

For example, outcomes assessment begins with developing a shared vision and aligning resources with that vision. Next, chairs must shape the conversation about the mission and goals of the department. Together, faculty must determine what knowledge, skills, attitudes, and values students should have acquired when they have completed a major, or a single course, and then develop procedures that measure the degree to which students have achieved these criteria. A team that has learned how to problem solve and handle conflict can handle this process most effectively.

Revision of the curriculum so that it incorporates state-of-the-art or cutting-edge technology requires significant effort and input from all members of the department who know how to listen to and appreciate one another's point of view. Departmental discussion of standards of performance—what faculty expect of students—would prevent the sometimes wide variability that students face as they take different courses in the same department or compare with their friends what is required by different faculty members teaching different sections of the same course.

But there is also a downside to functioning as a team. It takes time, and time is a precious commodity in academe. Being a team leader, initiating problem-solving meetings, making decisions by consensus, and deciding on strategies for handling conflict all take time. Yet there are many tasks that can be performed only when everyone has ownership in the mission and goals of the department. The other extreme is faculty who all work at protecting their own turf.

"A team is a small number of people with complementary skills who are committed to a common purpose, performance goals, and approach for which they hold themselves mutually accountable" (Katzenbach and Smith, 1993, p. 45). Many organizations have used Jon Katzenbach and Douglas Smith's book *The Wisdom of Teams* as a kind of bible for developing teamwork. The insights about small group dynamics that the authors discuss can certainly be applied to university life. Members of a team need to develop expertise in creating a climate of trust and support, using active listening, managing conflict creatively, problem solving and decision making, and cultivating interpersonal effectiveness in small groups. Not all members of a team will possess all of these skills at the outset; some will develop them in the course of working together.

Although a chair can use some interventions to enhance team effectiveness, a chair is not the right person to conduct team building. Some departments are quite dysfunctional, fragmented by unhealthy conflict, and strongly vested in protecting their own turf. When such a situation exists, it is prudent to bring in an outside consultant—perhaps someone on campus who has expertise in this area—to undertake a team-building experience with all members of the department. It simply does not work for chairs to try to do this in their own departments, even if they have the necessary skills.

PRINCIPLE 3. Shared goals are developed.

Getting everyone on board begins with creating a shared vision in the department. Based on this vision, faculty develop or revisit the mission statement and finally generate strategic goals and implementation or action steps. Departments in which everyone has participated in the development of a vision, a mission statement, strategic goals, and action steps tend to be more effective, partly because commitment is generated. Finally, for alignment to occur—that is, for everyone to be more productive because they are all moving in the same direction—faculty goals must be aligned with departmental goals.

To many academics, the visioning process smacks of a touchy-feely approach that sounds anti-intellectual and anti-everything-else that the scholarly world values. However, visioning or scenario building is the first step in thinking creatively about possibilities for the future. Authors of problem-solving strategies have suggested that all individuals are creative, but what keeps them from exercising their creativity more often is that they have been taught to be critical of their own ideas, as well as of the ideas of others. When that censorship intrudes too early in the thinking process, it limits the number of ideas that are generated and results in reducing the number of alternatives to be considered.

New ideas are fragile and often die aborning because they are not given a chance to be developed before they are critically examined. Creative thinking frequently builds on the ideas of others. Interaction of individuals in an uncritical atmosphere is what helps create a vision that is intellectually and emotionally stimulating.

Without creativity, plans are frequently prosaic and mundane and the alternatives that are examined become limited. In a group trained only to be critical, creativity is cut off, partly because individuals are reluctant to express ideas for fear that they will be viewed as unrealistic, unscientific, illogical, or foolish.

There are several useful guides for developing a vision, mission, strategic goals, and action steps. Peter Senge and his colleagues (1994, p. 20) have developed a series of questions that chairs can easily adapt for use with faculty members to encourage them to imagine the possibilities for their department, such as the following: What would you like to see your department become and what reputation would it have? What values would it embody? How would people work together? How would people handle the good times and the bad? What do you have to do, and what resources do you need to make this happen?

Walter H. Gmelch and Val D. Miskin (1993, pp. 35–62) have presented a comprehensive procedure for departmental planning that includes developing a vision, mission, and goals. In my book *Strengthening Departmental Leadership* (Lucas, 1994, pp. 54–59), I have described how to plan for and obtain buy-in for a visioning meeting from the faculty, and I have provided a list of questions that a chair can use to unleash the creative thinking needed to develop a vision and mission statement.

An example of the positive effect that revisiting a mission statement can have occurred in a management department. The old mission statement defined the department's work as having an impact only on industrial organizations. Two people in the department were doing solid research on public health organizations and one was doing research on institutions of higher education. None of the three people was given any release time for research because their work was deemed to be tangential to the mission of the department. When the faculty revisited the mission statement, a few relatively small changes, including substituting the words *contemporary organizations* for *industrial and business organizations,* made the work of these faculty members legitimate. When they were able to receive research release time for the publications they were producing, their morale improved significantly because they felt affirmed and valued.

PRINCIPLE 4. All team members are motivated.

When individual group members feel valued, respected, and listened to by one another, the group becomes cohesive and attractive to its members. Individuals enjoy working with one another. Humor and informality become part of their interaction. They feel empowered, they are willing to take risks as they offer opinions, and professional development (opportunities for people to stretch themselves and grow) is ongoing. Individuals agree to take on tasks that must be completed by the group. They develop a can-do attitude. The task of the chair is to help create such a climate in the group.

Although the discussion here focuses on the motivation of individuals as team members, when faculty are not motivated to be reflective practitioners as teachers, or are not motivated to engage in scholarly activities, or are unwilling to do their fair share of work in the department, they certainly are not functioning as team players. If they are not working on their own professional development, or in other ways contributing to the department, they are not viewed as competent or thought to have anything to contribute to formulating or achieving the strategic goals of the department. Because they are not valued, their self-esteem is lowered. This dynamic is so dysfunctional that it is difficult for chairs to know how and where to intervene.

On the basis of self-report data from nearly 4,800 questionnaires from department chairs, I have found that less than one-third of chairs feel that they have been successful in motivating faculty—particularly faculty who are poor teachers or difficult colleagues—or in improving the overall quality of teaching in the department. Moreover, less than 40 percent of chairs rate themselves as successful in motivating midcareer or burned-out faculty members. The analyses, completed as part of needs assessment before campus visits, are remarkably consistent from one campus to another, regardless of the type of institution. Essentially they show that chairs do not feel they have been particularly successful in motivating faculty, particularly tenured faculty.

Although many chairs feel they have no power to motivate faculty, the reality seems to be that they simply do not know how to intervene when they recognize problems in the department. The faculty that chairs are most concerned about are those who are unproductive, who are ineffective teachers, who are not engaged in scholarly activities, and who fragment the department as they engage in divisive behavior. Whereas external groups may feel that the answer to some of these problems is simply to insist on mandatory retirement, sometimes triggered by post-tenure review, the truth is that many faculty members could become productive members of the department again, if they felt valued and appreciated.

However, when chairs deal with faculty who exhibit any of these problems, they often fall prey to a fundamental attribution error: when individuals perform poorly, the tendency of the observer is to label them unmotivated, or in academe, to say that they don't care because they have tenure. Conversely, faculty members tend to subscribe to the self-serving bias that if there is a failure in their own behavior, external circumstances are responsible. They may say, for example, "Doing research is pointless because it isn't expected and won't be rewarded," or "These students are not motivated. My job is to teach; motivation is their problem," or "Student evaluations are unjust. Students simply want to be entertained. I get poor or just average ratings because they don't want to work hard enough to meet my standards."

However, many of the poor teachers, some of whom were hired decades ago, others of whom are of relatively recent vintage, were given no assistance in becoming reflective about their teaching. In most departments, there have typically been few discussions of the literature on teaching and learning, about how defining course and class objectives is the basis for selecting the pedagogical approaches that will lead to the achievement of those goals. Although it is true that centers for teaching and learning have much to offer and have made some significant inroads by providing workshops and individual training on the use of experiential and collaborative learning, there has not been systematic training across university campuses. Workshops on these topics are usually poorly attended by those who need them most. The primary reason for this seems to be that when individuals have been teaching poorly for a number of years, they tend to use defenses such as blaming the students (Boice, 1992) and feel they do not need to do anything about their own teaching.

So, the dissatisfaction that comes up repeatedly on chair questionnaires I have collected relates to the need for revitalization of faculty. Complaints often focus on difficult faculty who seem unwilling to discuss teaching, who do not believe that students are capable of evaluating their teaching, who conclude that outcomes assessment is just another fad that will go away, who resist updating the curriculum, who regard peer or chair review of classroom teaching as an infringement on academic freedom—in other words, faculty curmudgeons who are not good team players. Chairs frequently feel powerless in the face of such circumstances, saying, "Faculty are tenured and cannot be motivated to change their behavior."

There are several basic approaches chairs can use, however, to motivate faculty to be more productive and to be effective team members. Annual goal setting and formal discussion of teaching at department meetings are discussed briefly here. Approaches that will increase scholarly engagement in the department can be found in *Strengthening Departmental Leadership* (Lucas, 1994, pp. 149–172).

Considerable research demonstrates that individual goal setting is one of the most effective methods of motivating individuals (Locke and Latham, 1990). Because the academic career ladder is short, and most departments do little to celebrate academic success, faculty receive little positive feedback from the department about their accomplishments. Individual goal setting with the chair is a powerful motivating tool when it is used not simply as more paperwork to be completed but as a dynamic process to stimulate faculty members' own career planning and to provide them with the opportunity to know they are valued by someone whose competence they respect. Affirmation of value and acknowledgment that faculty members have made a difference are scarce commodities in higher education. Poignant stories have often been told by faculty who receive recognition for their work on a national level yet feel unappreciated by their own institutions. It is when faculty feel they are not valued anywhere that stagnation occurs both professionally and personally and they just "put in their time" and try to find some satisfaction outside the institution.

If used as a dynamic process instead of as a paperwork procedure, annual goal setting creates a formal opportunity for valuing what faculty have accomplished and encourages them to think about, and increases their satisfaction in, their careers. During individual goal-setting interviews, chairs should ask questions that will help individuals be objective about their own careers and about the challenges they can pursue over the next one to three years. Sample questions might include the following:

- What would contribute to your professional development during the next year?
- What goals would you find intellectually and emotionally stimulating at this point in your career?
- If this were the best of all possible worlds and you could accomplish whatever goals you wanted, what would they be?

And for those midcareer faculty who seem to have lost their momentum:

- What were your goals and dreams when you began your career in higher education?
- To what extent have you achieved those goals?
- Are some of the goals you haven't reached ones that you can achieve now?
- How can I help you do that?

Because research has indicated that goals are most effective when they are specific, moderately difficult, acceptable to the faculty member, and aligned with the goals of the department; when they can be monitored; when they include time lines for accomplishment of action steps; and when they provide feedback, the role of chairs is to be certain that the goals set by faculty members satisfy these criteria. Of course some faculty members have already generated great momentum in their careers. They do not need much prompting from a chair. However, even highly productive faculty will be receptive to acknowledgment of their accomplishments during the annual review period by someone they respect.

The other major approach to motivating faculty, particularly in the area of teaching, is to discuss different topics related to teaching as formal agenda items at department meetings at least once a semester. When questions about teaching are raised at such meetings, the enthusiasm of faculty members who are excellent teachers is often contagious and generates ideas for the poor teachers to try in their own classrooms. Faculty can be asked to describe a "golden moment" or an experience in their teaching, an occasion on which they felt that student learning was really occurring. Then they can be asked, "What did you do to make this happen?" Afterwards, themes can be identified from responses given by several faculty members. The question, "What made the difference between a golden moment and a class in which you felt students were not learning?" can highlight that there are times when even excellent teachers experience discouragement. Instead of focusing on poor teachers, this approach identifies strategies that work in any classroom, and approaches that are unlikely to succeed. Other publications have provided some strategies for building discussions on teaching into department meetings (Lucas, 1994, forthcoming).

PRINCIPLE 5. Excellence is the standard against which performance is evaluated.

In teams in which high achievement is valued, chairs create opportunities for the development of the talents and skills of individual faculty members. Leadership is shared and people are given a chance to cultivate abilities that are important to them and to the team. When individuals demonstrate aptitudes in particular areas, occasions are generated that will allow them to develop their talents. For example, a faculty member with good listening skills can make an important contribution as a departmental ombudsman. Someone who has an interest in handling conflict can serve as a third-party mediator for the team. If appropriate, such individuals might be encouraged to attend workshops on related topics to enhance their competence. Individuals who care about creating a good image for the department might chair a public relations committee that collects information about faculty and team accomplishments and submits articles for publication in university newsletters or in local newspapers.

In such teams, contributions to the team are recognized and rewarded by team members. Faculty invest their energy in getting results, rather than in endless fruitless discussions about why what is asked of them cannot be done. Responsibility and accountability are built into the system. Peer pressure and confrontation are used when individuals or committees do not deliver what was promised by agreed-upon deadlines. However, when a committee does not achieve its objectives, unbiased evaluation of the process rather than attribution of blame helps the committee to save face while recognizing that colleagues are accountable to each other. A can-do attitude is characteristic of the department.

PRINCIPLE 6. A climate of trust is created.

In an effective team, communication is honest and open. A level playing field is created so that all faculty feel they have equal status in the group. New faculty feel welcomed and are not viewed by senior faculty members, who may have joined the college when teaching rather than scholarship was valued, as setting unrealistic standards for research and publication. Senior faculty are respected and valued. Particularly when they have not been productive scholars, they are assisted in thinking about the kinds of activities that will be both stimulating to them and helpful in reaching departmental goals.

In an effective team, information is shared with all team members, and individuals confront one another when there are problems rather than complaining about faculty members behind their backs. All members encourage feedback from others and appreciate the potential for professional growth and insight that feedback can provide. They remember that feedback is a gift, they summarize what they have heard to ensure that the message is understood, they thank the giver, and they ask for clarification if needed rather than defend themselves. Negative feedback can be accepted more easily when sincere, positive feedback is also shared generously and frequently. Members are also clever enough to know that the amount of negative feedback anyone can take at a given time is limited. They provide objective statements about behaviors, avoid assumptions about others' motivations, and refrain from personal attacks. The team leader is a role model in requesting, accepting, and providing feedback.

PRINCIPLE 7. Problem solving, rather than winning, is the basis for cohesiveness.

In effective teams, the purpose of problem solving is not for individuals to win points but for team members to find the best possible solution to a problem. The role of the chair is to help faculty understand the problem-solving process, to enlist their aid in making it work, and to experiment with using the process until faculty become good problem solvers. The steps in problem solving can be summarized simply:

- Identify the symptoms and define the problem.
- Generate many alternatives.
- Consider the pros and cons of the most viable options.
- Select an alternative everyone can live with.
- Experiment by trying this solution for a designated period.
- Select one or more people who will accept responsibility for reporting back to the group on how well the solution is working, evaluating its effectiveness in terms of specified criteria.
- If the solution works, or can be tinkered with to make it work, agree to continue it for an indefinite period.

All of this sounds deceptively simple. However, academicians are an independent group and enjoy divergent thinking, so agreement may not be reached easily. Also, many decisions affect different faculty members in different ways. When a particular decision is made, some gain but some lose. Input for problem solving and decision making cannot be wholly objective. The chair's goal, then, must be to have decisions made fairly and with the best interests of the department as well as of the individuals in mind.

PRINCIPLE 8.　Participative decision making is used whenever appropriate.

The team selects the right decision-making styles, choosing participative decision making whenever commitment is needed. Individuals are not likely to work to implement someone else's decisions. The statement "Nobody ever washes a rental car" suggests that individuals are not willing to make investments in what they do not own. The chair deliberately raises constructive conflict when decisions are made based on premature closure. When the group makes a decision too quickly, or without having thought a problem through, the chair can acknowledge that one point of view has been clearly articulated and then ask a specific individual to summarize the arguments against that perspective so that the group can consider all sides of the question. This process makes it more likely that comprehensive decisions that satisfy everybody will result.

PRINCIPLE 9. The team leader has good facilitation skills.

Meetings are most satisfying when they have a clear purpose, when they are used for problem solving rather to convey information that could have been distributed in writing, when members feel they have status in the group and are listened to, and when conflict is encouraged in order to come to a comprehensive decision that most people feel is equitable. For a group to work effectively, attention needs to be given to two functions for which both the group leader and the members have responsibility. These are the task and relationship aspects of a group. Individuals who exercise task roles select, define, and work toward achieving the goals or purposes for which the group is organized. Relationship roles, which contribute to the group working well together, deal with small-group dynamics; that is, they determine whether all individuals feel respected by the group, have a sense of inclusion, and feel free to express their opinions. Meeting audits can be used to check on faculty satisfaction with what was achieved at a meeting and how it was accomplished. Two books on conducting productive meetings are recommended: *We've Got to Start Meeting Like This* (Mosvick and Nelson, 1987), a helpful, basic book; and *The Skilled Facilitator* (Schwarz,1994), a fairly sophisticated book that not only integrates group facilitation theory and practice but also includes principles that chairs can use to help individuals develop innovative solutions to complex problems.

PRINCIPLE 10. Conflict is managed effectively.

Effective team leaders know that conflict in teams is predictable. They develop strategies for handling conflict within the team. To facilitate reaching better decisions, the leader's responsibility is to prevent dysfunctional conflict and introduce constructive conflict deliberately when a group has come to a decision too quickly without exploring at least two major sides of the issue.

Conflict is a predictable stage of any team's development. Bruce Tuckman and Mary Jensen (1977) have labeled the four stages of a group's existence *forming, storming, norming,* and *performing*. These stages are usually repeated when a department has a new chair. In the forming stage, individuals are polite, keep feelings to themselves, and try to determine how involved they will become with the group. The storming stage is full of conflict about leadership, goals, how decisions will be made, and how conflict will be handled. Some departments become stagnated in this stage for years. The norming stage includes acceptance of others' opinions, sharing information, and determining the rules by which the group will operate. During the performing stage, individuals understand and accept their roles and work effectively both independently and interdependently. It is useful for chairs to recognize that conflict is a normal part of a team's development. Providing structure to the discussion while being a supportive leader, a chair helps the group decide how it will function and make decisions. The group can also be encouraged to develop a set of guidelines for how they will handle different kinds of conflict. William W. Wilmot and Joyce L. Hocker's *Interpersonal Conflict* (1998) is a good, basic book on managing conflict that chairs would find useful.

PRINCIPLE 11. The team monitors its own functioning.

A chair could begin the process by inviting members of the department to evaluate the way they function together, to savor their successes, and to identify opportunities for team development. A form can be constructed that lists the principles that have just been discussed and team members can be asked to rate how the team is doing on each of the characteristics of effective teams. Faculty members can add other items, such as expectations faculty have of the chair and of each other and expectations the chair has of faculty, individual recognition of team members, the degree of support team members provide for each other, satisfaction with procedures used by the team, and the time the team takes to renew itself. Each of these items can be placed on a continuum labeled strongly agree, agree, neither agree nor disagree, disagree, and strongly disagree. Faculty members would then sit in a circle or U and a copy of this form would be given to each person. They would complete the form individually, placing an X on the continuum for each characteristic. It is important that all of the items be written as positive statements so that all items with which faculty agree are positive and all statements with which faculty disagree are negative. This will greatly facilitate interpretation of the results.

Faculty would then share with the group three characteristics with which they strongly agree. They should be asked to give examples of positive events that illustrate why they feel this is one of the team's strengths. Enough time should be spent on this so that faculty can savor their success in several areas. After this, team members can develop several alternatives in two areas that represent opportunities for ongoing team development—in other words, positive characteristics of effective teams that they disagree or strongly disagree are characteristics of their team. It is not advisable to spend too much time giving examples of weakness. This could too easily become a gripe session. It is better if the group focuses on suggestions to enhance the team's functioning.

Checking on how the team is doing can be handled simply and more frequently by using a meetings audit (Lucas, 1994, pp. 185–186). A form can be distributed during the last five minutes of a meeting that asks participants what was handled well, what they felt dissatisfied with, and what suggestions they can provide for handling dissatisfactions more productively at future meetings. These forms, which are completed anonymously, are summarized at the beginning of the next meeting. Enough time is taken to savor what is being done well and then suggestions are entertained for handling opportunities for improving meetings.

PRINCIPLE 12. Chairs develop increased self-awareness.

Chairs who want to become good team leaders must first look at themselves. Self-monitoring and self-evaluation in interactions with others is the platform on which leadership skills can be built. Daniel Goleman's *Working with Emotional Intelligence* (1998) is a good source of information on heightening self-awareness. Time and stress management require knowledge and attention (Lucas, 1994).

Chairs need to view their role as that of leader, not paper pusher. The self-fulfilling prophecy is powerful. If chairs think of themselves as merely administering trivia, that may be all they will accomplish. Chairs must take charge of their own lives and continually develop themselves as leaders. If they do only the things they are good at, they will not grow. They must take some risks, set some "Big Hairy Audacious Goals (BHAGs). Like climbing a big mountain or going to the moon, a BHAG may be daunting and perhaps risky, but the adventure, excitement, and challenge of it grabs people in the gut, gets their juices flowing, and creates immense forward momentum" (Collins and Porras, 1994, p. 9). Chairs who have not failed lately have not been taking enough risks. They should consider creating a support group made up of all the chairs in their college. A book such as this one or one on chair leadership (for example, Lucas, 1994; Gmelch and Miskin, 1993) can be used as a guide. Chairs can read a chapter, integrate their own experiences on the topic, and then share their insights at regularly scheduled meetings. Only in academe are in-service programs, particularly in leadership, underutilized. Role-playing, discussion of issues that chairs are facing, problem solving, brainstorming—all of the strategies that will work for group members can become part of these meetings. The group can set goals, be supportive, and reward other chairs for achieving them.

Change Is a Team Effort

For several years, the American Association for Higher Education and the PEW Higher Education Roundtables have argued that the responsibility for change rests with the academic department and that it is the department chair who must bring about change. "More than any other figure within the department, it is the chair who must convene those faculty conversations that, precisely because they raise tough questions, evoke meaningful answers defining the nature of the community's work" (Zemsky, 1996, p. 10).

> We turn to the academic department, precisely because it,
> more than any other unit within the academy, has the power
> to organize and make accessible what is known and what is to
> be taught by whom. It is the department that provides the

foundation to support both disciplinary study and interdisciplinary efforts that span complex issues and problems.

It is the department that provides the foundation to take broad responsibility for the quality of the services it provides. A department should be held accountable for the quality of teaching its members deliver, for the coherence of its major, for its contributions to the general education curriculum, and for the supervision and rewarding of its individual faculty members.

For most faculty, it is an academic home, a place of identification, support, and camaraderie. And we believe, it is the academic department that provides those who seek change the place from which to launch the process of renewal [Zemsky, 1996, p. 5].

In order to maintain stability yet respond to change, chairs will need to examine carefully their role as team leader. Ongoing personal and professional development in qualities such as integrity, commitment, hard work, and the willingness to listen to and accept the ideas of faculty are essential. This chapter has laid the foundation for self-reflection by chairs and departments by presenting the characteristics of effective teams and by discussing how chairs as team leaders can help shape the ways in which teams function.

To thrive as team leaders, chairs must develop insight about the impact of their behavior on others. It is not whether what leaders do is good or bad but rather how such behaviors affect others. (This statement is not a negation of morality; rather, it refers to increasing sensitivity, or being able to view a situation from another's perspective.) These leadership skills can be learned. "Gone forever—at least in our eyes—is the debilitating perspective that the trajectory of a company [organization] depends on whether it is led by people ordained with rare and mysterious qualities that cannot be learned by others" (Collins and Porras, 1994, p. xiv).

Sharing positive feedback, caring about people, and encouraging and supporting others all create the kind of climate in a department that can accomplish the impossible. In *The Wisdom of Teams,* Katzenbach and Smith (1993) repeatedly make the point that teams of people working together can realize more than individuals working alone can realize. "Unbridled enthusiasm is the raw motivating power for teams" (p. 265). People can generate such enthusiasm much more easily in groups than as single individuals. When the goal is to overcome barriers to change, unleash the power of faculty as they generate a vision of what is possible, and take responsibility for making it happen, such an achievement is the way any chair might like to be remembered.

References

Arnold, C. K. "Land-Grant Colleges." In L. C. Deighton (ed.), *The Encyclopedia of Education,* Vol. 6. New York: Free Press, 1971.

Arreola, R. A. "On the Tightrope: The Department Chair as Faculty Evaluator and Developer." *The Department Chair,* 1997, *8*(1), 3–5.

Barr, R. B., and Tagg, J. "From Teaching to Learning: A New Paradigm for Undergraduate Education." *Change,* 1995, *27*(6), 12–25.

Bennett, M. J. *When Dreams Came True: The G.I. Bill and the Making of Modern America.* Washington, D.C.: Brassey's, 1996.

Boice, R. *The New Faculty Member: Supporting and Fostering Professional Development.* San Francisco: Jossey-Bass, 1992.

Collins, J. C., and Porras, J. I. *Built to Last: Successful Habits of Visionary Companies.* New York: HarperCollins, 1994.

Diamond, R. M. "What It Takes to Lead a Department." *The Department Chair,* 1996, *6*(4), 1, 20, 23.

Giles-Gee, H., and Lucas, N. *Survey Summary: University of Maryland System Survey of Faculty Roles and Rewards in Higher Education.* Adelphi, Md.: University of Maryland, Dec. 1994.

Giles-Gee, H., and McMahon, M. J. "System-Wide and Institutional Development Programs for Chairpersons." *The Department Chair,* 1997, *8*(1), 1, 18–19.

Giles-Gee, H., and McMahon, M. J. "Faculty Evaluation: Role of Chairpersons in Addressing Faculty Development and Accountability." *The Department Chair,* 1999, *9*(3), 7–9.

Gmelch, W. H., and Miskin, V. D. *Leadership Skills for Department Chairs.* Bolton, Mass.: Anker Press, 1993.

Goleman, D. *Working with Emotional Intelligence.* New York: Bantam Books, 1998.

Katzenbach, J. R., and Smith, D. K. *The Wisdom of Teams: Creating the Higher-Performance Organization.* Boston: Harvard Business School Press, 1993.

Kerr, C. "Expanding Access and Changing Missions: The Federal Role in U.S. Higher Education." *Educational Record,* 1994, *75*(4), 27–31.

Locke, E. A., and Latham, G. P. *A Theory of Goal Setting and Task Performance.* Englewood Cliffs, N.J.: Prentice Hall, 1990.

Lucas, A. F. *Strengthening Departmental Leadership: A Team-Building Guide for Chairs in Colleges and Universities.* San Francisco: Jossey-Bass, 1994.

Lucas, A. F. "Reaching the Unreachable: Improving the Teaching of Poor Teachers." In L. Hilsen and E. Wadsworth (eds.), *Professional and Organizational Development Handbook for New Practitioners*. Bolton, Mass.: Anker Press, forthcoming.

McAdams, R. P. "Revitalizing the Department Chair." *AAHE Bulletin*, Feb. 1997, pp. 10–13.

Mosvick, R. G., and Nelson, R. B. *We've Got to Start Meeting Like This*. Glenview, Ill.: Scott, Foresman, 1987.

Rice, R. E. "Foreword." In A. F. Lucas, *Strengthening Departmental Leadership: A Team-Building Guide for Chairs in Colleges and Universities*. San Francisco: Jossey-Bass, 1994.

Schmidt, P. "States Increasingly Link Budgets to Performance." *Chronicle of Higher Education*, July 24, 1998, p. A26.

Schwarz, R. M. *The Skilled Facilitator: Practical Wisdom for Developing Effective Groups*. San Francisco: Jossey-Bass, 1994.

Senge, P. M., and others. *The Fifth Discipline Fieldbook: Strategies and Tools for Building a Learning Organization*. New York: Doubleday, 1994.

Tuckman, B. W., and Jensen, M.A.C. "Stages of Small-Group Development Revisited." *Groups and Organization Studies*, 1977, *2*, 419–442.

Wilmot, W. W., and Hocker, J. L. *Interpersonal Conflict*. (5th ed.) New York: McGraw-Hill, 1998.

Zemsky, R. (ed.). "Double Agent." *PEW Higher Education Roundtable Policy Perspectives*, 1996, *6*(3), 1–11.

Recommended Reading

Bland, C. J., and Bergquist, W. H. *The Vitality of Senior Faculty Members: Snow on the Roof, Fire in the Furnace*. ASHE-ERIC Higher Education Report, vol. 25, no. 7. Washington, D.C.: George Washington University Graduate School of Education and Human Development, 1997.

Edgerton, R. "Community and Commitment in Higher Education: An Interview with Parker J. Palmer." *AAHE Bulletin*, Sept. 1992, pp. 3–7.

Hackman, M. Z., and Johnson, C. E. *Leadership: A Communication Perspective*. Prospect Heights, Ill.: Waveland Press, 1996.

Higgerson, M. L. *Communication Skills for Department Chairs*. Bolton, Mass.: Anker Press, 1996.

Kouzes, J. M., and Posner, B. Z. *The Leadership Challenge: How to Keep Getting Extraordinary Things Done in Organizations*. San Francisco: Jossey-Bass, 1995.

McCauley, C. D., Moxley, R. S., and Van Velsor, E. (eds). *Handbook of Leadership Development*. San Francisco: Jossey-Bass, 1998.

Tichy, N. M. *The Leadership Engine: How Winning Companies Build Leaders at Every Level*. New York: HarperCollins, 1997.

Wergin, J. F. *The Collaborative Department: How Five Campuses Are Inching Toward Cultures of Collective Responsibility.* Washington, D.C.: American Association for Higher Education, Forum on Faculty Roles and Rewards, 1994.

Chapter Two

A Collaborative Model for Leading Academic Change

Ann F. Lucas

Responsibility for making decisions about how a discipline will respond to change rests with department members, who can best generate needed transformation by working together as a team rather than as independent entrepreneurs. A chair who knows how to be an effective team leader is in the best position to help faculty examine how they function together so they can create a cohesive department that will be able to control its own future rather than have it determined for them.

Performance-based management, which has already been adopted by half the states for their public colleges and universities, allocates budgets on the basis of indices of the success achieved by educational institutions (Schmidt, 1998, p. A26). Such a policy is one way of getting the attention of academics, for it means that higher education no longer has the luxury of changing slowly. If academics do not direct and shape reform, they will be passive bystanders to transformations mandated by someone else.

Academics find themselves caught in a trap, because although they value autonomy, governors and boards of trustees demand accountability (Green, 1997, p. 13). The ensuing conflict, accompanied by the slow process of shared governance in academe, has tested the patience of elected state officials who feel that their most viable option is to legislate change.

Although some faculty members have tried to stand their ground, insisting that they will not let external constituencies determine their lives, state or trustee control of the budget forces cooperation. Under these circumstances, the chair's role is to help faculty understand that resistance simply reduces their power, whereas their power is increased when they decide how policy will be implemented—for example, when they determine what performance indices should be adopted rather than have them imposed. Clearly there is little that faculty can do to change a governor's decision. What they can do is define the policy in a way that makes sense to them.

When effective teams exist, it is much easier for the chair to lead change effectively and to deal with the resistance that change inevitably triggers. When teams are experienced in problem solving and decision making, in managing conflict, in listening to one another, and in valuing every member of the team, managing change is easier. Sometimes chairs feel helpless when they contemplate changes that need to be implemented. However, even when the climate is toxic, even when attitudes are generally negative, it is possible for chairs to be effective change agents. Under such circumstances, the focus should be on changing behavior, not on changing the climate and the poor attitudes. All of the activities described in Chapter One that help shape team behavior should be the chair's highest priorities. It will then be possible to lead discussions in a cohesive team with two common goals: reflecting continually on the way the team functions, and transforming its work of designing learning experiences for students.

Launching Change

In addition to knowing how to develop the characteristics of an effective team, chairs need to know how to undertake the process of change. Yet the literature on change is both voluminous and confusing. I have therefore selected one effective change model and illustrated it here with several examples of departments that have launched significant and successful change efforts. Given the wide diversity of the literature on change, it should not be surprising that all of the contributing authors of this volume have not necessarily used the same paradigm.

I have chosen John P. Kotter's (1996) comprehensive eight-stage change model because (1) it is based on his extensive experience with organizations and has thus been demonstrated to work; (2) it reflects the elements deemed essential by most authors of the literature on change, but it goes beyond the work of other researchers by integrating these elements in a natural progression that provides useful guidelines; and (3) my own experience in consulting with universities that have been unsuccessful in their change efforts has convinced me that they failed to succeed because several of these processes were not implemented.

The Eight-Step Change Process

Change is more likely to be successful when the following stages are used as guidelines (Kotter, 1996, p. 21):

1. Establishing a sense of urgency
2. Creating the guiding coalition
3. Developing a vision and strategy
4. Communicating the change vision
5. Empowering broad-based action
6. Generating short-term wins
7. Consolidating gains and producing more change
8. Anchoring new approaches in the culture

The first example is an eight-year project in the Department of Management and Marketing at Fairleigh Dickinson University (FDU), a large private university in which student enrollment had been declining, as was true at schools across the country, because fewer students were choosing business as a major. A number of faculty had become stagnant, discussions about teaching seldom occurred, several faculty members had received poor student evaluations, the curriculum had not been updated in years, and a large percentage of faculty were not engaged in scholarly activity. A few members of the department felt strongly that some changes had to take place.

Although there is a tendency for many academics to feel that nothing constructive can happen until a university's culture is changed, my experience, supplemented by the wisdom found in the rich literature on change, demonstrates that change must begin with a modification of behavior and attitudes. The process used to make this happen at FDU is discussed in the following paragraphs using the stages in Kotter's change process to illustrate what was done by the management faculty.

1. *Establishing a sense of urgency.* This is a crucial step that is often neglected by those who want to bring about change. Given that individuals tend to want to preserve the status quo—even if it is a painful situation—unless there are some cogent reasons for change, they will resist. Typically, faculty who oppose change will think, What do I stand to lose if change takes place? I know what I have now; what will I have to give up? Therefore, those who want to lead change must get others on board by identifying both potential crises and the opportunities that will not come about unless change occurs. In some institutions, faculty have become very skeptical about purported crises. Therefore, although urgency can be demonstrated, greater emphasis should be placed on the opportunities that will be generated for faculty as a result of the change.

At FDU, a few faculty members, under the leadership of one individual, decided on their own that they would like to develop the Center for Human Resource Management Studies (CHRMS). They felt that this new program could be the answer to many of the department's problems. It could provide students with marketable skills; link faculty more closely with outside organizations by partnering with business; increase research projects; enhance consulting possibilities, thereby increasing both the departmental budget and faculty income; and revitalize faculty. These were the messages that were repeated to create a sense of urgency and to emphasize opportunities for professional development in an otherwise complacent faculty.

2. *Creating the guiding coalition.* Enough people must be involved at this stage to get the change project rolling. They must demonstrate commitment and be willing to devote time and energy to the project. Synergy, cohesion, and attractiveness of group membership will generate sustained excitement about the project.

At FDU, initially only about six of thirty-two faculty members were involved in the CHRMS project under the leadership of Daniel Twomey, an ex-chair of the management and marketing department. These individuals, who felt dissatisfied with the stagnation in the department, began meeting on a regular basis. They received no additional compensation or release time for their work in program development.

3. *Developing a vision and strategy.* There was excitement in FDU's management and marketing department as individuals involved in the project envisioned what developing such a program could do for the department, the students, the faculty, and the college. The vision was to transform management education through academic-business partnerships, application-oriented learning methods, and state-of-the-art learning technologies. Partnering with industry would create an updated curriculum that would attract and educate more and better graduate students and provide stimulating new courses to teach, more research projects, and more consulting opportunities for faculty. The mission statement for the program became, "The Center for Human Resource Management Studies is a partnership between education, industry, and the community, creating a learning environment committed to the development of knowledge and leadership in the management of human resources."

Whereas a vision can excite and stimulate faculty intellectually and emotionally, it leads nowhere unless participants take the next step of developing strategic goals and action steps. The strategic objectives for the CHRMS were as follows (CHRMS Staff, 1994):

1. To be the standard of excellence and innovation for partnering with business
2. To be a leader in integrating scholarship with practice
3. To be a leader in an integrated learning community
4. To be global in perspective, organization, and activity
5. To serve societal needs and foster economic development

The action steps for meeting these goals are discussed shortly, in the section on empowerment, which is stage 5 of Kotter's change model.

4. *Communicating the change vision.* It must be possible to communicate the vision as an "elevator speech," that is, in the time it would take an elevator to travel between floors. The vision must be simple yet exciting. The FDU faculty found the mission of transforming management education through partnering with industry to be a stimulating prospect that would make their lives more

interesting professionally. A newsletter was developed to discuss the new enterprise with colleagues and business partners. Ongoing conversations with others, both in the department and in the College of Business, and frequent progress reports at meetings at a later stage spread news of the vision. The dean, who was supportive, was kept informed.

5. *Empowering broad-based action.* Groups that act as change agents must be given the authority to act in ways that move the change effort forward. In FDU's management and marketing department, the change agents empowered themselves while keeping the dean apprised of developments so that the dean could be certain that the change agents were functioning within the scope of their responsibility and authority. At this stage, the committee decided on the following action steps to implement their strategic goals. They

- Formed an advisory committee of faculty and the vice presidents of human resources from various external organizations
- Conducted focus groups with vice presidents of human resources and with graduate students at the university
- Conducted a curriculum survey of all other colleges of business that offer programs in human resources
- Interviewed individually some human resources people from several organizations
- Ran monthly breakfast meetings with the vice presidents of human resources from external organizations
- Formed committees with vice presidents to develop an innovative, cutting-edge curriculum (the vice presidents felt this was their greatest contribution)
- Created a subcommittee of the advisory committee to discuss research and consulting possibilities
- Developed other subcommittees that focused on noncredit short courses to be attended by individuals from business, and on the use of advisory committee members as guest lecturers in classes or as adjunct faculty

6. *Generating short-term wins.* As Rosabeth Moss Kanter (1988, p. 94) points out, "everything looks like a failure in the middle." Persistence and some indication that their efforts had been suc-

cessful were needed after the change agents had expended so much effort on planning and implementation steps. Some of the management group's tangible accomplishments were as follows:

- The new human resource development curriculum was approved by the educational policy committee and by the dean.
- Four one-day noncredit courses for individuals employed in human resources grossed about $15,000 during the first year. The money went into the budget for the CHRMS.
- Two more graduate assistants were hired, which doubled the previous number.
- A video on the human resources program that could be used for publicity purposes was produced, gratis, with significant professional expertise provided by a company represented by one of the advisory board members.

The rewards for faculty included that they were able to teach innovative courses and engage in some research and consulting projects. Rewards for students included a new program that offered marketable skills, closer contact with faculty and high-level business partners, more internships, summer employment, and excellent job-placement opportunities at the completion of the program.

As Terrence E. Deal and M. K. Key (1998) make so clear in their book *Corporate Celebration,* celebration infuses life with passion and purpose. Ceremonies that commemorate accomplishments can put spice back into lives, create excitement, revitalize, and rebuild commitment to counteract burnout by reminding individuals of how far they have come toward reaching goals that were once so energizing.

7. *Consolidating gains and producing more change.* Once a certain level of achievement has been attained, accomplishments must be integrated and new goals set. It was now possible for the new human resources program to be staffed all day, five days a week. Research and consulting projects with external organizations were initiated. The following steps were also taken:

- An executive-in-residence joined the department as a full-time affiliate whose salary was covered by industry.

- A utility company invited the program director to develop an employee evaluation program.
- A prestigious organization invited the faculty to develop an employee satisfaction program.
- A third organization requested a survey to determine regional salaries for a particular industry.
- Another graduate assistant was added to assist in research conducted by the human resources center.
- The program continued to offer short courses and became institutionalized as a funding source for the department.

8. *Anchoring new approaches in the culture.* When a new culture is developed, it must be embedded in the organization so that it becomes a permanent part of the structure. Others in the organization need to recognize that the change is effective and is being rewarded. Some indications of success at FDU were as follows:

- Annual joint presentations by faculty, members of the advisory committee, and leaders in the field of management were made to professional organizations, such as the Academy of Management.
- Monthly breakfast seminars were offered by leaders from industry.
- Business ethics roundtables were hosted by academics and business partners.
- Human resource law roundtables were held four times a year.
- Diversity roundtables were presented four times a year.
- Executive scholars program for students were held monthly by business partners.
- Research papers and discussions were presented monthly by faculty.
- Eight new faculty members were hired who brought important skills and in turn received ongoing faculty development in the area of human resource management.
- Student enrollment in the CHRMS program tripled.
- The number of internships for students more than doubled, and graduates of the program were hired by companies that had grown to know their work.

- Faculty felt revitalized by their participation in the program.
- Research and consulting with industry became an ongoing part of the culture.
- Executives from the advisory committee now teach as adjunct faculty or lecture in classes in which they have special expertise.
- Planned social activities have solidified the relationships among faculty, students, and members of the advisory committee.
- Additional faculty have become involved in research and consulting with organizations represented by members of the advisory committee.

An interesting positive side effect occurred in the rest of the management department as the CHRMS demonstrated visible signs of success. Over a ten-year period, eight faculty members retired, another seven voluntarily left the university, three were discontinued, and two died. The department faculty members seemed quite aware that standards were being increased, that more would be expected of them, and that their performance would look bad by comparison. Faculty not involved in the CHRMS began to note their own strengths and identify opportunities for new programs that could be built around them. Committees were formed to discuss curriculum revision and outcomes assessment. Colloquia on teaching effectiveness and increasing faculty scholarship were offered. Junior faculty began presenting some of their own research, and these new faculty members also helped revitalize the department. Without any deliberate attempt on their part, the faculty who made up the critical mass of change agents also triggered renewal that took the form of changed behavior and attitudes in the rest of the department.

Although this change process was used in a management and marketing department, the dynamics of change are the same in any department. A leader is needed, one who can manage resistance and conflict so that the department is strengthened and faculty are revitalized rather than demoralized by the process. A courageous department chair who is knowledgeable about the steps to take and what to expect at each stage is the ideal person to launch such a change, which can transform a department. If change is to be permanent, planning and long-term management are required, and the change must be rewarded by central administration.

Two Other Successful Change Projects: Downsizing and Merging

Two additional successful change projects are described here briefly. One involved faculty downsizing in a unionized university. Based on the number of full-time equivalent students, one hundred buyouts and terminations from 527 full-time faculty was the goal. The downsizing program was successful for a number of reasons: the union was involved from the very beginning, communication with the faculty about the need for the program was excellent, a generous buyout package was provided, assistance was given to faculty in the form of support groups and the teaching of self-marketing skills, and newsletter reports on successful job searches by faculty who left the university were given to the faculty who remained. Success was defined as faculty getting other positions that they enjoyed as much as or more than their faculty position at the university within six months of the decision to leave. The success rate was 94 percent (Lucas, 1990).

The success of this program can be accounted for by looking at the first seven steps in Kotter's model: establishing a sense of urgency, creating the guiding coalition, developing a vision and strategy, communicating the change vision, empowering faculty to assist those who would be leaving, generating short-term wins (the first newsletter announcements about faculty who secured other satisfying positions), and consolidating gains and producing more change (the first successful project was followed by assisting forty administrators and professional staff in many of the same ways and retraining an additional fifty-seven faculty members in the cutting-edge knowledge of their fields). The eighth step, embedding the change in the culture, was not necessary once the downsizing project was completed.

Probably the one step that was given insufficient attention was step 3, creating a vision and strategy. In this situation, there were not enough students for the full-time faculty to teach, and the sense of urgency was so strong that the vision was simply that down-sizing would help the institution to survive and that most colleagues who would be leaving would go voluntarily, receive a generous buyout package, and be assisted in furthering their careers as they moved to equally or more satisfying positions.

A second successful change project (Lucas, 1988), involving the restructuring of colleges within a large, private, multicampus university, was undertaken as part of an overall strategy to cope with a 25 percent drop in student enrollment. Two of the colleges at this university, located on campuses ten miles apart, were merged into one. Two biology departments, one from arts and sciences and the other from a liberal arts college, were not only combined but also moved into a college of science and engineering. Thirty faculty members with different experiential and learning histories, different cultures, and different methods of solving problems had to compete to teach advanced and graduate courses, and to problem solve about limited laboratory and office space and other limited resources. Another factor that created high faculty resistance to the move was the biologists' perception of a condescending attitude among the engineering faculty, who were significantly more successful in generating external funding. Called a "dynamics-of-merging project," this successful enterprise can also be examined in terms of Kotter's leading change model.

The sense of urgency was clear. The decision to merge was made at the top by the president and the deans. When the department requested a meeting with its dean to discuss space allocation, the dean's response was interpreted as, "If you want something from me, show me that you are a quality department—write, publish, secure some grant money." When asked about what they wanted to do about the situation, the participants said they wanted to prove to the dean that they were a high-quality department. The chair and thirty faculty members became a highly motivated critical mass of change agents who had created a vision of quality. They enthusiastically approached the tasks of strategic goal setting, and as they said later to the facilitator, "The dean has provided the stick. You have provided the carrot."

Throughout ensuing meetings, the change agents reminded one another of their change vision—to prove to the dean and their new colleagues in the College of Science and Engineering that they were a quality department. They listed their short-term wins as follows:

- We have a better appreciation of those factors that affect our survival. We feel ready to address these factors, set goals and implementation steps, and assign priorities.
- We have pooled resources. We now know that we can accomplish specific things if we want to. Some positive goals have been developed, and we know there are steps we can take to become more productive and change our image.
- We have appreciated other people in the department as people, and we are aware that we are colleagues and that we should listen to one another. We have formed a bond.
- We feel more cohesive because we all have the same agenda: to benefit the department.
- There is a changed atmosphere here. Things have been said that have not been said before. There has been no adversarial feeling in these meetings, unlike when we used to meet together as a department. Even the tone of voice and the quality of contributions are different. We seem more focused; there is not so much extraneous behavior. We feel less threatened than we did at department meetings. Maybe it is because we have been breaking into smaller groups and have an equal opportunity to speak. Maybe it is because we have been sitting in a circle and can see one another's faces. At department meetings we sat in rows as if we were students and saw the backs of one another's heads.

These comments typify the sense of empowerment and the generation of short-term wins, although because the dynamics of how the department functioned together were so positive, these were also long-term benefits. Because a small group of the change agents reported back to the dean on their progress in developing a new joint innovative curriculum and grant applications, the dean also empowered them and provided resources. When the department achieved its first sizeable funding for a grant, a standard was set for consolidating their gains, producing more changes, and anchoring their new approaches in the culture.

Why Change Efforts Fail

When one or more steps in Kotter's change model are ignored, the desired goals are not achieved. Moreover, chairs must be brought on board from the very beginning of the change process. Their hard work, their conviction that they are not well trained either for their leadership role or for dealing with the variety of problems they confront almost daily, their considerable frustration when there are expectations from administration and faculty for which they are not given the tools or resources they need, their inability to motivate faculty, and their belief that they are not appreciated leave them feeling left out of the loop when important plans and decisions are made in the university.

In one fairly prestigious private university, the provost and deans, faced with problems of declining enrollment, high attrition, poor teaching, and decreasing scholarly activity, decided that they needed to offer innovative programs, develop more income from research funded by grants, improve teaching effectiveness, and involve more faculty in research. However, they felt that being successful in their plans would be a long, uphill struggle because faculty were very resistant to change. They believed that too few faculty were interested in innovative programs and that most were content with the status quo. Less than half of the faculty were engaged in research or developing grants. Based on students' evaluations, a number of faculty were perceived to be poor teachers.

Self-report data from fifty-five chair questionnaires showed results that I have found to be fairly typical of many universities. Less than 30 percent of the chairs reported any degree of success in improving the overall quality of teaching in the department and in motivating difficult colleagues or poor teachers, less than 40 percent reported any success in motivating midcareer and burned-out faculty, and less than half reported success in increasing scholarly activity in their faculty. Only 18 percent reported an ability to keep up with their own scholarly work. Comments from chairs' questionnaires about their frustrations, which are interesting because the same problems appear in many institutions, included the following:

Not trained for a leadership role

- I am a natural teacher and scientist. I am not a natural manager. I don't like being a department head.
- Time. Also lack of training. The attacks of one professor on my leadership [are] a constant drain on my energy. I don't handle [them] well.

Inability to motivate faculty

- There is little leverage over tenured full professors. Academia may be the closest thing we have to a caste society.
- Not being able to motivate two very bright research-oriented faculty to become truly engaged with departmental and institutional matters. One was denied tenure because he came to campus only two afternoons per week.
- Working with faculty who resist change, [who] do not want to do anything more than teach nine hours a week, who are tenured and doing little or nothing in professional development, and who make no contributions to the department or college.
- Motivating faculty who are "retired on the job."

Increasing pressures on the chair

- Greater responsibilities, innumerable meetings, little creative time, little opportunity for teaching
- Inability to obtain real commitments to research and publication
- Long time required to do almost anything
- Never having enough time to complete tasks with deadlines
- Amount of paper work

Difficulty getting cooperation from administration

- Dissatisfaction in working with administration; getting firm commitments from them.
- The dean who does not appreciate the contribution of this department.

- Lack of trust and respect toward chairs from upper administration: We are micromanaged to death. New ideas are shot down unless they conform to the "flavor of the month." The creativity and energy of full-time faculty [are] thought to be wholly replaceable by adjuncts without concern for erosion of quality.

No appreciation for hard work

- Recurrent feelings that no one cares.
- Faculty come to me with every problem, from broken marriages to demands that I see to it that their wastepaper baskets are emptied. It is not easy to lead, reconcile, and be a father-confessor. At the end of the day, no one—not the faculty, the dean, or the vice president—no one says, "Thank you."

The administrative leadership in this institution was frustrated by the perceived lack of faculty cooperation but they felt they could go ahead on their own and make the changes that would help their institution be more competitive. Until the needs assessment was conducted that brought to light these perspectives, the academic administrators seemed oblivious to the problems that chairs were facing. They seemed not to know that sharing their own sense of urgency and developing a critical mass of chairs and informal leaders among faculty could generate the change they wanted to launch. It did not seem to occur to administrators to bring chairs into the loop through leadership development and other interventions that could help chairs work with administration and handle problems that the chairs were experiencing with faculty. The primary concerns of administrators were that enrollment was declining and that they were losing a considerable number of good students to another university within easy commuting distance, a university that offered innovative programs and had funding for expensive equipment because it had developed more grants. When I asked what opportunities would be created for faculty if they obtained greater funding from grants, there was a long pause. After an apparent shift in their thinking, the provost and deans indicated that faculty could engage in research that would revitalize the faculty, could have more research assistants and better equipment (not having state-of-the art equipment was a source of frequent complaints from faculty), could teach new courses, and could develop some consulting under university auspices, which would add to their incomes. However, when I asked if they had communicated any of this to their chairs and faculty, they answered that these things should be apparent to them.

The administrative leadership at this institution did not have a clear sense that change is a process. Ignoring the first six steps in Kotter's change model, the provost and deans were concerned with putting in place a plan that they would develop and hand down to chairs and faculty. They had not created a sense of urgency or indicated opportunities, had not developed a critical mass that included chairs and faculty, had not created a shared vision and a strategy that could be communicated to generate enthusiasm and a sense of direction and purpose, had not empowered others to act, and had not generated short-term wins. They had felt that the situation was so bad that they had simply mandated change. Because neither the deans nor the administrators understood how to launch an effective change effort, their progress was limited, and faculty and programs continued to stagnate.

In this same university, there was no emphasis on accountability. (In Kotter's model, accountability is included in stage 6, generating short-term wins, although the emphasis is on reward.) All faculty were given three-credit release time for scholarly activities. However, they were never asked how they used that release time. Eventually it became an entitlement, although it was still labeled time spent on scholarship. Unless feedback and accountability are included in any change project, the desired goals will never be achieved.

Several of Kotter's stages were then put in place, beginning with creating a sense of urgency and sharing opportunities for faculty, developing a critical mass of change agents that included chairs and some key faculty, and developing and communicating a shared vision. Leadership development and team building were part of training those who would be involved in the change efforts. During the next three years this institution generated considerable grant money and developed two innovative programs as they partnered with industry, which generated funding from industry and increased student enrollment.

Failure to Communicate Decision-Making Style

Several other points are worth emphasizing. In academic institutions, chairs and faculty, both formal and informal leaders, must be included in the change process, but the nature of what will be done with their input must be clarified. The example that follows is of a toxic climate that was created at the university level, but chairs could as easily fall into the same trap in their own departments.

In a large state university in which a workshop for chairs was conducted, the chairs confided at the first coffee break that there was a lot of conflict in their institution. They concluded that the conflict was due to their new president and vice president being disingenuous, or as they put it, "phonies." The chairs said that the vice president, acting on behalf of the president, had come to them individually to ask their advice on certain changes that might be inaugurated. The chairs said that although they had given their carefully considered advice to the vice president, the following week the president announced a decision that was 180 degrees away from what they had recommended. Although it could be said that the vice president had tried to involve a critical mass of chairs and faculty in developing a vision and strategic goals, what he had not done was indicate to the chairs and faculty the process he was using in developing his plans. The vice president's perception was that he was using a consultative style of decision making, that is, that he was trying to broaden his own perspective by discovering how a number of individuals felt about the issue and how different outcomes would affect them. The chairs he interviewed, however, thought that he was employing a democratic decision-making style and that if most of them recommended a particular course of action, that is the action the president would take. Given the two different perceptions of the process, dissatisfaction with the outcome was inevitable. Erosion of the relationship between the chairs and faculty and the administration began at this point.

If the president had explained the process used in making the decision, the chairs and faculty would more likely have accepted it. Instead of simply announcing the decision, the president should have indicated to the chairs that he had asked the vice president to solicit their advice and that he appreciated the perspectives he had gathered. Then he could have summarized what these perspectives were. Next he could have indicated the pros and cons of each alternative, and finally what he had chosen to do, but he should have explained that he also had to consider his responsibility to the board of trustees, and why he felt, given all the information he had collected, that the decision made was the best option. It is when advice is requested and apparently ignored that people feel used and distrustful. The point is that if chairs are asked for input by the vice president, or if faculty perspectives are requested by the chair, that input must be taken seriously if a change effort is to be successful. Chairs and faculty must be informed about the process to be used—in this case consultative, not democratic—in the final decision-making process, and how the decision is aligned with the mission and strategic goals.

The other complaint of the chairs in this state institution was that the president was inaugurating change for the sake of change and that all of the change he was instituting was arbitrary and capricious. When the top administrators in this university were interviewed, they stated that the president had announced the new mission and strategic goals at his inaugural address two years before. However, he had not alluded to them since that time. This is a good example of the need to repeat the vision and mission at every opportunity so that everyone in the university or department is clear about the direction in which the institution is moving, how each change is related to the mission, and what steps will be required to get there.

Failure Resulting from Not Involving a Critical Mass of Faculty

Another illustration of a poorly managed change program is a small private college whose chief academic officer had felt for some time that the school should be involved in distance learning. In the course of hiring an individual for an administrative position, the vice president discovered that the applicant had a great deal of experience running distance learning programs in a state university. So the university hired the applicant and asked that she develop a distance learning program for the school. The problem was that the administration had not gotten faculty on board, and although the administrators were convinced that distance learning would be good for the college, the faculty were concerned that the introduction of distance learning might jeopardize their positions. The college spent considerable money on technical equipment, only to discover that when they finally held open meetings for faculty on the project that had been put in place, nobody came. The administration had to go back to square one and involve faculty in the decision-making and planning process.

Other schools have tried to introduce technology and have failed, not because there was something wrong with the idea or because the technology did not work, but rather because there was no development and communication of a shared vision. In one college, faculty were skeptical about technology and its interference with their rapport with students. In another school, insufficient thought was given to teaching faculty how technology can be used in teaching, and no incentives were given for using technology. In one university a small group of faculty was encouraged to volunteer for training but were told that after they had learned how to integrate technology with their teaching they would have to teach the course on alternate weeks on two campuses thirty-five miles apart. This amounted to a disincentive, and very few faculty volunteered for training.

Dealing with Resistance

As was discussed in Chapter One, higher education has been quite adaptable to change stemming from large social forces, such as the land grant provisions and the G.I. Bill. However, higher education has also been quite resistant to change. As Madeleine Green (1997, p. 4) has written about higher education, "its mission is to conserve; to embody the timeless values of scholarly inquiry and the transmission of knowledge from one generation to the next." So a certain amount of resistance has helped to preserve what is good about higher education.

People will always resist things that they perceive to be not in their best interest. Moreover, even when the current situation is painful, individuals feel they know what they have and they believe that the results of change could make matters worse. So change is usually resisted—either actively, through protests or sabotage, or passively, with an expectation that the request for change is simply a whim of some administrator who will simply move on in time to another institution. Anyone who initiates change must be prepared, therefore, to deal in a positive fashion with this resistance.

Resistance needs to be handled respectfully. Instead of defending the need to change, change agents have to be prepared to do a lot of active listening. Chairs leading change need to get behind the eyes of the person doing the objecting. When chairs are able to view the situation from another person's perspective, they can frequently discover some real problems that need to be addressed, some barriers that may not have occurred to them. This may cause chairs to change some parts of what they will do and how they intend to launch and implement the change. Also, a willingness to listen builds a relationship with the other person or persons. In turn, the person or persons being listened to often also become more willing to listen to another perspective. It helps to ask them how they would solve the problem that the change is intended to manage. In this way, some individuals who resist an alternative may begin to appreciate that they cannot think of a better solution. When this occurs, they are often more willing to go along with what chairs have proposed. Or chairs may be able to collaborate in developing a better plan of action. This approach, though it clearly takes time, is more likely to contribute to success and bring others on board. A good source on handling resistance is Rick Maurer's *Beyond the Wall of Resistance* (1996). Also, Sandra Cheldelin discusses resistance to change and offers a number of practical suggestions for handling it in Chapter Three of this volume.

Throughout the rest of this book, the authors address some of the greatest challenges with which chairs will have to cope in the next decade. It is important to keep Kotter's eight-stage model in mind in leading change in any of these areas. Although the topics are varied, the strategies that work are quite similar. It is helpful to recognize that if a change project seems to be failing, a good strategy is to check on whether one of these stages has been overlooked or not thought through carefully. The stages do not necessarily follow one another in a linear fashion, so there are times when it is necessary to skip a stage or backtrack to discover which steps have been neglected. Change is a challenge. Remember also that change is a team sport.

Individuals can passively accept change, they can resist it, or they can help shape it. Transformational leaders determine the trajectory that change will take; caretakers passively accept change. Chairs who are team leaders will, in collaboration with their faculty, anticipate change in their disciplines, think more imaginatively about the future, create shared visions and new meanings for their department, and develop ownership and commitment to these new realities.

References

Center for Human Resource Management Studies Staff. *CHRMS Strategic Plan, Attachment A.* Unpublished document. Madison, N.J.: Fairleigh Dickinson University, 1994.

Deal, T. E., and Key, M. K. *Corporate Celebration: Play, Purpose, and Profit at Work.* San Francisco: Berrett-Koehler, 1998.

Green, M. F. *Transforming Higher Education: Views from Leaders Around the World.* Phoenix, Ariz.: American Council on Education and Oryx Press, 1997.

Kanter, R. M. "Change-Master Skills: What It Takes to Be Creative." In R. L. Kuhn (ed.), *Handbook for Creative and Innovative Managers.* New York: McGraw-Hill, 1988.

Kotter, J. P. *Leading Change.* Boston, Mass.: Harvard Business School Press, 1996.

Lucas, A. F. "Strategies for a Team-Building Intervention in the Academic Department." *Journal of Staff, Program, and Organization Development,* 1988, *6*(1), 21–32.

Lucas, A. F. "Redirecting Faculty Through Organizational Development: Fairleigh Dickinson University." In J. H. Schuster, D. W. Wheeler, and Associates, *Enhancing Faculty Careers.* San Francisco: Jossey-Bass, 1990.

Maurer, R. *Beyond the Wall of Resistance.* Austin, Tex.: Bard Books, 1996.

Schmidt, P. "States Increasingly Link Budgets to Performance." *Chronicle of Higher Education,* July 24, 1998, p. A26.

Recommended Readings

Bunker, B. B, and Alban, B. T. *Large Group Interventions: Engaging the Whole System for Rapid Change.* San Francisco: Jossey-Bass, 1997.

Dolence, M. G., and Norris, D. M. *Transforming Higher Education: A Vision for Learning in the Twenty-First Century.* Ann Arbor, Mich.: Society for College and University Planning, 1995.

Jacobs, R. W. *Real-Time Strategic Change: How to Involve an Entire Organization in Fast and Far-Reaching Change.* San Francisco: Berrett-Koehler, 1994.

Karr, D. K., Hard, K. J., and Trahant, W. J. *Managing the Change Process: A Field Book for Change Agents, Consultants, Team Leaders, and Reengineering Managers.* New York: McGraw-Hill, 1996.

LaMarsh, J. *Changing the Way We Change.* Reading, Mass.: Addison-Wesley, 1995.

O'Toole, J. *Leading Change: Overcoming the Ideology of Comfort and the Tyranny of Custom.* San Francisco: Jossey-Bass, 1995.

Senge, P., and others. *The Dance of Change: The Challenges to Sustaining Momentum in Learning Organizations.* New York: Doubleday, 1999.

Tushman, M. L., and O'Reilly, C. A. III. *Winning Through Innovation: A Practical Guide to Leading Organizational Change and Renewal.* Boston: Harvard Business School Press, 1997.

Chapter Three

Handling Resistance to Change

Sandra I. Cheldelin

Because of all the department-based change initiatives that occur year after year, we know it can be done. We also know that such change is not easy. Department chairs, in their unique role, experience the difficulties more than most. When change is initiated within the department, chairs must sell the interests of their department colleagues. When it is initiated outside the department, chairs are responsible for obtaining support from the department. Change often involves adding more tasks to already full schedules, responsibilities, and workloads. New initiatives seldom replace existing ones, and priorities are often not clear. Will faculty be rewarded if they engage in the initiative? Are the previous activities and responsibilities no longer important? Does everyone understand the significance of the initiative? These questions and issues begin the discussion of why change is hard. Chairs feel squeezed. To engage themselves purposefully in most new initiatives seems, at first blush, masochistic. With this in mind, this chapter provides chairs with a tool kit of knowledge, skills, and intervention strategies for initiating change, coping with apathy or resistance to change, and working with the conflict that inevitably emerges because of change.

Chairs as Linking Pins

There are many initiatives and changes well under way across American higher education today that are common and shared experiences. A population bubble is moving through as senior faculty face retirement or find creative ways of slowing down. Ann Ferren (1998) addresses this in her timely working paper *Senior Faculty Considering Retirement*. As a group, the successors of these faculty are dramatically different in gender, ethnicity, background, and even values. In profound ways they are challenging some of the historical canons of what it means to be a college professor and what it means to be a member of a department. Senior faculty—university citizens who have traditionally been leaders of faculty senates and volunteers for governance and community development assignments, beyond the call of duty—will need to be replaced. Their replacements will need to be empowered by chairs, deans, and provosts. Chairs are already finding themselves caught between these junior and senior faculty groups. Senior faculty must think about letting go and mentoring younger faculty to engage in these important roles. Chairs carry the burden of encouraging this to happen.

Some of the most persistent conflicts in any organization involve the changing nature of its membership. Departments are becoming more inclusive of women and minority groups. Chairs ultimately have to check for bias in selection, recruitment, promotion, and the more subtle ways in which groups are excluded. Differences in styles, approaches to work, problem solving, and values must be embraced, supported, and nourished. Chairs are responsible for bringing a balanced representation into the department, for advocating and modeling attitudes and behaviors that are inclusive and pluralistic. The important working paper of R. Eugene Rice (1996) *Making a Place for the New American Scholar* addresses these issues at length.

Robert Bellah (1997) reminds us that the membership changes in the academy are not limited to changes in gender and race. He moves the conversation into discussion of the growing class and cultural wars that are occurring within the university today. The increasingly diverse membership in departments will at some point likely surface society's struggles with deeply rooted and enduring sexism, racism, classism, and homophobia. If these problems are not enough, add the changing nature of student bodies across the country. Colleges and universities now enroll more women than men. Traditional-aged students are no longer the majority. Increasingly classrooms are filled with older students, working full-time and part-time, who have insufficient financial support to complete their education without acquiring large debts.

The Additive Nature of Change Initiatives

Other national initiatives, common and shared experiences on campus, place the chair in an untenable situation of adding to already full workloads by creating more work for department chairs and faculty. For example, there is an ongoing shift of focus from the work of faculty—teaching—to the work of students—learning. Taken seriously, this shift has enormous impact on the role of faculty, on how they think about the acquisition of knowledge and on how they know if students are learning.

The national assessment conference agenda of 1998, "Architecture for Change: Information as Foundation," sponsored by the American Association for Higher Education, gave universities a new metaphor and professors a new charge: serve as architects to create the best learning environments for students. Other national initiatives are involved with rethinking faculty priorities, roles, and rewards, including post-tenure review and developing alternative employment arrangements. Richard Chait's *Where Tenure Does Not Reign: Colleges with Contract Systems* (1997) and Judith Gappa's *Two Faculties or One? The Conundrum of Part-Timers in a Bifurcated Workplace* (1997) further explore these changes. In addition to publishing working papers, organizations are also presenting annual institutes and academies that are bringing together planning teams consisting of faculty, administrators, and in some cases, students, for weeklong intensives held off-campus.

The massive influx of technology and the creation of the virtual university are other examples. The yellowed lecture notes are nearly history. This is illustrated no more dramatically than in recent books on transforming higher education that are designed to help colleges and universities move into the so-called knowledge age (Apps, 1994; Harvey and Knight, 1996; Rendon and Hope, 1995). A remarkably provocative issue of the *AAHE Bulletin* (May 1998) is devoted primarily to Theodore Marchese's documented examples of academy competitors in distance learning, "Not-So-Distant Competitors: How New Providers Are Remaking the Post-secondary Marketplace." Many departments offer on-line courses, and faculty and student advising and mentoring are significantly influenced by these parties having electronic access to one another.

The forces for change initiated within the academy cannot be divorced from the pressures outside its walls. In less than two decades, the academy has experienced a dramatic public image crisis. What was once one of the most prestigious of occupations—being a college professor—is now often spoken of with contempt and disdain. When job security and massive layoffs occurred in the 1980s, tenure and life-time employment for faculty and department chairs seemed to the greater public at least unfair and often irrelevant to the demands of a rapidly changing society.

Remarkably, college and university faculty and administrators have managed with some success to address many of these current change agendas. Unfortunately, the responses are incremental shifts that result in adding tasks to chairs' and faculty members' already full schedules and responsibilities. This additive model needs to be replaced with a transformative one that requires rethinking everyone's roles and responsibilities, and the way in which the culture within which everyone works can be changed. When chairs engage in their own change initiatives, they must consider the extent to which they are willing to let key actors in the change process eliminate some of their current responsibilities in order to take on new projects. Without this allowance, faculty will perceive the change—and no doubt rightfully so—to be in the context of a multiple-priority full workload in an already dramatically shifting environment. This will result in apathy, resistance, or outright hostility.

Principles of Transformative Change

Transformative change occurs best in the context of a collaborative department. Edward Marshall (1995, p. 4) punctuates this idea with his belief that "collaboration is the premier candidate to replace hierarchy as the organizing principle for leading and managing the 21st century workplace." Clearly there has been a redefinition of the role of leader in organizations: the coach, mentor, and steward replace the autocratic ruler and charismatic decision maker (Senge, 1990).

The important change from command-and-control to collaboration brings a shift of power, authority, status, and decision making. David and Frank Johnson (1997) take the premise that universities are dependent on building relationships. "Social interdependence is at the heart of all human interaction and cooperation is at the heart of all small group efforts" (p. 72). The academy is ahead of most organizations in its culture of shared governance. There are lessons to be learned, nevertheless, in building a collaborative culture, the essential ingredient for transformative change.

With new initiatives, chairs need not only take into account the impact of increased workload, but they must also consider some of the principles known about change that apply directly to department business. Walter Sikes (1989), a pioneer in the organization development field and a professional of the National Training Laboratories, has developed twelve basic principles of change in organizations. Four of these principles are particularly relevant and easily adapted to departments in the academy.

1. *We cannot change just one element of a system.* Chairs certainly understand the concepts embedded in systems theory. Two examples illustrate this important point. How often have we witnessed the acquisition of computers across campuses without sufficient ongoing budgetary support for software, training, upgrading, integrating, and long-term repair and replacement? Similarly, most universities are involved with creating required, accreditation-driven assessment plans. The departments can no longer report faculty and student evaluations as sufficient outcome data. The chairs and their faculties must expand their criteria. In both cases, the university-wide initiatives have an impact on each department.

2. *Colleagues will resist anything that feels like punishment.* Full cooperation requires faculty to feel excited about and rewarded for change initiatives. When people feel punished, they exert unnecessary energy in resisting. It is predictable that the extra work faculty willingly do, with only intrinsic rewards in return, may come to a complete stop if they perceive themselves as "suckers." Punishment may change an immediate behavior, but it will also likely result in long-term aggression.

3. *Change always generates stress.* Human behavior is remarkably predictable. We establish enduring sequences and patterns of interaction. Whether change is positive or punishing, stress is generated if we have to develop new patterns. Those who feel that they are unable to control what is happening to them will experience the most stress. This principle is well illustrated when a new member joins a department. There is an immediate change in group dynamics. Though the candidate is likely to have been selected by department colleagues, adjusting to the new person takes time and creates stress. Chairs need to help faculty maintain a sense of control, and they need to provide support and stress-management activities.

4. *Participating in setting goals and devising strategies reduces resistance to change.* The key here is to involve all the people most affected by the change initiative. This means including faculty in the initial brainstorming to generate ideas. Allow them to help gather and analyze data for decision making and to be central in decision making about how to proceed.

Along with awareness of these basic principles, there is greater likelihood of support if the essential ingredients of successful change are provided: a thorough understanding of the implications of the change and a careful alignment of the change and the values held by department members. Chairs will receive support if faculty believe that the benefits of the change initiative are worthwhile, and if they know what impact the change will have on their lives, including on their workload, relationships, and stress level.

Resistance to Change

The tenth edition of Merriam Webster's Collegiate Dictionary says that to resist is to take a stand or to exert force in opposition. We have all been resisters and we have all experienced resistance. The process has been at least partially unpleasant. So why do even the best and most logical ideas and plans for the most reasonable initiatives that involve the most rational and well-intended people still encounter opposition and often overt blocking?

William Bridges (1980) makes an important and useful distinction here. He says that most resistance is not about resistance to *change* but rather about resistance to *transition*: "Change occurs when something new starts or something old stops, and it takes place at a particular point in time. But transition cannot be localized in time that way, since it is the gradual psychological process through which individuals and groups reorient themselves so that they can function and find meanings in a changed situation" (p. 17).

Change is situational and starts with a new beginning. Transition is psychological and starts with an ending. Transition means letting go of old attitudes, old behaviors, old ways of doing department business. Unmanaged transitions are likely to be a significant source of resistance to any change initiative and might be the key to understanding resistance when chairs least predict it. The following case helps illustrate this point.

A department of a large state university recently approved significant curricular revisions for both their masters and doctoral programs. The year-long planning resulted in nearly unanimous support from faculty, students, and staff. Now that the plan is in the implementation phase, it is surprising to many that grumblings are occurring in hallway conversations and faculty meetings. As new students are advised of the new requirements, faculty are in a transition between their old curricula and the new. They all know old course numbers. Most of them know the old course content. Students are asking about courses that have just been created or that are still being designed. Faculty are left feeling less competent and frustrated by not being able to answer students' questions. In Bridges's paradigm, the new beginning—or in this case, the new curriculum—is the last step. At an advising session, it was clear that faculty had not let go of the old program:

> Well, that used to be Conflict 613 but the new number is Conflict 713 because both masters and doctoral students can take it. It is now only three credits instead of four, but I don't know what has been cut or changed. It used to be a requirement but it isn't anymore. Instead you must select between these four alternatives—I think. Oh, I don't know. I hate these new changes. I don't know what to tell you. I knew this wasn't a good idea to shift this course. I'm not even sure it is a good idea to change the curriculum at all. Nothing was really wrong with it before.

This transitional phase is predictable and will last for a considerable time until all members of the community come to terms with the changes and reintegrate the new with the old. In the meantime, this phase of the transition is what Bridges calls the "neutral zone"—when things are still ambiguous and people have not sorted out all their feelings about letting go, much less about embracing something new. Getting comfortable with this neutral zone is the key to coping with resistance. Getting comfortable means allowing time for change without premature closure. Getting comfortable means living with the ambiguity, because it may prevent escaping or abandoning a new plan, and it is an opportunity for people to think creatively about how to make the anticipated changes work.

An excellent strategy when initiating any change project is to think about the transitional issues. Transitions have three phases. They begin with letting go, followed by the neutral zone (between the old and the new), and finishing with a new beginning (the change initiative). In the previous example, faculty could "end" the old curriculum with a group storytelling about what it was like to be a part of that program. They could spend the next few months sharing their experiences wrestling with the newly designed program: what is working, what is difficult, and what creative and successful ad hoc strategies are being used. Until then, they will not take full ownership of the new masters and doctoral programs, the final phase of this transition and the beginning of the change itself.

Faces of Resistance

Being able to identify when resistance is occurring, viewing it as a natural process instead of as something wrong with one or both of the parties, providing support for faculty to express their concerns directly, and not taking any of this personally are all keys to beginning an intervention on any resistance. Sometimes it is not easy to know when resistance is present because it is often well disguised. These indirect methods of expressing resistance are hard to recognize because they seem quite rational and logical. Peter Block (1981) calls these indirect strategies "faces of resistance" that are often misread and yet are powerful ways to block one from proceeding. Seasoned chairs will find these faces familiar as they reflect on their own experiences: Faculty may request more details before they are willing to consider the initiative, or (the corollary) they may flood the chair with details that are unnecessary, irrelevant, or hard to understand. Colleagues may identify the real problem as time—too many demands are already imposed on them—or they may outline the impracticality of the proposed change and why it will not work in this department or with these students. Other faces could be a continual state of confusion after the proposal is explained multiple times, or intellectualizing by spinning multiple theories and keeping the discussion at a nonimplementable stage. Faculty may identify all the methodological problems, including what is wrong with the data collection, data, or data analysis that is the basis for the change.

At the root of much resistance are issues of power, control, and vulnerability. Chairs have positional power and although the academy is steeped in cultures of shared governance and consensual decision making, hierarchies still prevail. If faculty oppose the change and chairs are heavy-handed, faculty will likely feel powerless, victimized, and vulnerable, and will probably behave accordingly. As a result, chairs are likely to feel punished and resentful. This all has a familiar and unpleasant ring. At this point, overt conflict is likely to erupt. All parties will experience helplessness, alienation, and confusion.

To intervene, chairs need to encourage department members to engage in authentic dialogue, to get out of their respective roles as much as possible, to clarify the issues, and to identify what is needed. Letting people say what is on their minds, without retaliation, is essential to beginning any repair process.

Levels of Resistance

The conflict resolution literature often speaks of a *nested* framework for understanding both the location and the sources of conflict. The nested framework is useful, too, in understanding resistance. Resistance and conflict at one level of the college or university may be caused by, and will certainly be affected by, other parts of the college or university. A nested model for chairs means the following: individuals within the department also work within the college or division, within the university (perhaps a multiuniversity system), and within the greater academy—within both a discipline and higher education at large. Resistance can be nested at any of these levels. Although one level may be the *location* of the resistance—for example, the department—it may not necessarily be the *source* of the resistance.

Chairs typically experience resistance at the intrapersonal, interpersonal, and departmental levels (which will be elaborated on shortly). Nevertheless, the current climate of change in the academy has sources of resistance, too, at higher levels. The declining public image of the academy's role in and usefulness to society is one example. The source of this resistance is the public domain, but it may be located in intrapersonal issues of identity. Another common example is resistance to university-wide assessment initiatives for accreditation purposes. The source of this resistance is the accrediting commission, but it emerges among department members.

Intrapersonal Level of Resistance

Human beings have wonderful physiological and psychological capacities for maintaining health. Sometimes these capacities are dramatically challenged, especially during periods of considerable change. Some form of intrapersonal resistance by individual members of the department will develop and chairs will be in the special predicament of trying to understand these responses, which are likely to be as varied and numerous as there are members of the department. Illness and defense mechanisms are common responses. Chairs may want to seek skilled human relations training or use outside consultants to help reduce these kinds of barriers.

A helpful way of thinking about individual responses beyond defense mechanisms is informed by the work of Edgar Schein (1990). His concept of *career anchors* reflects a phenomenon that occurs within each of us that combines our sense of competence, our orientation toward our work, and the values we are most reticent to relinquish. Schein believes that most professionals are guided by one dominant anchor that "hooks" us to what is important, highly valued, and a significant part of our self-images.

Schein conducted a longitudinal study of graduates of the Sloan School of Management. He learned that the actual events of the graduates' career histories were highly variable, but the reasons they gave for their choices of work and the pattern of their feelings about their work proved to be consistent. After several hundred career-history interviews of college graduates at various career stages, he identified eight career anchor categories:

- Technical/functional competence
- General managerial competence
- Autonomy/independence
- Security/stability
- Entrepreneurial creativity
- Service/dedication to a cause
- Pure challenge
- Lifestyle

Faculty, like other professionals, have individual anchors that can reflect any of the eight identified by Schein. The socialization process of becoming an academic professional strongly supports the autonomy/independence anchor. Schein (1990, p. 26) describes this one as follows:

> Some people discover early in their working lives that they cannot stand to be bound by other people's rules, procedures, working hours, dress codes, and other norms that almost invariably arise in any kind of organization. Regardless of what they work on, such people have an overriding need to do things in their own way, at their own pace, and against their own standards. They find organizational life to be restrictive, irrational, and intrusive into their private lives; therefore, they prefer to pursue more independent careers on their own terms.

It is predictable that resistance is likely to occur when faculty with autonomy/independence career anchors are asked to be part of department or college-based change initiatives. The first response is that responding to such a change will distract them from their own agendas.

A second important intrapersonal component to resistance is the faculty members' definitions of what it means to them to be a professional (Rice, 1996). Professional identities are very complex and always involve locus-of-control issues, particularly in relationship to the origins of any change. The most likely source of intrapersonal resistance on Rice's list is the faculty's sense of time and who "owns" their time. An open dialogue about what impact the change will have on their lives allows space for faculty with internal loci of control to articulate their concerns.

Interpersonal Level of Resistance

The most common behavior manifested at the interpersonal level of resistance is conflict between individuals within the department. The determination of whether and when it is important to intervene is a judgment call. Initiating change can be the excuse for unresolved interpersonal departmental conflicts to reemerge. Engaging the peacemaker in the department may be useful. That is, a member of the department can serve as a trusted ally, reconnecting the two colleagues, often behind closed doors, by listening, supporting, nurturing, and providing third-party intervention. These informal peacemakers provide support, help reframe issues, and help colleagues understand how each party is making meaning of the incident or incidents. The chair has formal authority to do this, but other members of the department who have no differential power base can also be influential at this informal level.

When interpersonal contention exists, chairs should watch for challenges to colleagues' self-images and offer face-saving measures. Bert Brown (1977, p. 278) found that face-saving is essential when colleagues need to "resist undeserved intimidation in order to guard against the loss of self-esteem and of social approval that ordinarily results from uncontested acquiescence of such treatment." Under intimidating conditions, colleagues may profess that they will not be treated this way. Face-giving, then, is what the chair needs to do to support the faculty members' public and private images. Articulating the person's role or confirming the individual's relationship and alignment in the department are ways to do this. Similarly, identifying and supporting members who have peacemaking skills will intervene and help build department cohesiveness at the interpersonal level.

Intradepartmental Level of Resistance

Resistant behavior may well manifest at the intradepartmental level as destructive conflict, especially when it diverts attention from important issues and activities or undermines the good feelings generally found within the department. This kind of conflict can fracture cohesiveness, polarize members, and create factions. As a result, chairs will experience less cooperation, openness, and honest participation by members. Unresolved differences in the values of colleagues in the department may reemerge, get reinforced, and deepen convictions about who is right and wrong. Worrisome at this stage is behavior that may later be regretted.

Intradepartmental resistance need not be destructive, however. Such resistance can serve as a catalyst to encourage open discussion of issues, allowing for full exploration of all department members' concerns, needs, values, and interests. It can provide space for releasing emotions that do not have to result in hostile behaviors. It can increase department involvement by representing diverse interests and by defining and resolving problems as they emerge. It can also build members' cohesiveness and confidence in one another and support authentic communication among department members. For this to happen, the chair's role is critical. The chair needs to create ways that conflict can be expressed and frame resistance in catalytic ways to begin real dialogue within the group. Members of the department who have excellent process skills can help chairs accomplish this.

Escalation of Resistance to Overt Conflict

When resistance emerges, it is important to anticipate potential conflicts. Chairs should have access to a process for dealing with predictable conflicts, from the informal strategies of peacemaking, negotiation, and mediation, to more formal steps involving legal interventions. Begin by thinking carefully about such questions as, What are the issues? What is the climate? Who are the personalities involved? What are their histories with these issues?

When conflicts do arise, identify and acknowledge them. Though many people prefer an avoidance model—hoping that with enough time the conflict will just go away—it is nevertheless important for chairs to name the issues when they surface. This demonstrates that they are aware there are concerns and that they are listening and interested in being helpful. It may be important for chairs to consider asking a third party—the department peacemaker or an inside or outside facilitator, negotiator, or mediator—for help.

Even the most thoughtful chairs with the best information on how to manage resistance will sometimes find that resistance has escalated once the change initiative is well under way. When preventive measures do not work, it is time to initiate overt intervention strategies. There are predictable stages in any escalation process just as there are specific sources of the conflict. Knowing both the conflict stage and the conflict source can help in the design of an intervention.

Escalation begins with the parties involved having *misperceptions* or ascribing *attributions* that move them to a level of *commitment* to their own positions. For example, "There they go again. This administration is always imposing another thing for us to do that is just busywork! We have to stand firm."

This comment is often followed by advice about how chairs ought to proceed (or not proceed): "Let's call a meeting and develop a position paper as to why this won't work. We've already been down this path and it is high time they got off our backs!"

Such an approach can result in *entrapment,* whereby members of the department spend far too much energy, time, and resources locked into preventing the group from proceeding or analyzing the problem to justify not proceeding. The emotional response to this is some kind of *arousal* or *aggression* that is demonstrated by sarcasm, hostility, joking, or scapegoating. By now the parties feel justified in harming those who have harmed them with *reciprocal* behaviors that tend to be mean-spirited. Finally, there are usually identifiable formations of *coalitions*—we versus they.

Christopher Moore (1996) and his colleagues at CRD Associates identify five possible sources of conflict and describe behavior that may well be manifested because of escalated resistance. The five sources are *relationship* conflicts, *value* problems, *data* conflicts, *interest* problems, and *structural* conditions. As chairs listen carefully to the language and metaphors used in the stories presented by aggrieved parties, they can make a fairly good assessment about the predominant source. The usefulness of this analysis is that it allows chairs to consider a tailor-made intervention. For example, most value-based conflicts reflect differences in beliefs, cultures, and worldviews. Chairs do not need more accurate data. They need to understand how the parties are making meaning of the situation. Similarly, data conflicts often occur because of inadequate or uneven access to information. The intervention should provide pertinent data rather than focus on improving the relationship.

Intervention Strategies

At any time throughout the change initiative, resistance can emerge. It requires immediate attention or it will likely escalate quickly. Chairs have multiple options. They can avoid the entire situation (the preference of most, but usually not successful). They can use coercion, but this is likely to increase hostility dramatically within the department. Following are some useful alternatives.

Private and Informal Forms of Conflict Intervention

Private and informal strategies are too often underappreciated in terms of the quality of department maintenance work that occurs. Whenever chairs engage or support others to engage in private chats outside meeting rooms, in coalition-building over lunch, and in opportunities to vent and explain concerns, an intervention on resistance has begun. Gossip sessions in the halls and counseling behind closed office doors allow colleagues to form coalitions that often result not in conflict but rather in letting off steam. The personal skills and characteristics of informal peacemakers in the department are very useful. If such persons are respected, have a history of integrity, are transparent in their motives, and demonstrate good interpersonal and communication skills, they have the foundations for reestablishing trust and for affording members a safe environment in which to allow the truth to be told.

Whether or not the informal phase is done on an individual or small-group level, or if an invited third party facilitates a conversation or conducts a negotiation or more formal mediation, these processes provide the aggrieved party with a significant amount of self-control. It is when chairs shift to administrative decision making and use attorneys and forced coercive acts that the locus of control for the change of behavior moves from the self to another person. These tactics require very careful and thoughtful processes, and chairs will probably need assistance from university legal advisors.

Addressing conflicts early in the process, providing opportunities for problem solving, and depersonalizing the process are ways to resolve the concerns with minimal outside intervention.

Interest-Based Strategies

Some of the seminal work in dispute resolution came from the Program on Negotiation (PON) at the Harvard Law School. This program introduced the importance of helping parties reframe conflicts away from personal attacks and toward individual interests. The usefulness to chairs of this approach is a shift in thinking about the conflict. The strategies of placing blame or determining who is most powerful are used too often. The PON method attempts to reconcile each party's interests (their needs, desires, concerns, and fears). Interest-based strategies find ways to diminish power relationships and maintain the rules and order of the system, but they focus predominantly on identifying the people's interests and then moving to problem solving. Finding common ground is the essential strategy.

Overcoming Overt and Persistent Conflict

Ideally, the informal strategies will result in getting colleagues back on board and working collaboratively. Sometimes department chairs initiate change driven by a need to do business in a different way because the current way is not working. If this is the case, there are preliminary analytical steps that should be taken prior to initiating change that consider both structure and process. Structure involves the complexity of beliefs, attitudes, and images that colleagues have about one another. Chairs will need to envision some kind of structure that alters the current adversarial relationships. This could include finding ways to work collaboratively on team projects, changing workload assignments, allowing members to work independently, providing access to decision-making processes, and so forth.

Process takes into account the interests and activities of all stakeholders—both advocates and adversaries—over a long period. Christopher Mitchell (1996) identifies a number of elements essential to the treatment of conflict processes for intractable conflicts.

Although his intended audience is involved in violent and unresolved regional conflicts, such as those in Afghanistan and Burundi,
Chechnya and Sri Lanka, it is interesting to note that these keys
are quite applicable to departmental wars and long-standing conflicts that sit simmering until another opportunity—in this case,
imposed change—presents itself and brings the overt hostilities to
the foreground once again.

If there is a long history of conflict in the department, it will
be necessary for chairs to commit to a long-term process in order
for change to be lasting. This process requires patience and persistence. One important element is the involvement of all the
stakeholders. The most obvious stakeholders are the aggrieved parties; others could include students, staff, and members of other
departments affected by the conflict. A stakeholder analysis will
identify all levels involved in the department conflict. In the search
for a solution, consider structural changes such as collaborative
goal setting and strategic visioning. More and more departments
are utilizing Future Search Conferences (Emery and Purser, 1996;
Weisbord, 1993; Weisbord and Janoff, 1995) as useful multiparty
interventions that involve all stakeholders.

In addition to structural changes, many processes must take
place, at multiple levels, for overall change to be successful. Chairs
need the dean and provost or vice president on board, along with
other chairs or division heads. They need to build support from
faculty, students, and staff within the department. Because conflict
resolution is an interactive process, chairs must also take into
account the lingering pain suffered in the change process. If they
do not consider the faculty's pain, latent feelings will linger and
present themselves at other times.

Mitchell (1996) encourages us to replace the "culture of
revenge" that exists in protracted conflicts—in this case, long-
standing disputes in the department—to a "culture of reciprocity."
The existence of unresolved issues over time means that colleagues
have probably suffered greatly. This requires a level of forgiveness
as an integral part of any solution. To move to a culture of reciprocity, there must be joint acceptance of responsibility for the past
and acknowledgment of the damages and wrongs that have
occurred. This needs to be followed by mutual apologies. For genuine reconciliation to occur, it is necessary to move away from

declaring who is at fault and toward finding new and common ground.

Conflict resolution is not an end state but rather a process that is ongoing. As change initiatives get under way, conflict is likely to occur. Interventions allow chairs to move ahead with a clearer understanding that resistance and perhaps outright conflict will likely occur in the future. When colleagues have a history of resolving such conflicts and getting on the other side of hard feelings, change will seem less scary and conflict can be framed as refreshing and honest dialogue about differences. Change may be hard but it is also continual. To lessen the burdens, chairs need to reflect thoughtfully on their entire initiative and on its impact on individuals and the group at large. Engagement of all parties involved from the beginning increases success. Change can revitalize a department. Creative ways of managing apathy, resistance, and outright conflict are some of the delightful fringe benefits of the job.

References

Apps, J. *Leadership for the Emerging Age: Transforming Practice in Adult and Continuing Education*. San Francisco: Jossey-Bass, 1994.

Bellah, R. N. "Class Wars and Culture Wars in the University Today: Why We Can't Defend Ourselves." *Academe,* July–Aug. 1997, pp. 22–26.

Block, P. *Flawless Consulting*. San Diego: Learning Concepts and Universities Associates, 1981.

Bridges, W. *Transitions: Making Sense of Life's Changes*. Reading, Mass.: Addison-Wesley, 1980.

Brown, B. R. "Facing-Saving and Face-Restoration in Negotiation." In D. Druckman (ed.), *Negotiations*. Thousand Oaks, Calif.: Sage, 1977.

Chait, R. *Where Tenure Does Not Reign: Colleges with Contract Systems*. AAHE New Pathways Working Paper no. 3. Washington, D.C.: American Association for Higher Education, 1997.

Dolence, M. G., and Norris, D. M. *Transforming Higher Education: A Vision for Learning in the Twenty-First Century*. Ann Arbor, Mich.: Society for College and University Planning, 1995.

Emery, M., and Purser, R. *The Search Conference: A Powerful Method for Planning Organizational Change and Community Action*. San Francisco: Jossey-Bass, 1996.

Ferren, A. S. *Senior Faculty Considering Retirement: A Developmental and Policy Issue*. AAHE New Pathways Working Paper no. 11. Washington, D.C.: American Association for Higher Education, 1998.

Gappa, J. M. *Two Faculties or One? The Conundrum of Part-Timers in a Bifur-cated Workforce.* AAHE New Pathways Working Paper no. 6. Washington, D.C.: American Association for Higher Education, 1997.

Harvey, L., and Knight, P. *Transforming Higher Education.* Bristol, Pa.: Open University Press, 1996.

Johnson, D. W., and Johnson, F. P. *Joining Together: Group Theory and Group Skills.* (6th ed.) Needham Heights, Mass.: Allyn and Bacon, 1997.

Marchese, T. "Not-So-Distant Competitors: How New Providers Are Remaking the Postsecondary Marketplace." *AAHE Bulletin,* 1998, *59*(9), 3–7.

Marshall, E. M. *Transforming the Way We Work: The Power of the Collaborative Workplace.* New York: American Management Association, 1995.

Mitchell, C. "Conflictos Cronicos: Claves de. Tratamiento" [Intractable Conflicts: Keys to Treatment?]. Paper presented at the VI Jornadas Internacionales de Cultura y Paz, Gernika, Spain, Apr. 22–26, 1996. Available upon request from Christopher Mitchell, Institute for Conflict Analysis and Resolution, George Mason University, Fairfax, Virginia.

Moore, C. *The Mediation Process: Practical Strategies for Resolving Conflict.* (2nd ed.) San Francisco: Jossey-Bass, 1996.

Rendon, L., Hope, R., and Associates. *Educating a New Majority: Transforming America's Educational System for Diversity.* San Francisco: Jossey-Bass, 1995.

Rice, R. E. *Making a Place for the New American Scholar.* AAHE New Pathways Working Paper no. 1. Washington, D.C.: American Association for Higher Education, 1996.

Schein, E. H. *Career Anchors: Discovering Your Real Values.* San Francisco: Jossey-Bass, 1990.

Senge, P. M. *The Fifth Discipline: The Art and Practice of the Learning Organization.* New York: Doubleday, 1990.

Sikes, W. "Basic Principles of Change." In W. Sikes, A. Drexler, and J. Gant (eds.), *The Emerging Practice of Organization Development.* Alexandria, Va.: National Training Laboratories Institute for Applied Behavioral Science; and San Diego: University Associates, 1989.

Weisbord, M. R. *Discovering Common Ground: How Future Search Conferences Bring People Together to Achieve Breakthrough Innovation, Empowerment, Shared Vision, and Community Action.* San Francisco: Berrett-Koehler, 1993.

Weisbord, M. R., and Janoff, S. *Future Search: An Action Guide to Finding Common Ground in Organizations and Communities.* San Francisco: Berrett-Koehler, 1995.

Chapter Four

Transforming Departments into Productive Learning Communities

Thomas A. Angelo

Caveat lector: The references to *transformation* in the title and throughout this chapter are not made casually. Transformation denotes significant, qualitative change, not merely tinkering with, adding on, or moving bits about. Given its transformative perspective, this chapter will not be of much use to readers looking for simple, quick, and easy solutions. Instead, it is written for chairs with vision, change agents who are dissatisfied with the status quo and convinced that their departments can and indeed must provide more effective teaching, produce more and better learning, foster more meaningful scholarship, and operate in a more collaborative fashion. At the same time, it is written for chairs with high but realistic expectations, those who recognize that meaningful improvement typically requires years of well-conceived, well-led, sustained effort.

The chapter begins by arguing that many recent efforts at academic reform, though well-intentioned, have resulted in relatively little lasting improvement. It offers a diagnosis of the problem and suggests an alternative vision of academic departments as productive, scholarly learning communities. It then discusses seven transformative ideas that are central to that vision and offers seven research-based guidelines for putting these transformative ideas into practice within departments. Throughout the chapter, the emphasis is on helping chairs think differently about change so they might act more effectively to bring it about.

Since the beginnings of the current higher education reform movement in the mid-1980s, thousands of department chairs have promoted change under the banners of assessment, continuous quality improvement, active learning, strategic planning, distance education, and other related movements. Much has changed as a result of these efforts and much has improved, of course. Nonetheless, there are still surprisingly few well-documented examples of significant, lasting gains in student learning at the departmental or institutional level. Similarly, nearly thirty years of organized faculty development efforts nationwide have reaped rather modest rewards, if evidence of improved student learning is the relevant indicator.

Why haven't we made more progress? Why do the vast majority of well-intentioned change efforts seem to result in little or no long-term improvement in student learning? Peter Ewell (1997, p. 3) offers two compelling reasons: "They [the change efforts] have been implemented without a deep understanding of what 'collegiate learning' really means and the specific circumstances and strategies that are likely to promote it. They have [also] for the most part been attempted piecemeal both within and across institutions." This chapter suggests an additional reason: Most academic change efforts have not acknowledged or addressed faculty's legitimate reasons for resisting change. Simply put, many faculty fear that attempts to increase productivity and promote learning-centered practice will undermine scholarship and academic freedom, two deeply held values in academic culture.

If this diagnosis is correct, then chairs who simply rededicate themselves to working harder—doing more of the same—are unlikely to reap better outcomes than their predecessors did. Instead, it may be time to rethink—and even to replace—traditional ideas about academic change and improvement and the strategies that flow from them if we are to move from tinkering to transformation.

Key Assumptions

The remainder of this chapter rests on five key assumptions. First, it assumes that a central, if not the primary, goal of academic departments is to provide high-quality instruction—to help students learn more effectively and efficiently than they would on their own. Second, it assumes that a department will more likely succeed in providing high-quality teaching and producing high-quality learning if its students, faculty, and chair explicitly agree on that goal and work together toward realizing it. Third, it assumes that effective collaboration toward shared goals is still far from the norm in most colleges and universities. To make it so would require a transformation in the ways faculty and students think about and carry out their daily work. Fourth, it views departments as the most promising units of instructional reform and chairs as the natural leaders in transforming departmental cultures. And fifth, it asserts that academics collectively know a great deal about promoting effective teaching, learning, collaboration, and change in higher education, and that guidelines based on this knowledge from research and practice can orient our efforts toward success.

Seven Transformative Ideas

This chapter draws together a diversity of perspectives, theories, concepts, terms, and strategies from a range of literatures—among them cognitive science, higher education, psychology, and management. It distills seven *transformative ideas:* the social construction of knowledge, mental models, the learning paradigm, learning productivity, learning communities, the scholarship of teaching, and assessment. Taken seriously, these ideas have the potential to help us transform our mental models and standard practices. They can help us construct a new and transformative vision, or metaphor, of academic departments as productive, scholarly learning communities. In this vision, a productive department is one that helps students and faculty to produce demonstrably high-quality learning. The scholarly aspect of the vision is well-expressed by Ernest Boyer (1990, p. 24): "What we urgently need today is a more inclusive view of what it means to be a scholar—a recognition that knowledge is acquired through research, through synthesis, through practice, and through teaching." In a learning community, students and faculty collaborate to achieve shared, significant learning goals (Angelo, 1997, p. 3).

The Social Construction of Knowledge

Simply put, the constructivist view of learning is that humans learn not primarily by receiving and copying impressions and information from the world but rather by constructing and reconstructing our own mental conceptions *of* the world. As Jean Piaget (1975) and many others have noted, we often force and distort new information and experience to fit our existing conceptions—or reject them outright if they do not fit. Social constructivists agree that meaning is largely internally constructed, but they stress that shared meanings—socially constructed and negotiated—are necessary for human communication and society. An academic discipline, with its (largely) shared concepts, dialect, and culture, is a paramount example of socially constructed and continually reconstructed knowledge.

Constructivism is arguably the dominant model of human learning in educational psychology today. The transformative power of social constructivism inheres both in its rejection of the traditional "transmission of knowledge" and "banking" metaphors and in its assertion that learners must construct knowledge and understanding *for* themselves *through* interaction and negotiation with the world and other humans—including faculty, other students, and authors living and dead. (See Chapter Seven in Belenky, Clinchy, Goldberger, and Tarule, 1986.) For faculty, this means that students, in order to learn deeply, must become active partners in the construction of their learning. Similarly, chairs intent on change must engage their colleagues in constructing or adapting new, shared, contextually relevant concepts rather than presenting faculty with imported, prefabricated mental models for adoption.

Mental Models

In *The Fifth Discipline*, Peter Senge (1990, p. 8) defines *mental models* as "deeply ingrained assumptions, generalizations, or even pictures or images that influence how we change the world and how we take action." Senge argues that building a "learning organization" requires us to reflect on, make explicit, reconsider, and sometimes redesign these implicit mental models (1990, pp. xiv, xv).

The transformative implication here is that our existing mental models must often be socially *de*constructed before change can occur. In relation to the corporate world, Senge notes, "Many insights into new markets or outmoded organizational practices fail to get put into practice because they conflict with powerful, tacit mental models" (p. 8). For the department chair as for the classroom teacher, acknowledging and making explicit these implicit mental models is a necessary first step toward new learning. For example, many teachers and students still tacitly believe that learning occurs by transmission—thus the continuing appeal of the noninteractive lecture.

The Learning Paradigm

In a widely read and discussed article, Robert Barr and John Tagg (1995) argue that American higher education is undergoing an industrywide "paradigm shift," a transformation from a faculty-and teaching-centered model to a student-and learning-centered model. As Barr and Tagg see it, the primary purpose of higher education—and by extension, of academic departments—in this new paradigm will be to produce learning, not to provide instruction. By shifting the focus from a means (teaching) to the intended end (learning), Barr and Tagg redefine classroom teaching as only one of several possible means for producing learning.

Inherent in the learning paradigm is a radical shift from the usual quantitative, credit-hour, and head-count–based models of undergraduate education to a more qualitative competency- and mastery-based view. If institutions can be thought of as producing learning, then raising questions about their levels of learning productivity—and not just about numbers of graduates or credit units generated—begins to make sense.

Learning Productivity

The phrase *learning productivity* has multiple and overlapping meanings (Poulsen, 1995), starting with the dreaded "doing more with less." In this chapter, however, learning productivity means promoting more, deeper, and better learning with the resources available. It requires that we work more cost- and time-efficiently to the extent that we can without sacrificing learning quality. To be useful, a model of learning productivity requires that we develop clear goals, criteria, and standards for learning production, as well as means to assess and measure outputs. (See also Johnstone, 1993.)

Learning Communities

Although there are various definitions of *learning communities,* most center around a vision of faculty and students working together systematically toward shared significant academic goals. Collaboration is stressed, competition is deemphasized, and both faculty and students must take on new, often unfamiliar roles. The faculty member's primary role shifts from delivering content to designing learning environments and experiences, and to serving as coach, expert guide, and role model for learners. In a learning community, the student's role changes as well, from relatively passive observer of teaching and consumer of information to active coconstructor of knowledge and understanding (see Angelo, 1997; Cross, 1998; Gabelnick, MacGregor, Matthews, and Smith, 1990; Tinto, 1997).

The Scholarship of Teaching

Although this phrase originally referred to only one of the four categories of scholarship that Boyer (1990) promoted in *Scholarship Reconsidered* (the other three were the scholarships of discovery, of integration, and of application) it soon became shorthand for expanded and diverse visions of faculty roles. The transformative thrust of the idea comes both in valuing a broad range of activity (Rice, 1991) and in finding ways to assess and evaluate scholarly contributions that cannot simply be counted—as publications and grants usually are (Glassick, Huber, and Maeroff, 1997).

Assessment

Catherine Palomba and Trudy Banta (1999, p. 4) define assessment as "the systematic collection, review, and use of information about educational programs for the purpose of improving student learning and development." Central to this model is the belief that assumptions about learning outcomes should be empirically tested and that claims should be based on evidence. Take a look at the unsupported claims made in almost any college's or university's public relations material and you will see how far institutions are from this goal.

Guidelines for Transforming Departments into Productive Learning Communities

Drawing on the seven transformation ideas just discussed, this section offers chairs seven practical guidelines for transforming their departments into more productive scholarly learning communities and provides specific suggestions on how chairs can promote scholarly collaboration among students and faculty in order to improve learning.

GUIDELINE 1. *Build shared trust.* Begin by lowering social and interpersonal barriers to change.

Most of us learn little of positive or lasting value from people we do not trust. To form a productive departmental learning community, then, faculty must come to trust one another and their chair. The same is true of student-student and student-faculty relations. Admitting that this is often *not* the case will doubtless make many readers smile. Nonetheless, it is possible, with time and effort, to create a positive climate for improvement in most departments. Helpful resources exist. For example, in Chapters Eight and Nine of *Strengthening Departmental Leadership*, Ann Lucas (1994) provides many practical suggestions for team building and conflict management with faculty. In Chapters Three and Twenty-Two of *Teaching Tips* (1994), Wilbert McKeachie and others provide analogous ideas for building classroom community with students.

As a simple first step in building trust—before turning to problems, tasks, and issues to be resolved—take time to highlight what faculty members are already doing well and to share successful strategies. Encouraging faculty to provide an example of successful teaching allows them to present their best face and demonstrates that each faculty member is a smart person with ideas to contribute for the good of the whole.

Sharing Lessons Learned from Successful Teaching

Directions: Focus on a specific unit, lesson, concept, or skill that you teach particularly well. With that successful experience in mind, take the next five minutes to jot down answers to the following six questions. Then prepare to explain your example to your colleagues in the small group in no more than three minutes.

1. From what course is your example taken?
2. What exactly were you trying to teach? That is, what was your main teaching goal or objective?
3. How did you teach it? That is, what specifically did you do that promoted success?
4. How did you know that your students had learned it? That is, how did you assess or evaluate their achievement of your goal?
5. What did you learn, as a teacher, from the experience?
6. What "big lesson" (general principle) about effective teaching and learning does your example illustrates? Put another way, why did what you did work so well? How would you explain it to a beginning teacher?

   Once you have answered the questions, break into five- to seven-person groups. Each person should take no more than three minutes to tell his or her story, and everyone is encouraged to look for common themes among the examples. The common themes can then be mined for lessons in a whole-group discussion. With discipline, this exercise can easily be completed in a half-hour. More ambitious chairs may want to capture and document the good examples to share more widely.

Whatever the means, the point here is to start not with problems and debate but by attending to faculty members' needs to feel respected, valued, safe, and in the company of worthy, smart, well-intentioned peers.

GUIDELINE 2. *Build shared motivation.* **Collectively determine goals worth working toward and problems worth solving—and consider the likely costs and benefits.**

Once a working level of shared trust has been established, a chair can begin to develop a shared learning-improvement agenda.

Most people work more productively if they have clear, personally meaningful, reasonable goals toward which to work. Students in courses and faculty in departments accomplish more when they share some learning goals. Although both students and faculty members have goals, they can rarely articulate clearly what those goals are, they rarely know how well their goals match those of their peers, and their goals rarely focus on learning. Faculty goals often focus on what they will teach rather than on what students will learn and how, and students' goals often focus on "getting through." Thus, because goals powerfully motivate and direct behavior (Stark, Shaw, and Lowther, 1989), developing a set of shared learning goals is a logical next step in building a productive learning community.

There are many techniques for determining goals (see, for example, Palomba and Banta, 1999, Chapter Two), but the key for faculty is to find or develop some learning-related goals in common. The Teaching Goals Inventory developed by K. Patricia Cross and myself (Angelo and Cross, 1993) is a (noncopyrighted) quick, self-scorable questionnaire for helping faculty identify their most important instructional goals. An even simpler approach is to ask faculty to list two or three things they would like to learn in the coming year or that they would like to make certain the department's students learn well before graduating, and then to look for common goals across the lists. Whatever the shared goals are, to be useful they must be clear, specific, linked to a time frame, feasible, and most important, significant.

Goals are not always sufficient to motivate people to learn. After all, if the status quo is not problematic, why change? But neither do all problems provide useful starting points. As Peter Ewell (1997, p. 4) notes, "Maximum learning tends to occur when people are confronted with specific, identifiable problems that they want to solve and that are within their capacity to do so." It is critical, in any case, to connect and frame problems within a larger vision of shared goals, so that energies and resources are not dissipated in myriad efforts that add up to little or no improvement.

Here is a three-step thought exercise for faculty and students to use to identify promising problems:

1. Once you have a problem in mind, write down what you think the best solution would be.

2. Assuming that this is the solution, could the group actually implement it?

3. Even if the solution could be implemented, would the group choose to do so?

If the answer to either of the latter questions is no, it is probably not a problem worth taking on. If the answer is yes, then it is time for a cost-benefit analysis, however informal, of the proposed solution. I recommend trying to "guesstimate" the following types of costs before committing to a problem: costs in human time and effort, costs in financial resources, costs in political capital, and opportunity costs. That is, what other important problems will you not be able to tackle if you follow this path?

GUIDELINE 3. *Build a shared language.* Develop a collective understanding of new concepts (mental models) needed for transformation.

Given that most of us assume we are speaking standard English, it is surprising how often we fail to understand one another. In fact, however, even those of us who are native English speakers regularly use disciplinary *dialects,* such as environmental biology, literary studies, and social psychology, as well as unique, personal *idiolects.* Building a shared vision for transformative change requires shared mental models and shared language for describing and manipulating these models. This often requires building a shared group dialect, or at least some shared vocabulary. In other words, before faculty can collaborate productively, they must establish what they mean by key terms such as *learning, community, improvement, productivity,* and *assessment.* Taking this step will allow them to make explicit any implicit conflicts among their mental models so they can work them out.

A simple strategy for uncovering different mental models is to ask faculty to describe and define in writing what they mean by one of the terms that is central to departmental goals. Say the term is *assessment.* Collect the responses and discuss them or create a concept map from them, making visually apparent the areas of agreement and difference. You may find that to various individuals *assessment* means standardized testing, student ratings of faculty, grading, institutional research, and time wasted.

Rather than contesting these preexisting definitions, suggest the adoption of an additional, shared working definition, much like adding another meaning after a word listed in a dictionary. This add-on strategy does not require that individuals give up their existing mental models, which many will resist. Instead, it requires only that they acknowledge differences between their own models and meanings and those of the group's other members, and that they use the shared model when collaborating.

GUIDELINE 4.   *Design backward and work forward.* Work backward from the shared vision and long-term goals to determine outcomes, strategies, and activities.

Backward design simply means starting with the desired end, goal, or overall vision, then determining the related outcomes and the best means to reach them. Typical departmental curricula, for example, have been designed forward—or more accurately, built forward. That is, faculty usually decide which courses they want to teach and how they want to teach them, then pile up all their courses and try to construct a curricular rationale for the lot. Grant Wiggins and Jany McTighe (1998, p. 9) propose, as an alternative, a three-stage backward design process: "(1) Identify Desired Results, (2) Determine Acceptable Evidence, and (3) Plan Learning Experiences and Instruction." Backward design—which is basically the same model as that which underlies the assessment process and strategic planning—presupposes shared trust, goals, and mental models.

GUIDELINE 5.   *Think and act systematically.* Understand the advantages and limitations of the larger systems within which you operate, and seek connections and applications to those larger worlds.

Senge (1990, p. 68) writes, "Systems thinking is a discipline for seeing wholes. It is a framework for seeing interrelationships rather than things, for seeing patterns of change rather than static 'snapshots.'" The main point here is that all of us operate within larger contexts that affect and are often affected by our actions. It is relatively common in academic life for individuals or departments to make decisions and changes independently that end up causing ripples, or crises, throughout the larger organization. How many of us, for example, have found our daily working lives unexpectedly affected by decisions made by the campus's information technology managers?

Academic departments, of course, are systems within systems. Consequently, there are some limits to the amount and type of change an individual department can initiate or maintain. For example, few departments could, on their own, move to a totally qualitative, competency-based curriculum without dramatically compromising their students' likelihood of graduating.

Ewell (1997, p. 6) notes that systems thinking "first demands a comprehensive audit of current and contemplated policies, practices, and behaviors. It also requires a detailed analysis of current values and rewards and how these will inhibit or support desired changes." One simple way to begin this auditing process is to draw a diagram of all those within, and perhaps outside, the university with whom the department engages and to determine the likely impact of proposed changes on each entity. It is often enough to rate the impact on each person or office using a scale from −3 (large negative impact) to 0 (no impact) to +3 (large positive impact). A quick look at the score distributions and totals will help you gauge in advance the wisdom of proceeding and the likelihood of succeeding.

GUIDELINE 6. *Practice what you preach.* Use what you have learned about individual and organizational learning to inform and explain your efforts and strategies.

Those who teach by example and live their own lessons have the most lasting impact on learners. In a list of six big-ticket items that promote learning, Ewell (1997, p. 5) includes "approaches in which the faculty constructively model the learning process," such as apprenticeships and guided practice. He also notes, "Change requires people to relearn their own roles" (p. 6), suggesting that faculty cannot hope to transform the teaching and learning process for students unless they learn and transform their mental models and behavior.

Given the research on effective collegiate learning, a very fruitful endeavor for many departments would be to develop faculty members' own skills at working cooperatively toward shared aims. In other words, train faculty in group work. Research findings show that cooperative learning is one of the most effective learning approaches available. As faculty grow more skilled at effective teamwork, they not only increase their likelihood of success in transforming departments, but they also enhance their ability to help students learn to collaborate effectively.

GUIDELINE 7. *Do not assume; ask.* Make the implicit explicit. Use assessment to focus on what matters most.

At heart, assessment is not about measurement tools and analytical techniques; it is first and foremost about asking the right questions. Whatever faculty assess (evaluate, measure, judge, grade, and so forth) is what those being assessed will likely pay more attention to and do more of. Thus, assessment is a powerful tool for focusing faculty attention and efforts. But attention and effort, like time and energy, are limited resources. So faculty must be mindful to focus assessment efforts only on what matters most or they will waste those precious resources.

At the same time, the ways in which faculty and students are assessed can promote or preclude change by affecting their motivation and fortunes. Recognizing the key role of assessment in change efforts, the Carnegie Foundation for the Advancement of Teaching realized that departments and institutions interested in implementing the recommendations in Boyer's *Scholarship Reconsidered* (1990) would need a workable framework for assessing the scholarship of teaching. That framework, presented in *Scholarship Assessed* (Glassick, Huber, and Maeroff, 1997) will be of use to all change-minded chairs. Barbara Walvoord and Virginia Anderson (1998) have written a similarly useful book, *Effective Grading,* on transforming the assessment and evaluation of student work.

This takes us back to the second and fourth guidelines. Faculty must first decide what their key shared goals are, then determine how they will know if they have achieved them, and only then decide on the instructional and assessment methods and techniques to be used. Throughout the process, of course, tacit differences or misunderstandings can be uncovered by using assessment methods to ask questions that will make the implicit explicit. Once a department has developed its transformative, learning-centered vision and goals, several general assessment resources may be of use, including books by Angelo and Cross (1993); Lion Gardiner, Caitlan Anderson, and Barbara Cambridge (1997); and James Nichols (1995).

In Summary: Five Modest First Steps

All long journeys begin with a single step, the proverb reminds us. This chapter may be summarized in five first steps in the journey toward departmental transformation. These five steps mirror Senge's (1990) five disciplines: personal mastery, mental models, shared vision, team learning, and systems thinking.

First, as a step toward personal mastery, resist the understandable urge to rush the change process. It rarely works. Experience shows that most successful academic innovations have taken years to bear fruit—as many fruit trees actually do. You will save time and grief later in the process if you take time at the front end to develop shared trust, shared language, and a small number of shared goals.

Second, to explore mental models, in addition to building trust, begin by sharing examples of successful teaching experiences, definitions of meaningful learning, and examples of exemplary student work. In other words, start with success.

Third, building on the first two steps, work with faculty to develop a shared vision of what students should know and be able to do at the end of a course, a sequence, or the major, and thus make possible backward design.

Fourth, from the beginning promote group work and team learning in your department. Because the quality of group process largely determines the productivity of the group, you may need to engage an expert facilitator to teach faculty how to work together effectively as a departmental learning community before they can do the same with students.

Fifth, apply systems thinking to departmental planning. Ask how what you are envisioning fits within the institutional structure and agenda, as well as how it fits into existing systems—both faculty roles and rewards and students' academic careers.

References

Angelo, T. A. "The Campus as Learning Community: Seven Promising Shifts and Seven Powerful Levers." *AAHE Bulletin,* 1997, *49*(9), 3–6.

Angelo, T. A., and Cross, K. P. *Classroom Assessment Techniques: A Handbook for College Teachers.* (2nd ed.) San Francisco: Jossey-Bass, 1993.

Barr, R. B., and Tagg, J. "From Teaching to Learning: A New Paradigm for Undergraduate Education." *Change,* 1995, *27*(6), 12–25.

Belenky, M. F., Clinchy, B. M., Goldberger, N. R., and Tarule, J. M. *Women's Ways of Knowing: The Development of Self, Voice, and Mind.* New York: Basic Books, 1986.

Boyer, E. L. *Scholarship Reconsidered: Priorities for the Professoriate.* Princeton, N.J.: Carnegie Foundation for the Advancement of Teaching, 1990.

Cross, K. P. "Why Learning Communities? Why Now?" *About Campus,* 1998, *3*(3), 4–11.

Ewell, P. T. "Organizing for Learning: A New Imperative." *AAHE Bulletin,* 1997, *50*(4), 10–12.

Gabelnick, F., MacGregor, J., Matthews, R., and Smith, B. L. (eds.). *Learning Communities: Creating Connections Among Students, Faculty, and Disciplines.* New Directions for Teaching and Learning, no. 41. San Francisco: Jossey-Bass, 1990.

Gardiner, L. F., Anderson, C., and Cambridge, B. L. *Learning Through Assessment: A Resource Guide for Higher Education.* Washington, D.C.: American Association for Higher Education, Assessment Forum, 1997.

Glassick, C. E., Huber, M. T., and Maeroff, G. I. *Scholarship Assessed: Evaluation of the Professoriate.* San Francisco: Jossey-Bass, 1997.

Johnstone, D. B. "Enhancing the Productivity of Learning." *AAHE Bulletin,* 1993, *46*(4), 3–5.

Lucas, A. F. *Strengthening Departmental Leadership: A Team-Building Guide for Chairs in Colleges and Universities.* San Francisco: Jossey-Bass, 1994.

McKeachie, W. J., and others. *Teaching Tips: Strategies, Research, and Theory for College and University Teachers.* (9th ed.) Lexington, Mass.: Heath, 1994.

Nichols, J. O. *A Practitioner's Handbook for Institutional Effectiveness and Student Outcomes Assessment Implementation.* (3rd ed.) New York: Agathon Press, 1995.

Palomba, C. A., and Banta, T. W. *Assessment Essentials: Planning, Implementing, and Improving Assessment in Higher Education.* San Francisco: Jossey-Bass, 1999.

Piaget, J. *The Development of Thought: Equilibration of Cognitive Structures.* New York: Viking Penguin, 1975.

Poulsen, S. J. "Describing an Elephant: Specialists Explore the Meaning of Learning Productivity." *Wingspread Journal,* 1995, *17*(2), 4–6.

Rice, R. E. "The New American Scholar: Scholarship and the Purposes of the University." *Metropolitan Universities Journal,* 1991, *1*(4), 7–18.

Senge, P. M. *The Fifth Discipline: The Art and Practice of the Learning Organization.* New York: Doubleday, 1990.

Stark, J. S., Shaw, K. M., and Lowther, M. A. *Student Goals for College and Courses.* Report no. 6. Washington D.C.: School of Education and Human Development, George Washington University, 1989.

Tinto, V. "Universities as Learning Organizations." *About Campus,* 1997, *1*(6), 2–4.

Walvoord, B. E., and Anderson, V. J. *Effective Grading: A Tool for Learning and Assessment.* San Francisco: Jossey-Bass, 1998.

Wiggins, G., and McTighe, J. *Understanding by Design.* Alexandria, Va.: Association for Supervision and Curriculum Development, 1998.

Part Two

The Collaborative Role of the Chair in Departmental Change

New faculty are entering academe in larger numbers, and department chairs often assert that their arrival has revitalized the department. However, senior faculty in many comprehensive universities have frequently become disgruntled because they feel the rules of the game are changing. They had felt valued as teachers, but now the ground seems to be shifting under them. First, the role of the teacher has been redefined to that of designer of student learning, but many senior faculty are still more comfortable with the lecture approach. Second, although scholarship has been redefined so that it is much broader in scope, many senior faculty who are full professors know that if they now had to apply for promotion to the highest rank of the professoriate, they would not quality under the new norms. Consequently, they often feel demoralized and demeaned by colleagues in their own departments.

How department members function together was examined in the first four chapters of this book. Respect, recognition of contributions, and valuing each individual were discussed as essential to forming productive learning communities. The next three chapters present concrete guidelines for developing departmental structures and policies that shape the way the department views itself and sets priorities. Joint formulation of these policies by all members of the department will help new faculty become clear about what is expected of them if they are to earn tenure and promotion. Senior faculty will have an opportunity to help determine the direction the department should take if it is to move forward, and they will learn to set their own goals in ways that make sense in terms of the department's mission.

The clearer the department promotion and tenure document is, the easier will be the role of the department chair. Robert M. Diamond, in Chapter Five, describes the value and functions of this document and its role in making apparent to others in the institution how scholarship is defined by the discipline. Diamond delineates the conditions that make work scholarly. Most helpful are his guidelines on what elements departments should consider as they formulate a promotion and tenure document.

When the department's promotion and tenure document has been developed so that it is a jointly agreed-upon and clear statement, annual faculty reviews can be well conducted. Good evaluations include goal setting for the following year. When these reviews are handled effectively, faculty take charge of their own professional development. Post-tenure review then has a firm platform on which to build.

Post-tenure review, although now mandated in more than three-fifths of state colleges and universities, is still a formidable task for many chairs. Once again, this process, and the criteria to be used, needs to be developed by department faculty members who have learned to collaborate on difficult issues. The choice is not whether to use post-tenure review—that decision has already been made in more than thirty states for public institutions. The questions are, What kind of structure will be set up? What will the criteria be? Who will participate? and How will the review be implemented? In addition to performing tasks and resolving questions, teams also need to evaluate periodically how well the process is functioning, to look at what each individual expects of others on the team (including the team leader), to develop and then revisit their mission statement and strategic goals, to look at their decision-making processes, and to assume responsibility for group endeavors. These issues are presented in Chapter Six by Christine M. Licata, who is one of the leading figures in the post-tenure review movement.

"Few issues in academic life are as controversial and as potentially damaging to institutional collegiality as the faculty reward system," asserts Howard B. Altman in Chapter Seven as he looks at the department chair's role in rewarding faculty. The multifaceted aspects of reward systems and the implications for faculty are thoughtfully explored in this chapter. Whereas chairs are in the best position to evaluate a faculty member's work, and thus to be advocates for faculty as recommendations for tenure, promotion, and merit increases are made, the downside is decreased cohesiveness in the department characterized by hostility and resentment when some faculty do not receive as high merit increases as others. Altman examines the complexities for the chair of the various kinds of rewards that are important to individual faculty, the chair's role in rewarding faculty, and the role of the chair in faculty development. Finally, Altman explores the factors that will increase the credibility of the chair's recommendations as personnel decisions are considered by others in the university structure.

In reading these chapters, chairs will have an opportunity to consider the ways in which the departmental structure and policy can affect the department's functioning, and the kinds of issues that need to be explored jointly by chairs and faculty members to improve significantly the ways in which they operate together. Recommendations and guidelines for implementing these processes are included in each chapter.

Chapter Five

The Departmental Statement on Promotion and Tenure

A Key to Successful Leadership

Robert M. Diamond

Few documents will affect your role as chair more directly than the faculty reward statement of your department. Written well, it can help foster cooperation and collegiality among your faculty, articulate to others on campus the priorities of your unit, and provide guidelines for the future growth of your unit while reducing the stress associated with faculty rewards and assessment. Conversely, a poorly crafted statement can lead to conflict, confusion, a decrease in your effectiveness as an academic leader, unneeded hours of meetings, and even lawsuits. Unfortunately, until recently, well-crafted departmental promotion and tenure statements were nonexistent on most campuses. Given current pressures to safeguard fair treatment of faculty who perform different roles within an academic unit, departmental guidelines for promotion, tenure, and review are attracting renewed attention. Crafting careful and comprehensive guidelines is a challenge, but it is worth the effort. The better the statement is that your department drafts and agrees to support, the easier will be your job and the more effective you will be in the difficult and challenging position of department chair.

Functions of the Promotion and Tenure Document

A comprehensive, well-crafted faculty reward statement should be far more than a procedural guideline.

- It should clearly articulate the criteria that will be used to determine the quality of a faculty member's work, providing the candidate and faculty review committee with a clear indication of not only the review process but also the documentation that is required.
- It is the ideal vehicle for describing the mission and priorities of your department and how they relate to the mission and priorities of the institution. In the best of all worlds this statement would be the basis on which you, your unit, and your faculty would be judged.
- It is the ideal vehicle for describing to others what scholarly, professional, and creative work is in your unit and discipline. One of the major challenges you will face as chair is communicating to those in other fields this aspect of the work done in your department.
- It can play an important role in communicating to potential and new faculty members the priorities of the unit and institution. It can reduce the problems associated with new faculty expecting one thing and finding another—thus increasing the potential for long-term personal growth and productivity.

Finally, the development of the statement itself can have a number of benefits. If the process involves the entire department, drafting your guidelines can help build community and provide the basis for developing a shared vision of priorities—two essential components in a strong academic unit.

The School, College, or Institutional Statement

The departmental statement, while usually the most detailed of all promotion and tenure documents, does not exist in isolation. It must function in a cohesive way with the institutional guidelines (on larger campuses, with school or college statements, and on unionized institutions, with the collective bargaining agreement).

Such a fit with existing documents requires that before work on a department statement begins, those involved must review these other statements in detail. The other documents may provide guidelines that can be most helpful. You will also have to identify those areas in existing documents where specifics are already in place as well as topics that you will have to include as a result of omissions in the broader document. Unfortunately, these statements may also limit your ability to address issues that should be addressed or to develop guidelines that are sensitive to the unique characteristics of your department. What is most important is that the departmental statement be consistent with the school, college, and institutional statements and policies.

What to Look for

Among the issues addressed by institutional and school or college statements, such as procedures, time lines, and so forth, there are several that are most important from your perspective as department chair:

- *The recognition that there is no single definition of scholarship and that the reward system must recognize the differences among the disciplines.* Fortunately more and more institutional statements are stressing the need to be sensitive to these differences and are encouraging departments to include in their promotion and tenure documents a description of their priorities and a definition of how, in their field, scholarship, professional, and creative work are described. Although the institutional statement may include a clear statement of the common characteristics of scholarly and professional work, it should be up to your unit to decide what the range of scholarly work in your department should be. Although some disciplines are comfortable with the four forms of scholarship articulated by Ernest Boyer (1990) and R. Eugene Rice (1991), others are not. Thus this decision should be made at the department level (more on this later). In addition, it should be stressed that teaching and service activities can and should, under certain conditions, be considered scholarly, creative, and professional work.

- *Stopping the tenure clock.* One element that is often overlooked in promotion and tenure guidelines is the inclusion of a policy that permits the tenure and promotion clock to be stopped for purposes other than maternity leave or illness. There are situations in which a faculty member is given an assignment (a project, course, or curriculum design, or on many campuses, the role of department chair) that will preclude devoting the time needed to meet the requirements for tenure. In such cases, either the tenure clock must be stopped or the criteria for promotion and tenure must be modified. If such a policy does not exist at your institution, discuss with your dean, chief academic officer, or both the possibility of including it in your departmental statement.

• *A clear statement of institutional mission, vision, and priorities.* Hopefully your institution has a well-developed statement of its mission and vision. If the institutional mission statement is vague or general, be proactive and develop a clear priority statement for your unit that is approved by your dean. Statements at the departmental level are typically more specific than institutional mission or vision statements. Make sure that your departmental statement fits within the institutional mission and that the articulation between institutional mission and departmental priorities is made explicit. The departmental mission and priority statement serves as a guide for policies and procedures related to faculty rewards.

What to Include

In developing your departmental promotion and tenure guidelines, it is important to keep in mind that the audience for the document will include administrators and faculty from other disciplines who may have little understanding of what faculty in your academic area do. Your departmental guidelines provide a perfect opportunity for you to describe to others the characteristics of your discipline and the goals of your department. The writing must therefore be clean, concise, and light on disciplinary jargon. Several sections of the statement are especially important:

• *A description of scholarly, professional, and creative work in your field.* Faculty in one field often have little understanding of what faculty in other fields do, the nature of other disciplines, and the language and practices of other fields. This problem is compounded by the fact that historically, in every discipline, there is important work with all the attributes of scholarship that has not been appropriately recognized because it has not fit into the traditional mold of research and publication. In a report from the American Psychological Association, *Redefining Scholarship in Psychology: A Paradigm Shift* (1997, p. 7), a task force in the field of psychology addressed this issue:

> We value traditional research and recognize that without it there are no academic disciplines. On the other hand, scholarship can include more than the traditional definition of research, which usually means the collection of original data and publication of a peer-reviewed journal article in a recognized outlet with a high "impact" value. Our goal is to broaden the definition of scholarship so that it more accurately reflects the work of psychologists in creating, utilizing, and transforming disciplinary-based knowledge and recognizes alternative means of dissemination of the knowledge. We also want an operational definition of scholarship that is consistent with contemporary societal needs. The stakeholders in higher education—students, faculty, taxpayers, regents/trustees, state legislators, and prospective employers—want college graduates with the skills, abilities, ethics, and attitudes needed to participate in and lead our nation in a rapidly changing global context. The scholarly community must incorporate these critically important goals into academic job descriptions and the academy's hierarchy of values, or we are in danger of succeeding at scholarship narrowly defined, but failing the larger society that we serve.

Fortunately, a number of disciplines have addressed this problem directly and have developed—under a project at Syracuse University sponsored by the Pew Charitable Trusts, the Fund for the Improvement of Postsecondary Education, and the Lilly Endowment—statements that describe the range of faculty work in their fields. These statements were designed to be used by departments to develop their departmental policy guidelines. Written to be descriptive not prescriptive, the statements include a range of appropriate activities from which departments should select based on priorities at their institution. At this time, statements have been completed or are nearing completion in the following associations:

- American Academy of Religion
- American Assembly of Collegiate Schools of Business
- American Association of Colleges of Nursing
- American Association of Colleges of Teacher Education

- American Chemical Society
- American Historical Association
- American Library Association/American Council on Research Libraries
- American Psychological Association/The Society for the Teaching of Psychology
- American Society of Civil Engineers
- Association for Education in Journalism and Mass Communication
- Association for American Geographers
- Association of American Medical Colleges
- Association of College and Research Libraries
- Council of Administrators of Family and Consumer Sciences
- Council on Social Work Education
- Geological Society of America
- Joint Policy Board for Mathematics
- Modern Language Association
- National Council of Administrators of Home Economics
- National Council on Black Studies
- National Office for Arts Accreditation in Higher Education
- Landscape Architectural Accreditation Board
- National Architectural Accrediting Board
- National Association of Schools of Art and Design
- National Association of Schools of Dance
- National Association of Schools of Music
- National Association of Schools of Theater
- National Women's Study Association
- Society for College Science Teachers

If you do not have a copy of the statement from your discipline, it is available from the appropriate association. In addition, the American Association for Higher Education has published two collections of the statements under the title *The Disciplines Speak: Rewarding the Scholarly, Professional, and Creative Work of Faculty* (Diamond and Adam, 1995).

If such a statement is not available in your field, you will have to develop your departmental statement based on existing documents. (See Chapter Five in Diamond, 1999.) When speaking of definitions of scholarly work, some academic areas have been comfortable with the traditional categories—research, teaching, and service—while others have built on the work of R. Eugene Rice (1991, p. 9), who divides scholarly work into four components:

1. *The advancement of knowledge:* essentially original research
2. *The integration of knowledge:* synthesizing and reintegrating knowledge, revealing new patterns of meaning and new relationships between the parts and the whole
3. *The application of knowledge:* professional practice directly related to an individual's scholarly specialization
4. *The transformation of knowledge through teaching:* including pedagogical content knowledge and discipline-specific educational theory

It is up to you and your faculty to determine how best to describe the work of faculty in your field, and either approach presents a good place to start.

Documentation: What Makes the Work Scholarly

Even more important than the description of scholarship are the criteria that will be used to determine the quality of faculty work. Although the disciplines involved in the Syracuse Project could not agree on a definition of the term *scholarship,* they did agree that when the following six conditions exist, the work is scholarly (Diamond and Adam, 1993, p. 12):

- Requires a high level of discipline-related expertise
- Breaks new ground or is innovative
- Can be replicated
- Can be documented
- Can be peer reviewed
- Has significance or impact

In *Scholarship Assessed: Evaluation of the Professoriate,* a 1997 report from the Carnegie Foundation for the Advancement of Teaching, Charles E. Glassick, Mary Taylor Huber, and Gene I. Maeroff proposed a slightly different formulation that focuses more on the scholarly process than on the product of scholarship. Their six characteristics of scholarship include the following (p. 25):

1. Clear goals
2. Adequate preparation
3. Appropriate methods
4. Significant results
5. Effective presentation
6. Reflective critique

The best approach may in fact be a combination of the two approaches. If no existing institutional statements address the documentation issue, it will be up to your department to determine the characteristics of scholarly work that should be applied. This point is extremely important because it is these specific features on which the review committee should focus when considering the documentation a faculty member provides.

It should be mentioned that in order to achieve a campuswide quality standard, some institutions are proposing a set of characteristics to be applied across academic units. The department remains responsible for describing the range of activities that are appropriate for consideration as scholarly work.

The Professional Portfolio: What Should Be Included

Your departmental statement should describe in detail the range of materials that a candidate should submit and what should be included in a descriptive essay that provides context and cohesiveness for the selected documents. A selective portfolio is different from an accumulation of documents. Candidates are requested to document carefully three or four of their most important works so as to provide a more focused presentation of materials for review and consideration. In addition, the professional portfolio should include supportive materials on teaching and service. It should represent the full range of the work of the faculty members. As noted earlier, although some teaching- and service-related activities will meet the criteria of scholarships, others will not. These, however, should also be part of the portfolio.

The Contents of the Promotional and Tenure Guidelines

Exhibit 5.1 lists a number of items to be considered as you develop your statement. A more detailed description of the various levels of documentation, with examples from all kinds of institutions, can be found in *Aligning Faculty Rewards with Institutional Mission: Statements, Policies, and Guidelines* (Diamond, 1999).

Other Useful Resources

One of the paradoxes of higher education is that although the promotion and tenure system is vital to the health of an institution, departments and colleges tend to do very little to prepare adequately either the candidate or those who are serving on promotion and tenure committees for their roles in the process. The following practical guides were written to address this issue:

- *Preparing for Promotion and Tenure Review: A Faculty Guide* (Diamond, 1995)
- *Serving on Promotion and Tenure Committees: A Faculty Guide* (Diamond, 1994)

These guides include questions to be addressed, a number of checklists, and examples of how scholarly, professional, and creative work might be documented. Both guides are designed to facilitate the work of the candidate and the review committee.

There are several other references that you, as department chair, should have on your shelf:

- *Scholarship Assessed: Evaluation of the Professoriate* (Glassick, Huber, and Maeroff, 1997). This book presents a set of criteria for scholarly work and includes the data from a 1994 study of faculty work.
- *Scholarship Reconsidered: Priorities of the Professoriate* (Boyer, 1990). This work has provided a basis for much of the change in thinking about scholarship at colleges and universities.
- *Post-Tenure Review: Policies, Practices, Precautions* (Licata and Morreale, 1997). Post-tenure review should ideally be part of a seamless continuum of faculty development; unfortunately, in many instances it is not. This is a good place to start exploring the topic.

Exhibit 5.1. School and College Statement on Promotion and Tenure.

Considerations

1. Mission and priority statement: Rationale and how the school or college mission relates to the institutional mission.

2. Procedures and time lines: Who is responsible for what?

   • Are there procedures for early tenure decision?

   • What is the review process (that is, third year, and so forth)?

   • Can the tenure clock be stopped and under what conditions?

   • Are tenure and promotion decisions separate or are they combined?

   • Is collegiality a factor? If so, how is it defined and documented?

   • Are external reviews to be done and under what conditions? Is funding available to pay external reviewers?

3. Function or role of school or college promotion and tenure committee. Questions to consider:

   How will disciplinary differences be protected?

   How will differences in individual assignments be considered?

   How will individual strengths and interests be considered?

4. Features the committee should be looking for, that is, scholarly, professional, and creative work. What is the range of activities that if documented would meet these criteria?

5. Documenting scholarship: What will show evidence that work is scholarly, professional, and creative?

6. Documenting teaching: How will teaching be assessed? What methods will be employed (that is, review of course documents, class observations, student ratings, student performance assessment)?

7. When there are different recommendations at different levels, how will they be resolved? What is the appeal process?

Other Considerations

1. How do the recruitment, interviewing, and appointment processes for new faculty communicate the priorities of the school and college?

2. Is there a formal or informal mentoring plan for new faculty? If yes, how are assignments made?

3.   Is there a formal orientation program for new faculty?

4.   Is there a formal orientation plan for faculty serving on promotion and tenure committees?

Source: Diamond, 1999, p. 108.

• *Promotion and Tenure: Community and Socialization in the Academy* (Tierney and Bensimon, 1996). This book focuses on how faculty come to be socialized into the community of the academy. It includes many excellent references to the academic department and will sensitize you to issues that may make your life as department chair easier.

Summary

The more clearly and carefully articulated your promotion, tenure, and merit review policies and procedures are, the easier your role as department chair will be. Key among these policy statements are your department's and institution's mission and priority statements and guidelines for promotion and tenure, which define what is important to your unit and establish the criteria on which your faculty and your unit will be judged and rewarded. Such statements influence faculty priorities and go a long way in determining how they will spend their time. The better the match between your priorities for your unit and the priorities that are articulated by this document, the more effective you will be in your role as chair. It is your responsibility as chair to place the issues of documentation on the agenda of your department, to ensure that the needed scope and quality exist in the final document, and to negotiate the path of formal approval through the checkpoints in place at your institution. Clear and comprehensive guidelines can significantly reduce personnel problems, help with resource questions, and assist in negotiating departmental conflicts. In addition, the process of developing your department's statement can help build consensus and community. Strong, clearly articulated, and carefully designed guidelines will also make your job, which is extremely complex to begin with, more enjoyable and rewarding.

References

American Psychological Association. *Redefining Scholarship in Psychology: A Paradigm Shift.* Washington, D.C.: American Psychological Association, Society for the Teaching of Psychology Task Force on Defining Scholarship in Psychology, 1997.

Boyer, E. L. *Scholarship Reconsidered: Priorities for the Professoriate.* Princeton, N.J.: Carnegie Foundation for the Advancement of Teaching, 1990.

Diamond, R. M. *Serving on Promotion and Tenure Committees: A Faculty Guide.* Bolton, Mass.: Anker, 1994.

Diamond, R. M. *Preparing for Promotion and Tenure Review: A Faculty Guide.* Bolton, Mass.: Anker, 1995.

Diamond, R. M. *Aligning Faculty Rewards with Institutional Mission: Statements, Policies, and Guidelines.* Bolton, Mass.: Anker, 1999.

Diamond, R. M., and Adam, B. E. (eds.). *Recognizing Faculty Work: Reward Systems for the Year 2000.* New Directions in Higher Education, no. 81. San Francisco: Jossey-Bass, 1993.

Diamond, R. M., and Adam, B. E. (eds.). *The Disciplines Speak: Rewarding the Scholarly, Professional, and Creative Work of Faculty.* Washington, D.C.: American Association for Higher Education, 1995.

Glassick, C. E., Huber, M. T., and Maeroff, G. I. *Scholarship Assessed: Evaluation of the Professoriate.* San Francisco: Jossey-Bass, 1997.

Licata, C. M., and Morreale, J. C. *Post-Tenure Review: Policies, Practices, and Precautions.* AAHE New Pathways Working Paper no. 12. Washington, D.C.: American Association for Higher Education, 1997.

Rice, R. E. "The New American Scholar: Scholarship and the Purposes of the University." *Metropolitan Universities Journal,* 1991, *1*(4), 7–18.

Tierney, W. S., and Bensimon, E. M. *Promotion and Tenure: Community and Socialization in the Academy.* Albany: State University of New York Press, 1996.

Chapter Six

Post-Tenure Review

Christine M. Licata

Systematic evaluation of tenured faculty, commonly referred to today as post-tenure review, is one of the most controversial policy initiatives to emerge from the current national accountability movement. It is also one of the most significant new challenges facing department chairs. On many campuses, the mere mention of post-tenure review has spawned misunderstanding and conflicted expectations precisely because of what the term conveys. At first blush for some, the term is interpreted to mean a re-tenuring process; for others it suggests that there is a lack of performance evaluation beyond the award of tenure. Both conclusions are inaccurate, but they underlie some of the acrimony and uninformed debate on the issue. In fact, some campuses—including the University of Kentucky's College of Arts and Sciences, Arizona State University, Indiana University–Purdue University-Indianapolis, the State University System of Florida, and the University of Wisconsin—have sought other, less misleading terms to describe what is intended today to be a systematic process to review the performance and professional career goals of senior faculty, with the objective of improvement, enrichment, or both.

Even when described in this way, the initial reaction of faculty and chairs usually reflects some measure of defensiveness directed at why post-tenure review is now needed, and suspicion about

Information contained in the section on models and practices and in the discussion of Question 4 draws heavily on research conducted in collaboration with Joseph C. Morreale and reported in Licata and Morreale, 1997.

whether it will actually benefit individuals and institutions. On some campuses, such conversations are openly hostile and emotionally charged. Yet when campus discussions unfold, if they are framed carefully and involve a broad range of constituents, resistance can be reduced through reasoned consideration of the problems to be addressed and the academic tradition and values to be maintained. Chairs bring a critical voice to this examining dialogue because of their unique role with faculty and their knowledge of the existing institutional evaluation culture. Because of this voice, chairs are often able to pose the right questions and help strike the right balance.

As a group, chairs have a vested interest in how faculty performance issues, productivity measures, and vitality concerns are addressed, because in very practical terms chairs play pivotal formal and informal roles in giving meaning to these concerns and are most frequently entrusted to carry out and track accountability strategies.

So, although some chairs are apprehensive and perplexed about the idea of post-tenure review, others view it as no more than an additional component of the accountability culture and no less than another option within the evaluation continuum. When viewed in this way, post-tenure review is regarded as the extension of good human resource management that is begun the day a faculty member is hired. Carefully written evaluations by the chair, as described in Chapter Five by Robert Diamond, are important to both pre- and post-tenure faculty career development. Chairs can certainly be faculty advocates, but they are also in the best position to evaluate the work of colleagues. Because of this, the chair is rarely excluded from post-tenure review and is frequently the nexus for actions resulting from these reviews.

Taking faculty evaluation seriously and performing this responsibility well is not an easy assignment by any means, especially because most chairs are not selected or elected because of their evaluation expertise. This is a sphere that requires training and practice. For many chairs, faculty evaluation is the aspect of the job that carries the least amount of excitement. Yet because the trend toward requiring formal review of tenured faculty is on the rise and continues to catch the eye of legislatures, citizen-regents, and the public, chairs must be increasingly knowledgeable of underlying issues, aware of the inherent challenges, and proficient in the myriad skills that evaluation and development of senior faculty require.

Contemporary Context

Originally introduced by the National Commission on Higher Education (1982) as a critical issue to be faced by higher education, post-tenure practices have received focused and intense attention over the past five years. Although a few institutions reported early involvement with periodic review of senior faculty, the California State University system was the first large state system to endorse publicly and require such a review using a five-year cycle (Licata, 1986). Nevertheless, the work done by the American Association for Higher Education (AAHE) New Pathways I and II Projects indicates that post-tenure review activity is principally being pursued in the public sector and presently reported in well over thirty states (Miller, Licata, and Kavanagh, 1999; Licata and Morreale, 1997). (The states in which system policies have been established, where they are currently under consideration, or where selected state institutions have adopted post-tenure review are Alaska, Arkansas, Arizona, California, Colorado, Connecticut, Florida, Georgia, Hawaii, Idaho, Indiana, Iowa, Kansas, Kentucky, Louisiana, Maine, Maryland, Massachusetts, Minnesota, Missouri, Montana, Nebraska, New Jersey, New Mexico, North Carolina, North Dakota, Oklahoma, Oregon, Rhode Island, South Carolina, South Dakota, Texas, Utah, Virginia, Washington, West Virginia, Wisconsin.) Also, the impetus for this policy directive comes primarily from external calls for accountability, institutional needs for adaptability, the uncapping of mandatory retirement, and a general societal demand for assurance that tenure promotes quality and does not protect faculty from reasonable evaluation and opportunities for improvement.

What is different about the accountability climate of today is that it has taken on a new meaning—that is, it has the flavor of a higher order of accountability. Peter Ewell (1997) correctly characterizes this as a change from how we do our business to how well we do our business to what we actually do in our business. Fortunately, in some states the movement to abolish tenure has been interrupted, at least for the time being, by placing post-tenure review on the table as a way to persuade tenure critics that tenure itself is not the problem but reasonable oversight of the tenure covenant is. Public discourse about the meaning of tenure has actually helped to clarify what the proper role of senior faculty evaluation and development is within the context of traditional tenure tenets.

Consider the counsel of Donald Kennedy (1997, p. 22) on the fulfillment of academic duty: "That is a very large responsibility, and it is the essence of academic duty. But the instructions for fulfilling it are left vague even for the prospective practitioners. For this reason confusion and misunderstanding often prevail inside academia, and the public is equally confused. Thus understanding the professional responsibilities that constitute academic duty is important for those who will fulfill them. But it is equally important that they be understood in the same way by the public." Examination of academic duty helps deans, chairs, and faculty identify what tenure guarantees and what tenure demands, both on the part of the individual and on the part of the institution. Tenure then begins to be seen as a covenant that guarantees academic freedom and that appropriates due process protections but also requires sustained individual responsibility, quality performance, and continued professional development.

Evaluation of tenured faculty has always been allowable under the tenure doctrine. However, systematic efforts to enhance faculty vitality and demonstrate accountability, while not overly controversial in theory, are affiliated ideas that have required time to develop and pressure to adopt.

The original statement of Committee A of the American Association of University Professors (AAUP, 1983) on periodic review of tenured faculty was ultimately approved by the association's Committee on Academic Freedom and Tenure and included in their published policy documents and reports in 1995. The statement referred to such review as an overly burdensome process that would reap scant benefits, incur unacceptable costs, and erode collegial relationships. AAUP believed that post-tenure review was unnecessary in view of the long-standing review practices already in place and warned that it would be used to weaken tenure. Recently, however, given that post-tenure review policy mandates are on the rise, AAUP (1998) has weighed in again on the issue by reaffirming its 1983 position that post-tenure reviews should not be used as grounds for dismissal or disciplinary sanctions, and by advancing minimum standards of good practice to be used by faculty at institutions where post-tenure review is being considered. AAUP's standards suggest, among other things, that such a review should be a product of mutual negotiation, developmental in purpose, and supported by resources.

Models and Practices

Within most systems and on most campuses, the goals for post-tenure review include broad objectives, all aimed at fostering sustained quality and bringing focused attention to long-term career development. These objectives include:

1. Comprehensive assessment of performance utilizing multiple sources of evidence and reflective self-reporting
2. Significant involvement of peers in review and opportunity for collective departmental perspectives
3. Establishment of professional goals and consideration of career direction
4. Provision of meaningful feedback and opportunity for improvement, if necessary

With those objectives in mind, most policies established today include elements of both summative (consequential) and formative (developmental) evaluation. Rarely does one see a policy that is solely one or the other. Most plans, in fact, include provisions for improvement planning when performance warrants it, as well as opportunities for professional development planning for those who wish to redirect energies, refuel, or retool.

In general, external constituencies hold a more punitive view about what outcome should be expected from these reviews. A perception exists in boardrooms and legislative chambers that large numbers of tenured faculty are underperforming and need to be disciplined or dismissed as a result of these reviews. Based on experience to date, however, it is doubtful that these unrealistic and misinformed expectations about faculty performance will ever be realized through implementation of these review policies.

The question asked most frequently by faculty is, How does post-tenure review differ from the annual salary or merit review? Before responding, one must first recognize the institutional goals and identified needs in the area of senior faculty evaluation and development. Only after institutions agree on the problem or need that post-tenure review seeks to address can they rightfully determine if the annual review process is designed or could be redesigned to address that problem or need and whether current objectives suffice. A few institutions have chosen to modify their annual review process so that it effectively incorporates the four objectives mentioned earlier. However, the vast majority of institutions have elected to use either a periodic review for all tenured faculty or a selective review for some—both of which build on the annual review and do not replace it.

Periodic Review for All Tenured Faculty

This type of review places all tenured faculty on a periodic review cycle, usually five to seven years, and is designed to provide a prospective and retrospective assessment of how well faculty members meet institutional obligations and what developmental needs and goals emerge along the way. This approach is found within the state university systems of California, Florida, Hawaii, Georgia, Maryland, North Carolina, North Dakota, and Wisconsin, and at the University of Texas and the University of Iowa.

The most compelling rationale for adopting this approach is the belief that annual reviews tend to be pro forma and do not provide the opportunity for a focused conversation over time about career direction, career emphasis, and vitality preservation. Supporters of this approach point out that all faculty can benefit from a broadly focused assessment by peers that includes an opportunity to affirm the value of individual contributions, and that serious performance problems, if they exist, can best be addressed through a process that maximizes the annual review and complements it with a more comprehensive periodic review. Some argue, however, that requiring a comprehensive review of all faculty taxes the system in an inordinate fashion by placing additional responsibilities on peers and administrators, similar to the time and effort invested in tenure review. Some also assert that creating another review does nothing to fix the initial problems associated with the annual review or to alleviate factors that contribute to its perfunctory nature. Unfortunately, the actual costs of this approach are unknown at this point.

Selective Review for Some Tenured Faculty

Some institutions decide to use the annual review as a triggering agent for more intensive review when a person's overall performance or performance in the primary area of responsibility is judged to be below standard. The triggering can occur after one substandard review or after a number of consecutive unsatisfactory reviews. Once the problem has been identified, the faculty member moves to a more concentrated review in which peers render a judgment and recommendation regarding performance and needed improvement. Public institutions within Arizona, Colorado, and Montana; most public institutions in the commonwealth of Virginia; and Texas A&M University follow this model.

This approach places great importance on the annual review and is supported by some universities because it appears on the surface to require fewer resources and is seen as a way to maximize existing evaluation systems. The downside, however, is the perception that there is a second class of faculty—those whose performance is somehow deficient and requires institutional monitoring.

Choosing an appropriate model is a crucial step, but equally compelling is the need to establish a credible context within which the policy can be framed. Establishing such a context involves creating a set of design principles and unifying features. It is important for chairs to note that regardless of which of these two approaches is chosen, the annual review usually serves as either the foundation for a triggered approach or as a form of evidence in a periodic process. Because of this, the importance of the annual review is heightened and so too is the pressure on the chair to perform this evaluation duty with skill and fairness.

Design Principles and Features

Institutions that are successful in moving post-tenure review from concept to implementation share certain design principles in common. Exhibit 6.1 outlines these principles.

Exhibit 6.1. Post-Tenure Review Unifying Principles.

Principle	Description
Partnership in design	Faculty and administrators, including bargaining agents where appropriate, work together to design the process and the procedures. Without this collaboration, policy development is usually doomed.
Academic freedom	Protection of this cherished principle is affirmed and preserved in policy language.
Clearly articulated statement of purpose	Policy purpose and expected outcomes are communicated very clearly and articulated well with other institutional systems such as annual merit process, workload guidelines, and program review.
Flexibility and decentralized control	The local organizational unit is provided with reasonable latitude in determining specific review components, including criteria, standards, and sources of data.
Performance threshold	Establishing clear standards for satisfactory professional performance is critical, as is assuring that everyone will be judged fairly by peers, students, and administrators against such standards. Generally, performance standards follow established tenure criteria, promotion-in-rank criteria, or a collegewide or departmentally established threshold for satisfactory performance.
Accurate, defensible and useful information	Data collected and methods used to assess faculty performance are reliable and objective.
Peer review	Peers play a significant role in the review, usually in the form of a committee. Committee size and composition are influenced by overall unit scale. Usually the committee is composed of three to five members and selection is made by appointment or election. Often an existing committee (such as the department personnel committee) is used or a new committee is constituted, with representation from within and outside the immediate organizational unit.

Principle	Description
Professional development plan	A prospective professional development plan is highlighted and is used for a benchmark and referent for career transition planning and improvement.
Feedback	Documented feedback on both performance and professional development goals is usually provided to faculty through a meeting.
Institutional support	Support for faculty-development resources is evident and a priority within the institutional environment.
Reinforcement of evaluation skills	Opportunities to improve evaluation skills are provided to chairs and peers.

Source: Data based on research conducted by Licata and Morreale, 1997, and reprinted from Licata, 1998, p. 5.

In addition to these design principles, another key consideration on the minds of internal and external stakeholders centers squarely on process results and outcomes. Expected results vary from policy to policy but usually contain the following: provisions for affirmation of satisfactory performance, development of required improvement plan and guidance on length of time during which improvement should occur, development of a professional career plan, differentiated work assignments based on skills and interest, and sanctions (both required and allowed) when progress on performance is not forthcoming despite reasonable time and resources devoted to it. These sanctions typically include salary freezes, salary decreases, demotion, reallocation of support for research, probation, suspension, initiation of dismissal-for-cause proceedings, or some combination.

The experiences of department chairs in related types of assessment activities (including pre-tenure evaluation, merit compensation review, program review, sabbatical review, endowed chair review, and the like) can be extremely useful within this new post-tenure evaluation framework, In fact, there are several key stages in the process of policy development where chairs can make significant contributions.

Practical Recommendations for Chairs

What strategies can chairs use to help ensure that discussion related to post-tenure faculty review and development is informed by accurate information, enriched by pursuit of appropriate questions, and enabled by reasonable recommendations?

First, a bit of context. In principle, most chairs support the need for faculty review and development. What is particularly difficult and anguishing for chairs is that they perceive a lack of clarity and comfort about their role with tenured senior faculty. Chairs often wonder whether their actions to remediate and reward will be supported up the line and whether executive management has the resolve and commitment to follow through in difficult circumstances. In other words, chairs want to know whether they will be left holding the bag in situations where faculty improvement is needed. When chairs are left in the middle, the evaluation and development climate suffers dramatically because it is viewed as ineffective. Further, because chairs and faculty by and large believe that the academic vineyards should continually harvest high-quality fruit, they become demoralized by a lack of support.

Why is the institutional evaluation ethos so important? First, it establishes the context within which discussions of post-tenure review are initiated—it is where you begin; and second, the evaluation patina affects the tenor of discussions and the types of queries that result after the first post-tenure review breath is taken—it is where you must move from.

Developing a Sound Policy

Before a sound post-tenure review policy can be shaped, chairs should influence the policy discussion and direction in very specific ways.

• *Know the facts and don't be afraid to share them.* Chairs share a strategic position when it comes to knowing the successes and failures of the university system in motivating, rewarding, and enhancing the vitality of faculty. This leadership perspective is important because post-tenure review is one component of the overall university evaluation, development, and reward structure.

It must be viewed systemically, and chairs can stress the importance of taking such a systems view. In addition, chairs have easier access to and keener interest in information on the national accountability scene than most faculty do. Several recent publications and national reports (see Exhibit 6.2) examine current issues dealing with changing faculty roles, rewards, and review structures. It is incumbent upon departmental leaders to help enlarge and enrich campus dialogue by bringing these national perspectives into conversations, thus taking a broader view of the external and internal forces affecting the academy, including data and demographics on senior faculty. For example, demographic data show that even though 58 percent of all faculty are full-time, the number of full-time senior faculty is even higher (61 percent of full-time faculty are senior in rank); the average age is fifty-one, but by the year 2000, 50 percent of all faculty will be fifty-five or older. Also important is the fact that only 19.5 percent of this cohort group is predicted to retire in 2000 (National Center for Education Statistics, 1993). So, in effect, faculty who will be entrusted to lead and transform their institutions to meet the challenges of the next decade are tenured and quite secure in their positions and their careers.

These data help institutions focus on why they should be concerned about the energy and contributions of senior faculty. It is therefore important that policy deliberations benefit from a fuller understanding of the distinctive needs, concerns, and perspectives of senior faculty. Let us be clear. It is not a question of whether senior faculty are less productive or whether the quality of their work diminishes with age. Recent research has strongly challenged these presumptions and rendered them unfounded. It is really a matter of how changing priorities and interests that naturally accompany the progression of an individual's career can best be recognized, respected, and responded to. Daniel Wheeler and B. J. Wheeler (1994, p. 94) discuss career progression in a very practical way: "When a faculty member begins a new position, energy and drive can seem unlimited. Career concerns and getting ahead seem more important than anything else. As time progresses and many faculty begin to address personal issues, their priorities can change. Personal issues may include personal health

**Exhibit 6.2. Important Senior Faculty Resource Information
for Academic Leaders.**

American Association of State Colleges and Universities. *Facing Change:
Building the Faculty of the Future.* Washington, D.C.: American Association of State Colleges and Universities, 1999.

Bennett, J. B. *Collegial Professionalism: The Academy, Individualism and the
Common Good.* Phoenix: Oryx Press, 1998.

Bland, C. J., and Bergquist, W. H. *The Vitality of Senior Faculty Members:
Snow on the Roof—Fire in the Furnace.* ASHE-ERIC Higher Education
Report, vol. 25, no. 7. Washington, D.C.: George Washington University, Graduate School of Education and Human Development,
1997.

Chan, S. S., and Burton, J. "Faculty Vitality in the Comprehensive University: Changing Context and Concerns." *Research in Higher Education,* 1995, 36(2), 219–234.

Crawley, A. L. "Senior Faculty Renewal at Research Universities: Implications for Academic Policy Development." *Innovative Higher Education,* 1995, *20*(2), 71–94.

Diamond, R M., and Adam, B. E. *Changing Priorities at Research Universities: 1991–1996.* Syracuse: Center for Institutional Development,
1998.

Diamond, R. M., and Adam, B. E. (eds.). *Reorganizing Faculty Work: Reward
Systems for the Year 2000.* New Directions for Higher Education Series,
no. 81. San Francisco: Jossey-Bass, 1993.

Ferren, Ann S. *Senior Faculty Considering Retirement: A Developmental and
Policy Issue.* New Pathways Project Working Paper no. 11. Washington, D.C.: American Association for Higher Education, 1998.

Finkelstein, M. J., Seal, R. K., and Schuster, J. H. *The New Academic Generation: A Profession in Transformation.* Baltimore: Johns Hopkins University Press, 1998.

Glassick, C. E., Huber, M. T., and Maeroff, G. I. *Scholarship Assessed: Evaluation of the Professoriate.* San Francisco: Jossey-Bass, 1997.

Guskin, A. E. "Restructuring the Role of Faculty." *Change,* 1994, *26*(5),
16–25.

Heydinger, R., and Simsek, H. *An Agenda for Reshaping Faculty Productivity.* Denver, Colo.: State Higher Education Executive Officers and
Education Commission of the States, 1992.

Hubbard, G., and Atkins, S. "The Professor as a Person: The Role of Faculty Well-Being in Faculty Development." *Innovative Higher Education,* 1995, *20*(2), 117–128.

Karpiak, I. E. "University Professors at Mid-Life: Being a Part of . . . But Feeling Apart." In D. DeZure (ed.), *To Improve the Academy,* 1997, *16,* 21–40.

Licata, C. M., and Morreale, J. C. *Post-Tenure Review: Policies, Practices, and Precautions.* New Pathways Project Working Paper no. 12. Washington, D.C.: American Association for Higher Education, 1997.

Plater, W. "Using Tenure: Citizenship Within the New Academic Workforce." *American Behavioral Scientist,* 1998, 41(5), 680–715.

Rice, R. E. *Making a Place for the New American Scholar.* New Pathways Project Working Paper no. 1. Washington, D.C.: American Association for Higher Education, 1996.

Richards, M. P. "Preparing for Post-Tenure Review." *The Department Chair,* 1997, *8*(2), 2–3.

Sid W. Richardson Foundation Forum Task Force on Restructuring the University Reward System. *A Report by the Sid W. Richardson Foundation.* Fort Worth, Tex.: Sid W. Richardson Foundation Forum, 1997.

Tierney, W. G., and Bensimon, E. M. *Promotion and Tenure: Community and Socialization in the Academy.* Albany: State University of New York Press, 1996.

---

problems or those of the family or teenage children or aging parents whose demands seem relentless. . . . The efforts of the faculty member to address the myriad of professional and personal issues may sap the energy necessary to concentrate on one's career." Anyone in a chair position for any length of time has probably experienced this career progression with one or more department members. As the age of the professorate increases, so too will this progression. Carole Bland and William Bergquist (1997) suggest that recognizing changing needs and interests within the post-tenure review context can make it possible to facilitate the meshing of institutional and individual forms of vitality, and promote an integrated institutional approach that attends to the "varied needs of faculty at different stages of their careers and development" (p. 89). These same authors provide excellent background information on adult development theory, career development theory, and the factors that influence a productive campus environment. This information is invaluable in policy formation and implementation efforts.

Knowing the specific facts about the national post-tenure review movement is also important. Questions such as Why us? and Why now? are more easily answered when one is armed with solid data about reported models, practices, and results.

• *Be prepared for faculty questions and concerns.* Policy formulation is usually preceded by a series of questions that help identify areas of confusion and points of contention. Chairs should be ready for these frequently posed questions and help institutional leaders plan thoughtful responses. These questions will undoubtably include the following:

• What problem are we trying to address?
• Who is framing the problem?
• Why don't existing institutional policies handle the problem in an appropriate and fair way?
• If post-tenure review is established

   Will the annual review process be modified?

   With modifications, could the annual review process
      take care of the problem?

• What models and approaches carry the most benefit and the least burden?
• What will be the benefits of post-tenure review and what will be the costs?
• How does the institution currently judge the effectiveness of the annual review process and how will it judge the effectiveness of the post-tenure review process?

Working from these questions leads to one of the most important steps: obtaining clarity of purpose.

• *Be clear about policy objectives.* The purpose of post-tenure review must be clear because form follows function. Lack of clarity leads to conflicted expectations and unachieveable results. Chairs know this both intuitively and experientially from working with their faculty on other matters. The communication challenge most frequently faced by all academic administrators is being clear about what their message conveys.

It is through the process of clarifying policy purpose that discussions arise related to whether a policy can and should contain developmental or summative outcomes. If the policy goal has been identified and the other questions have been answered, this discussion is made much easier.

• *Invite broad participation.* People support what they help create. This fundamental notion is exceedingly important when laying the foundation for what has the potential to be a contentious policy initiative. Bringing all stakeholders to the table requires patience and time—but both are well spent when you get to the implementation stages. Chairs usually have good experience in strategies for consensus building, and this is a time to use them.

• *Establish underlying principles.* As described earlier, most post-tenure review plans today are guided by well-established policy principles. Institutions should review these carefully and also consider AAUP's guiding parameters before crafting policy that considers individual mission and context. Chairs can be helpful in reminding formulation groups of the importance of sticking to underlying purpose and principles.

• *Keep the process simple.* Much can be said about the virtue of design simplicity. But for those entrusted to oversee and carry out policy, the importance of keeping policy guidelines simple yet clear cannot be overstated. Many campuses elect to give great flexibility and autonomy to academic units to work out the myriad procedural details that are necessary. When this happens, chairs usually commandeer these unit deliberations and must be the voice of reason in the promotion of manageable procedures. Often the chair can save a unit from imposing overly elaborate review processes by asking, What is the opportunity cost here? In other words, what are the costs and benefits of this procedure versus another procedure?

Reports from the field (such as Licata and Morreale, 1997) indicate that one problem frequently noted by administrators is the amount of time, resources, and faculty documentation that are applied to the process. Chairs must continually drive this home and help colleagues resist the tendency to design overly burdensome and resource-intensive procedures. The resources issue should be raised in early discussion stages in order to explore what is reasonable, feasible, and affordable. Taxing an already overtaxed system will only result in general dissatisfaction. Reasonableness must prevail and chairs should insist on practicing a standard of reasonableness as policy and procedures are developed. The question that chairs must bring to the table is, How can we accomplish this goal and conserve scarce resources in doing so?

Insuring Reasonable Implementation

The devil is in the details. In post-tenure review, implementation details make or break a successful policy. Chairs and other academic administrators should devote copious attention to this aspect of the process and in particular strive to ensure that the following occur:

• *Reasonable implementation time lines are adopted.* Experience suggests that institutions underestimate the time required to implement a new policy. This has especially been true when academic units have been asked to determine the composition and selection method for peer reviewers, to define a satisfactory performance threshold within each performance criterion, to establish ranges of expected time lines for improvement plans, and to allocate reasonable funds for system implementation and faculty development. Chairs should not underestimate start-up time. The chair's rule of thumb on this might be two for one—that is, it takes twice as long as you think it will!

• *The review process is not made into a mystery.* Orienting departmental faculty to the purposes, procedures, and expected outcomes of post-tenure review is an essential leadership responsibility. Chairs are in the best position either to take this on themselves within the department or to persuade the dean to take it on. Ignorance is not bliss when it comes to the need for faculty to understand what the review entails and what the various roles of self, peers, students, administrators, and external evaluators are in the process.

Promoting Effective Outcomes

Efficient policy implementation is only one part of the equation. The other part is effective policy outcomes. Assessment of post-tenure review outcomes is a necessary component of policy over-sight. A concern expressed frequently is, How effective is the insti-tution's policy in achieving the desired objective and how do we know? This question must be answered because eventually it leads to policy modification and improvement.

Chairs and deans should maintain careful records of the process and keep an ear to the wall in order to assess faculty reaction and opinion regarding benefit. Some results will be in-dividually qualitative—that is, one-on-one celebration of accom-plishment, one-on-one discussion about career direction or redirection, and one-on-one candid yet sensitive feedback regard-ing needs for retooling or improvement. Although these results are primarily qualitative, they are as important as the quantitative data collected on faculty who receive a merit increment, are pro-moted, elect early retirement, or need improvement. Unfortu-nately, until very recently very little energy was directed toward reporting any of these results. However, efforts are now under way on some campuses and in some systems (for example, at the Uni-versity of Hawaii-Manoa, the Virginia System of Higher Education, and the University of Arizona and Arizona State Universities) to collect and report outcome data. Chairs and deans must be cham-pions of the need to do so. The AAHE New Pathways II Project has initiated a study of policy outcomes within institutional settings where such policies have existed for a number of years. The results of this study will help shed needed light on how well post-tenure review is working.

Challenges and Opportunities for Chairs

Post-tenure faculty evaluation poses challenges and opportunities for chairs. Good leadership entails understanding the needs and interests of departmental faculty, turning those interests into actions that benefit the individual and the department, and find-ing effective ways to reward faculty. Chairs, however, usually find this aspect of their work the most time-consuming and at times the most frustrating. Being the first among peers does not carry with it any preordained knowledge about performance evaluation. In fact, most chairs come to the job with little or no training or expe-rience in this area. Added to this lack of training is the additional conundrum that a rotating chair appointment presents—namely, that the person you evaluate this year may be evaluating you next year. Such factors can lead to casual and perfunctory faculty review strategies. Chairs must be willing to provide honest and fair evaluation. And as Deryl Leaming (1998, p. 39) cautions, "If you are unwilling to provide faculty members with honest appraisals of their work when it is less than satisfactory, you will face even more difficult tasks down the road." Most important, faculty need to have confidence in their chair's ability, preparation, and knowledge in the evaluation arena.

Overcoming Resistance

One challenge that chairs should expect to encounter is faculty resistance to the notion of additional performance review. As one faculty member put it, "If chairs and deans would just do to what they get paid to do, post-tenure review wouldn't be necessary." This riveting criticism of the system gives one pause, particularly if one is in an administrative position. Chairs can be an influential force in helping quiet some of this criticism by encouraging faculty to become involved in campus deliberations and policy development. Faculty fear that administrators will use post-tenure review to get rid of unconventional and controversial faculty. The best way to assuage this concern is for chairs to remain fair-minded, even-handed, and dedicated to promoting sound evaluation that includes appeal and due process procedures.

Nurturing Faculty Vitality

For many institutions, post-tenure review is not a new idea. In fact, if chairs already use techniques proven to increase faculty productivity (Bland and Bergquist, 1997), motivate special groups of faculty (Lucas, 1994), and enhance faculty performance through goal setting (Locke and Latham, 1990; Lucas, 1994), their responsibility for post-tenure review is only an extension of these practices. Most post-tenure faculty appreciate the opportunity to be involved in goal-setting interviews where annual goals are established, progress is monitored, and outcomes are evaluated. Ann

Lucas (1994) reminds us that such goal setting provides an opportunity to celebrate accomplishments, share failures with a supportive listener, and devote energy to thinking about life direction, and it enhances both accountability and productivity. Chairs must be supportive in the process and also forthcoming when goals are not met—a challenging role combination.

A promising option for chairs is to engage departmental faculty in assessment of individual vitality and well-being in order to better target areas where faculty development might be beneficial. Charles Walker (1998) of the Department of Psychology, St. Bonaventure University, offers such a faculty vitality profile inventory that can be self-administered and used as a catalyst to initiate conversations between the chair and the faculty member about future direction and development needs. The profile ties nine vitality dimensions to nineteen related faculty development practices and activities that can be useful as a first step in career planning. Conclusions from a study of the experiences of midcareer and older faculty (Karpiak, 1997) also offer useful recommendations for faculty development personnel and administrators to improve work-related aspects of faculty life. The study provides chairs with a unique construct for understanding how faculty react to career pressures and administrative expectations and how the university environment and the individual's perception of the environment help shape actions, expressions, and responses.

Promoting Departmental Mission and Collectivity

To survive or thrive as a department is the invitation extended to chairs when the option is given to insert departmental mission and collective responsibility for individual performance into the post-tenure review process. This can be a powerful opportunity. Jon Wergin (1994) describes it as a "culture of collective responsibility" (p. 16). He concludes that such notions gain meaning only when attention is paid to how to structure, evaluate, and reward work that reinforces the department as a "community of interest" (p. 16). Assessment thus becomes more collectively focused. "As assessment becomes more group focused, however, institutions will need to develop standards more appropriate to judging worth—that is,

standards to assess not only the inherent quality of faculty contributions but also the worth of these contributions to the mission of
the department and the institution" (p. 10).

An interesting example in practice of how to blend and reward
individual faculty work with departmental and university needs is
found in the annual departmental evaluation used in the College
of Liberal Arts and Sciences at Arizona State University. This evaluation demonstrates how units are contributing to student learning, enhancing and maintaining academic quality and reputation,
and attending to the various needs within the institution. Through
this annual unit evaluation, the department chair can "negotiate
faculty work assignments and responsibilities in ways that maximize
what is accomplished collectively by the faculty of a unit" (Krahenbuhl, 1998, p. 24). An example of this evaluation template is available at <http://www.aahe.org/change/nd98_table.htm>.

Supporting Peer Involvement

Departmental and institutional citizenship are grounded in strong
traditions of shared governance and peer review. Although the
level and scope of peer participation in departmental governance
and personnel processes vary greatly by institutional type and campus culture, most post-tenure review policies place peers in a pivotal judgment role with their colleagues. For many individuals, this
role carries a new sphere of influence that can be problematic. The
fear, of course, is that departmental reviewers, not wishing to bring
retribution on themselves, will go along to get along. This is one
reason that peer committees often involve members outside the
department and in some cases external to the campus. Regardless
of the composition of peer review committees, chairs can help
place this additional call to duty in the proper perspective by recognizing and rewarding reviewer competence as an important contribution to the department and university.

Common Concerns

Important concerns and lingering questions remain unanswered
in current post-tenure review conversations. As institutions
become more grounded in the post-tenure review process and

more experienced with procedures, anecdotal reporting will be replaced by systematic data. Nevertheless, preliminary review of more than one hundred policies and interviews of selected administrators within nine institutional settings suggest that most issues center on questions of impact, cost, and benefit (Licata and Morreale, 1997). Following is a discussion of these questions and the issues surrounding them.

QUESTION 1: What impact does post-tenure review have on the skills and preparation needed by chairs?

The adoption of post-tenure review ratchets up the array of skills that chairs must possess in order to move comfortably between the job of coach and judge, mediator and initiator, counselor and decision maker. As discussed earlier, chairs cannot be expected to know how to negotiate the boundaries of post-tenure review with faculty without additional opportunities for skill development. Chairs must be proactive in requesting support for training and development, especially in the following areas:

• *Writing factual and fair performance appraisals that are based on sound evaluation principles and solid evidence.* It is daunting for chairs to frame evaluation comments appropriately so they are based in fact and provide concrete examples of why a particular performance rating is assigned. Avoiding surprises in the appraisal is always good practice. Delivering positive evaluations is not the challenge; delivering bad news positively is. The tendency is either to write in an overly broad manner and skirt the tough performance issues or to focus only on the negative without also providing a balanced assessment of areas of strength. There are strategies, however, that can be acquired for saying what you mean without making the review characteristic of "vanilla" rhetoric or "red" journalism. Equity and objectivity must be the overriding principles.

When a chair faces a difficult evaluation situation, it often helps to seek help from another chair or someone at the next level in the administrative line. Asking for an objective review of the appraisal and for constructive comments on both content and tone can save one from painful exchanges later on. Faculty normally recoil at negative appraisals because of the inflammatory language used and the subjective comments made, not because of the performance in question. When the same points are made but expressed in an objective fashion, the reaction is less combative. Use facts and examples to illustrate your point and remember that judging how much to write is an acquired skill. Writing too much can be just as deadly as parsing words. Some excellent faculty evaluation resources are available today that chairs should have at their fingertips. See Exhibit 6.3 for a list of these materials. Chairs must remind themselves that the way in which one becomes skilled in writing appraisals is through on-the-job training and trial and error. Working smarter with appraisals is almost always a learned activity. As Mark Twain reportedly said, "Good judgment comes from experience. Experience comes from making bad judgments."

• *Counseling and negotiating strategies.* Chairs often do not possess the interpersonal toolbox that is essential in managing a range of conversations with senior faculty. Moving conversations with faculty about teaching performance, research productivity, or career direction into a productive, noncontentious dialogue can be aided by working from a firm base of knowledge and understanding about communication techniques and motivation theory. Again, these skills can be learned and practiced through simulation and scenario-based training, and through reference to good resource material. Faculty should leave an appraisal meeting with a clear understanding of how their performance has met or failed to meet clearly stated criteria and standards, and of what is expected of them in the future.

• *Strategic thinking and reality shaping.* In a departmental environment where differentiated work assignments and collaborative departmental planning are goals, the chair must continually think in a collective way, find occasions to bolster faculty enthusiasm, and offer new opportunities to contribute. Chairs accomplish this best when they have been exposed to strategic thinking and know how to introduce change into departmental affairs.

• *Assertiveness and sensitivity.* When it comes to evaluation, knowing when to "hold" and when to "fold" is not easy. It is helpful for chairs to have experience in role-play using assertive strategies and appraisal questioning techniques. Anticipating faculty reaction and being ready to respond in a sensitive but direct way to concerns, complaints, and questions are essential. So often what

Exhibit 6.3. Faculty Evaluation Resources.

Arreola, R. *Developing a Comprehensive Faculty Evaluation System: A Handbook for College Faculty and Administrators on Designing and Operating a Comprehensive Faculty Evaluation System.* Boston, Mass.: Anker, 1995. Chapters Eight and Thirteen provide information on evaluation protocol and issues in operating a faculty evaluation system.

Braskamp, L. A., and Ory, J. C. *Assessing Faculty Work: Enhancing Individual and Institutional Performance.* San Francisco: Jossey-Bass, 1994. Chapters Four through Eight discuss how to define and set performance expectations, collect and organize evidence, and prepare written assessment.

Centra, J. A. *Reflective Faculty Evaluation: Enhancing Teaching and Determining Faculty Effectiveness.* San Francisco: Jossey-Bass, 1993. Chapter Six focuses on the role of the department chair.

Hickson, M. III, and Stacks, D. W. *Effective Communication for Academic Chairs.* Albany: State University of New York Press, 1992. Chapters Six and Seven provide communication strategies for assessing performance and handling the appraisal interview.

Higgerson, M. L. *Communication Skills for Department Chairs.* Bolton, Mass.: Anker, 1996. Chapters Four, Five, and Six discuss techniques for conducting performance counseling, managing conflict, and implementing change.

Higgerson, M. L. "Strategies for Conducting Face-to-Face Faculty Evaluation." *The Department Chair,* 1994, *5*(2), 2–4. This article discusses steps chairs can take to make evaluation interviews productive and positive.

Lucas, A. F. *Strengthening Departmental Leadership.* San Francisco: Jossey-Bass, 1994. Chapters Seven through Ten discuss goal setting as a strategy to enhance faculty performance, ways to motivate faculty, and techniques for career planning.

Maurer, R. *Feedback Toolkit: Sixteen Tools for Better Communication in the Workplace.* Portland, Oreg.: Productivity Press, 1994. Part Two provides strategies for providing feedback on performance.

Murray, J. P. *Successful Faculty Development and Evaluation.* ASHE-ERIC Higher Education Report no. 8. Washington, D.C.: George Washington University, Graduate School of Education and Human Development, 1995. A section on the role of the department chair in the evaluation process provides recommendations for preparing reviews.

Murray, J. W., Jr. "Evaluating Faculty Performance: Will Your Decisions Withstand Challenge?" *Department Chair,* Fall 1998, pp. 1, 19, 20. This article provides advice on how to avoid legal pitfalls in evaluation.

we think we said in an appraisal interview and what the faculty member heard us say are not always perfectly synchronized. This problem is improved by scenario building in a training environment or even by practicing appraisal feedback with a colleague. It is imperative for chairs to focus on the performance itself and not on the individual's personality. It is important to provide specific examples of performance that characterize the evaluation criteria under discussion. Discussion of future goals, needed improvement, or ways to help ensure success is best cast by the chair in a suggestive fashion by posing questions that invite reflection and suggestions for change.

- *Understanding legal parameters.* Last but certainly not least is the need for chairs to understand the ramifications of improper evaluation. Knowledge is worth an ounce of prevention in such situations. Larry Braskamp and John Ory (1994) propose that chairs keep the following legal guidance in mind: base judgments on performance-related criteria and related evidence, rely on assessment of specific work outcomes, use individual rather than relative judgments of faculty work, provide honest feedback, and respect faculty appeal processes.

QUESTION 2: What impact does post-tenure review have on the method of chair selection?

The utility and viability of the rotating chair position are quickly coming under scrutiny. Post-tenure review is but one of the myriad additional responsibilities being placed on the shoulders of first-line academic leaders today. Readiness to accept a chair position requires more than merely interest and colleague support. In addition to responding to new external and legal mandates that affect departmental affairs, chairs are required to provide leadership in institutional planning for productivity, workload policies, outcomes assessment, merit-based compensation, program review, diversity, performance-based funding—and the agenda continues. All of these issues call into question whether longevity and continuity of effective departmental leadership are preferred to moving the responsibility along—a time-honored ritual of shared governance. Clearly because most post-tenure review policies integrate the annual review and long-term career planning into the process of chair leadership, stability and ability at the chair level seem critical coins of the realm. Today's pressures and expectations require a different skill subset than was necessary twenty years ago. The rotating chair position needs to be seriously reconsidered.

QUESTION 3: What procedural challenges can department chairs and members of peer review committees expect to confront as they work within the post-tenure evaluation environment?

Peer reviewers often feel just as ill-prepared for this new role with senior colleagues as chairs do. First, training is required in order for peer reviewers to understand the review process fully and to feel confident in providing appropriate constructive feedback on performance. Second, vagueness of criteria and standards often plagues reviewers and forces departments and units to revisit carefully the performance threshold that has been established. Third, the amount of documentation that faculty choose to provide can be excessive, unnecessary, and burdensome. When documentation begins to become excessive, additional documentation guidelines are warranted. Fourth, department chairs and deans struggle with what constitutes a reasonable improvement plan and what institutional resources should be provided. Establishing information sharing and providing guidance on these issues is essential. Variability in policy implementation across units within the same institution can be expected. However, the attention to detail provided is usually in direct proportion to the quality of departmental leadership.

QUESTION 4: What results can campuses expect from such a process?

By far the most significant question, and one that begs another, is, Why should we invest in such a review and what will be gained? Most reporting on this question is informal and anecdotal. It is incumbent on chairs to help their institution seek answers to this question and to help track the impact from such reviews on individual faculty contributions and on departmental productivity and accomplishment. When interviewed, senior academic officers from the University of Hawaii, the University of Maine, the University of Montana, and the California State University system generally agreed that the process was a "qualified success." Some referred to innovations that faculty members would not have initiated had they not been encouraged to do so through the review. Others talked about improvements that occurred in teaching and scholarship. Others pointed to the impact on retirements that the process seemed to generate because certain faculty preferred to retire rather than undergo a review or develop an improvement plan. No one talked about the occurrence of dismissal-for-cause.

After one review cycle at Georgia State University, administrators offer the following initial observations on the process (Abdelal, Blumenfeld, Crimmins, and Dressel, 1997, pp. 66–68):

> With very few exceptions faculty have entered into the conferences in a positive spirit. Those who were already doing well were gratified to have their accomplishments acknowledged and for that reason were all the more eager to identify ways to maintain or improve their performance. Faculty with difficulties were usually already aware of the problem and welcomed suggested remedies. Even those with serious deficiencies responded well to constructive ideas. Deans and department chairs were often able to show their good faith by providing incentives for improvement, and it was usually possible to reconfigure a faculty member's workload to take advantage of the things he or she does best. . . . Where faculty had not published in many years or simply had no enthusiasm for doing so, it was often possible to establish a mutually agreeable arrangement whereby the person would teach more and perhaps make a more substantial service contribution. . . . In fact, we were surprised at how willingly faculty enter into cooperative arrangements that we realign their talents and interests with department expectations. . . . Of course, the extent to which all such reconfigurations are possible depends upon departmental goals and the mix of faculty talents and other resources. Nevertheless, we have so far failed to encounter a case in which we were unable to devise a reasonable plan for improving faculty performance.

Only the University of Hawaii has tracked results over a ten-year period and is now able to show that of the 1,079 evaluations conducted, only ninety-two (8 percent) cases of deficiencies were noted and in these cases no dismissals occurred. The overwhelming majority of faculty satisfactorily completed the required development plan and 30 percent chose retirement (Des Jarlais and Wood, 1998).

Careful assessment of results and outcomes is needed in order to know exactly what the benefits are, what costs are incurred, and what changes are necessary. Chairs and faculty must be willing to participate in this tracking and provide their individual assessment regarding benefit and burden.

Although this need for tracking and improvement constitutes yet another responsibility for the chair to execute, the chair's voice is needed to create a more complete narrative regarding outcomes. On some campuses, attempts to seek out answers to these questions have been viewed as proof that policymakers are interested in knowing only what punitive sanctions have occurred. This view is shortsighted and, when carried to an extreme, constitutes a serious barrier for institutional attempts to assess overall policy effectiveness and impact. In this era of outcomes assessment, institutions must take the lead in reporting how well post-tenure efforts are progressing—even if the information is not what external stakeholders expect.

QUESTION 5: Does post-tenure review negatively affect department life and collegiality, obstruct pursuit of controversial research, or threaten academic freedom?

Many concerns and reservations of this sort have been voiced. However, no data exist to substantiate these reservations. Because most post-tenure review policies contain provisions that safeguard academic freedom and due process, one can only surmise that these concerns are grounded in fear rather than fact.

Another apprehension often expressed by faculty is that these reviews will be used by administration to make life uncomfortable for nonconforming and outspoken senior faculty. Again, no report from the field corroborates this apprehension. Chairs obviously play a large part in making sure that this does not happen.

QUESTION 6: Does post-tenure review have unintended consequences?

Although it is too early to know, early signals point to the fact that these reviews do in fact seem to produce unintended results. First, some campuses are finding that their system infrastructure is not fully developed and supportive of these reviews. For example, workload policy, reward structures, program review procedures, faculty development resources, and chairperson training—all necessary backbone to the process—are not always appropriately in place or linked to post-tenure review. When this happens, post-tenure review is hampered and unable to realize its full potential. Consequentially, in many instances institutions find themselves backpedaling to develop these affiliated processes before they can fully implement post-tenure review.

The effects of post-tenure review on pre-tenure review, recruitment of new faculty, and the method of chair selection remain unknown. Although it seems plausible that these processes will be affected in some way by increased attention to senior faculty review and development, the nature of the effect is still questionable. A trend that is finding increasing support is the push to have chairs and deans routinely evaluated by their own peers on their administrative work and in their faculty capacity. Some practitioners believe that this evaluation of administrators is a direct result of post-tenure faculty activities.

QUESTION 7: Will post-tenure review keep tenure viable?

No one really knows the answer to this frequently asked query. Some observers believe that if punitive results are not forthcoming, policymakers and taxpayers will interpret the reviews as nothing more than window dressing and subsequently unleash further attacks on tenure. Some question whether tenure is worth saving and seriously wonder if term contracts that are linked to effective evaluation and that assure academic freedom would be a better appointment option for the new millennium. Bland and Bergquist (1997) caution institutions that they should not evaluate what they cannot develop. And in that spirit, others proffer that if institutions use the post-tenure review platform to educate constituent groups about the meaning and measure of faculty worklife—thus advancing the position that the test of post-tenure review's success lies not in the number of faculty exiting a campus but rather in the ability of the process to promote positively an evaluation and development culture that attends to the vitality of faculty of all ranks—then policy effectiveness will be realized.

Herein lies the challenge as well as the opportunity—to provide stakeholders with a realistic lens through which to view tenure and accountability as mutually reinforcing principles, to reverse the misperception that the academic vineyards are replete with disengaged senior faculty, and to create a fluid evaluation and development continuum that keeps career renewal and professional vitality at the forefront.

Conclusion

As this chapter has pointed out, accountability as a higher education imperative, has brought issues of post-tenure faculty productivity and vitality to national attention. Although many universities and colleges are making major shifts in their missions, organizational structures, pedagogical approaches, and applications for technology, the faculty who are expected to implement these bold new ventures and select successors to move their institutions into the next century are entering the later years of their own careers. Career planning, if a part of post-tenure review, can have positive consequences for faculty and their departments with respect to how they address needs for career resiliency, reflection, redirection, and late-career transition planning. Post-tenure review can be a way of helping to maintain the vitality of our senior faculty.

Chairs play the most critical role of any institutional group in the eventual success of this policy mandate because they are essential agents for any type of change within higher education. Meaningful and effective senior faculty review and development are impossible without the engagement and support of department chairs. Quietly waiting it out or riding the tide on this policy issue just will not cut it for those in a department leadership role. All signs point to increased evaluation and development activity; all indications are that chairs, deans, and peers are central to successful policy implementation.

As Victor Hugo, reportedly, so provocatively reminds us, "Where the telescope ends, the microscope begins. Which of the two has the grander view." When it comes to various issues affecting faculty worklife, such as post-tenure review, chairs must be up to the task of helping faculty to see both views and find grandeur in them. This type of review is but another lens that helps reflective focus spawn self-directed change.

Chairs who use post-tenure faculty review as an opportunity to merge peer review with peer accountability and who stress the importance of individual faculty contributions to the collective departmental effort can actually manage the review process in a way that leads to individual and departmental renewal and excellence—goals well worthy of a chair's time, talent, and tenacity.

References

Abdelal, A., Blumenfeld, D., Crimmins, T., and Dressel, P. "Integrating Accountability Systems and Reward Structures." *Metropolitan Universities,* 1997, 7(4), pp. 61–73.

American Association of University Professors. "On Periodic Evaluation of Tenured Faculty."*Academe,* Nov.–Dec. 1983, 1a–14a.

American Association of University Professors. "On Periodic Evaluation of Tenured Faculty." *AAUP Policy Documents and Reports.* Washington, D.C.: American Association of University Professors, 1995.

American Association of University Professors. *Post-Tenure Review: An AAUP Response.* Washington, D.C.: American Association of University Professors, 1998.

Bland, C. J., and Bergquist, W. H. *The Vitality of Senior Faculty Members: Snow on the Roof, Fire in the Furnace.* ASHE-ERIC Higher Education Report, vol. 25, no. 7. Washington, D.C.: George Washington University Graduate School of Education and Human Development, 1997.

Braskamp, L. A., and Ory, J. C. *Assessing Faculty Work.* San Francisco: Jossey-Bass, 1994.

Des Jarlais, C., and Wood, M. "Post-Tenure Review Case Study: Ten Years of Faculty Evaluation at the University of Hawaii at Manoa." Presentation at the American Association for Higher Education Faculty Roles and Rewards Conference, Orlando, Florida, Jan. 31, 1998.

Ewell, P. T. "Assessment and Accountability in a Second Decade: New Looks or Same Old Stories?" Plenary address at the AAHE Assessment Forum, Miami Beach, Florida, June 1997.

Karpiak, I. E. "University Professors at Mid-Life: Being a Part of . . . . but Feeling Apart." In D. DeZure (ed.), *To Improve the Academy,* 1997, *16,* 21–40.

Kennedy, D. *Academic Duty.* Cambridge, Mass.: Harvard University Press, 1997.

Krahenbuhl, G. S. "Faculty Work: Integrating Responsibilities and Institutional Needs." *Change,* 1998, *30*(6), 18–25.

Leaming, D. *Academic Leadership: A Practical Guide to Chairing the Department*. Boston, Mass.: Anker, 1998.

Licata, C. M. *Post-Tenure Faculty Evaluation: Threat or Opportunity?* ASHE-ERIC Higher Education Report no. 1. Washington, D.C.: Association for the Study of Higher Education and Educational Resources Information Center, 1986.

Licata, C. M. "Post-Tenure Review: At the Crossroads of Accountability and Opportunity." *AAHE Bulletin*, 1998, *50* (10), 3–6.

Licata, C. M., and Morreale, J. C. *Post-Tenure Review: Policies, Practices, and Precautions*. AAHE New Pathways Working Paper no. 12. Washington, D.C.: American Association for Higher Education, 1997.

Locke, E. A., and Latham, G. P. *A Theory of Goal Setting and Task Performance*. Englewood Cliffs, N.J.: Prentice Hall, 1990.

Lucas, A. F. *Strengthening Departmental Leadership: A Team-Building Guide for Chairs in Colleges and Universities*. San Francisco: Jossey-Bass, 1994.

Miller, M. A., Licata, C. M., and Kavanagh, F. "The Status of Post-Tenure Review Within State Systems of Higher Education." Washington, D.C.: American Association for Higher Education, 1999.

National Center for Education Statistics. *National Study of Postsecondary Faculty*. Washington, D.C.: U.S. Department of Education, Office of Educational Research and Improvement, 1993.

National Commission on Higher Education. *To Strengthen Quality in Higher Education*. Washington, D.C.: American Council on Education, 1982.(ED 226 646)

Walker, C. *Faculty Vitality Profile Inventory*. Available from Dr. Charles Walker, Department of Psychology, St. Bonaventure University, St. Bonaventure, NY 14778. Phone (716) 375–2498; e-mail <cwalker@sbu.edu>.

Wergin, J. F. *The Collaborative Department: How Five Campuses Are Inching Toward Cultures of Collective Responsibility*. Washington, D.C.: American Association for Higher Education, Forum on Faculty Roles and Rewards, 1994.

Wheeler, D. W., and Wheeler, B. J. "Mentoring Faculty in Midcareer Issues." In M. A. Wunsch (ed.), *Mentoring Revisited: Making an Impact on Individuals and Institutions*. New Directions for Teaching and Learning, no. 57. San Francisco: Jossey-Bass, 1994.

Chapter Seven

Strengthening the Departmental Voice in the Faculty Reward System

Howard B. Altman

Few issues in academic life are as controversial and as potentially damaging to institutional collegiality as the faculty reward system. How a college or university chooses to recognize and reward faculty performance and what kinds of performance are deemed meritorious are divisive decisions that may pit faculty members against administrators and, not infrequently, faculty members against one another.

In many institutions, it is the department chair's responsibility to write the departmental recommendations for (or against) each faculty member's tenure, promotion, and salary adjustment. (In many departments, recommendations are also written by promotion and tenure committees.) These recommendations are in turn reviewed and either supported or overturned by collegewide committees, deans, and chief academic officers. Thus the chair is positioned squarely in the midst of the fray; his or her decisions can catch flak from all directions!

Defining Faculty Rewards

The concept of faculty reward is multifaceted. Indeed, what is valued as a reward differs for different people in academe. The three major categories of faculty rewards are usually *tenure, promotion in rank,* and *salary increases.* But changing institutional policies have modified these categories. (Some alternative categories are explored later in the chapter.) Not all higher education institutions award tenure to faculty, and increasingly colleges and universities are exploring alternatives to traditional faculty tenure. Promotion in rank is still viewed by most faculty as a significant institutional reward, but for the vast majority of faculty, promotion happens at most twice in a career that may span thirty years or more. Even the concept of a salary increase is no longer simple. Different policies may exist at unionized and nonunionized campuses. Some institutions award salary increments across the board, others mix across the board increases with merit raises, and still others provide raises solely for meritorious performance (Altman and Spangehl, 1991).

When salary increments in a department are distributed across the board, every faculty member usually gets either the same dollar amount or the same percentage increase. A less democratic variation is to use different percentage increases for faculty of different ranks, such as 5 percent for full professors, 4.5 percent for associate professors, and 4 percent for assistant professors, in an effort to enhance the salaries of more senior members of the department; or 5 percent for assistant professors, 4.5 percent for associate professors, and 4 percent for full professors, in an effort to compress salary ranges within the department. Across the board increases reflect the conviction that all members of the department are valued and are making contributions to the institution, as well as the reality that general environmental factors (such as inflation, increased medical costs, and so on) affect all faculty similarly.

In the approach labeled *across the board plus merit,* some (but not necessarily all) faculty in the department receive supplemental money (beyond the amount awarded across the board) for performance judged meritorious in some way. The underlying assumption here is that all faculty are valuable members of the department but some have demonstrated a higher level of performance (however defined) than their colleagues and deserve additional compensation in recognition of their outstanding work.

In the merit-only approach, some departmental faculty receive a salary increase while others receive nothing. Increases are based solely on the evaluation of performance according to predetermined and known criteria. Different systems exist. At some institutions, the *merit pool* may be allocated differentially (that is, high-, medium-, or low-merit increases) based on the assessment of faculty performance; at other institutions, all those who are awarded merit increments may receive the same number of dollars.

For the department chair, the need to recommend or allocate merit raises to faculty results in both potential problems and potential benefits. Among the potential problems are the following:

• *Decline in faculty collegiality.* A merit-based system may promote the hostility of faculty toward the institution, the department, colleagues, or the department chair. Jealousy and aggravated feelings are not uncommon among those denied a merit increase. Feelings of isolation and ostracism have been reported by those who receive increases far beyond those awarded to previously friendly colleagues.

• *Suboptimalization.* A merit-based system may promote individual faculty goals over departmental ones (or departmental goals over institutional ones). There is a danger that faculty may choose to do their own thing, thereby fragmenting and weakening the department as a unit.

• *Increased faculty stress and burnout.* The feeling that one's work is not highly valued by the department (when explicitly confirmed by a small merit increase or none at all) can be very stressful for a faculty member and can contribute to diminished vitality, productivity, and effectiveness.

• *Reward of short-term accomplishments over long-term efforts.* Merit systems usually reward what is accomplished within a specific time frame. If that frame is short—such as one or two academic years— such systems tend to discriminate against larger faculty projects that may take five years or more to bring to fruition (such as researching and writing a book).

• *Difficulty of quantifying behaviors that differ qualitatively.* Much of what faculty do is difficult to quantify, yet most merit systems require numerical measures of performance. How does the value of published articles compare, for example, with changing the lives of students? Chairs need to be aware that quantification does not, in itself, guarantee either accuracy or fairness.

Merit-only systems have potential benefits for the department as well:

- *Increased faculty productivity in those areas rewarded by the merit system.* Chairs need to be aware that there is likely to be a clear positive relationship between faculty rewards and faculty productivity, but only in those areas of faculty performance explicitly rewarded by the system. The corollary is obvious: those aspects of performance that are not rewarded may receive diminished attention from faculty.

- *Clear public articulation of institutional and departmental expectations for faculty activity.* The implementation of a merit pay policy presupposes that what constitutes expected and acceptable faculty performance has been determined and has been made known to and accepted by the faculty whose lives are affected by the policy. Much more is said later in the chapter about the need for explicit expectation statements for all departmental faculty.

- *Decision making about faculty salary levels may be done more carefully, more systematically, and more objectively.* Normally, a well-designed merit policy eliminates capricious and ad hominem decision making about faculty salaries. Objectivity and fairness are enhanced because the criteria, standards, procedures, and appropriate evidence to be used in judging performance have been clarified and understood.

To make the issue of faculty rewards even thornier, the purpose of rewarding faculty performance is not always clear. Is the justification for a salary increase a *judgment* on a faculty member's past performance, or an *incentive* to shape future performance? If the department chair wishes to provide an incentive to encourage a faculty member's efforts in teaching, for example, will an additional $500 raise (or any nominal sum, for that matter) serve that purpose? Clearly a new assistant professor, struggling to establish himself or herself financially at a starting salary, will view an additional $500 with considerably more gratitude than will a tenured full professor at the top of the salary schedule. For the latter, a far more effective incentive may be $500 worth of secretarial assistance or $500 worth of instructional software.

These suggested alternative rewards are two of a longer list of options that institutions and departments may wish to consider. Some of the ideas that follow may be far more appealing to some faculty than the current institutional approach to salary increases;

some may be viewed by other faculty as unattractive, heretical, or ridiculous:

- *Bonus to salary.* One-time-only bonuses, which do not become part of the person's base salary, may be a desirable reward, especially when the bonus is substantially larger than regular raises.
- *Reserved parking space.* There is never enough (or enough close-by) parking for faculty. On many campuses, a reserved space, if you can get one, may cost hundreds of dollars each year. If each department were given one close-by reserved parking space that could be awarded to a faculty member each year based on criteria determined by the department as a whole, and if a sign could be posted over that space identifying Professor X as the award winner for that year, the honoree would doubtless be far more grateful than he or she would be if given the cost of the reserved space as a salary increase.
- *Travel support.* Almost all departments have inadequate resources to cover all the requests for faculty professional travel. If compensated professional travel were viewed as a reward rather than as a perquisite of faculty status, those faculty awarded travel funds could be given what they need rather than only a portion of what they need to cover the costs of the trip. The types of compensated professional travel could be broadened to include faculty development travel, research travel (where one is not presenting a paper at a conference), and program development travel, as well as the more typical conference presentation travel.
- *Clerical assistance.* Most departments need more secretarial help. An award to a faculty member of, say, $1,000 in clerical support time, could make the difference between finishing a major project in the current academic year and not finishing it until the next year. Many faculty would find such an award extremely beneficial.
- *Research assistance.* What if a department pooled its student research assistants and awarded the use of an individual assistant to a faculty member for the duration of his or her research project, rather than assigning assistants to specific faculty members for the entire academic year? Assistants would be applied for and awarded competitively rather than on the basis of faculty seniority.
- *Released time.* This is one of the most costly rewards that a department can provide to a faculty member. Released time need not always be *from* teaching *for* research, but could be from any

aspect of faculty life for any other aspect. Released time should be viewed as a reward and should be awarded competitively.

• *Reassignment sabbatical.* A faculty member who wishes to teach in another field for which there is a need in the institution might be given a reassignment sabbatical to prepare himself or herself for the new teaching assignment. Such a sabbatical might be spent pursuing further formal graduate study at one's own or another higher education institution.

• *Faculty development sabbatical.* Sabbaticals can be awarded not only for research purposes but also to allow faculty to upgrade their skills and competencies, develop new curricula, learn new pedagogical techniques, and the like.

• *Office space.* What if the best office in the department (other than the chair's)—the one with the best view or the biggest floor space or the best furniture or location or office equipment—were awarded each year to the outstanding faculty member in that department (based on criteria the department collectively determined)? A plaque on the office door would identify this as the office of Professor X, outstanding professor for that academic year.

• *Scheduling and staffing of courses.* Courses belong to the department that offers them; they are not the private property of individual faculty members who happen to teach them. Chairs can use their authority to schedule and staff the department's courses as a way of rewarding deserving faculty, by assigning them the courses and schedules that best meet their needs and interests.

What many of these alternative rewards have in common is that they are likely to strengthen the institutional loyalty of recipient faculty, unlike traditional salary increases, which probably have little if any impact on a faculty member's loyalty to the institution (Altman, 1994).

As was suggested earlier, what is considered a reward may differ for faculty from different disciplines, for tenured and untenured faculty, for full-time and adjunct faculty, for junior and senior faculty, for male faculty and female faculty, for newcomers to the institution and those with fifteen or more years of service.

Tenure, promotion, and salary increases are all extrinsic faculty rewards. Many academics have argued, however, that it is the intrinsic rewards of faculty life that are the most satisfying. The opportunity to work with talented students, to spend one's time in intellectual pursuits, to have a flexible schedule, to be able to pursue research in one's areas of interest—these all contribute to the motivation to become and remain a faculty member. And while department chairs frequently play a major role in extrinsic faculty rewards, their ability to influence intrinsic satisfactions is also significant. By having some of the alternative rewards just suggested at their disposal, chairs may strengthen their impact on faculty members' intrinsic satisfactions.

Rethinking the Faculty Reward System

Traditionally, departmental decisions to reward faculty performance took a one-size-fits-all approach. Depending on the mission of the institution and department, there were similar, if not identical, role expectations for all faculty in the department. In research universities, all faculty were expected to be heavily involved in publishing, grantsmanship, or both. In teaching institutions, all faculty were expected to commit significant amounts of professional time to teaching and possibly also to advising. All faculty were evaluated on the extent to which they met these expectations. Although the one-size-fits-all approach simplified the evaluative work of the chair, it also led to considerable dissatisfaction and demoralization among those faculty whose own goals differed from those of the department or institution on which they were evaluated.

With the publication in 1990 of Ernest L. Boyer's important book *Scholarship Reconsidered: Priorities of the Professoriate* (1990), many higher education institutions began to take another look at the one-size-fits-all model for faculty careers. As Boyer wrote, "Today, on campuses across the nation, there is a recognition that the faculty reward system does not match the full range of academic functions and that professors are often caught between competing obligations. In response, there is a lively and growing discussion about how faculty should, in fact, spend their time" (p. 1). He goes on to pose the question, "Can we, in fact, have a higher education system in this country that includes multiple models of success?" (p. 2). The answer suggested by Boyer and by R. Eugene Rice (1996), whose research at the Carnegie Foundation for the Advancement of Teaching provided the theoretical underpinnings for this book, is an unequivocal yes.

As is well known today, Boyer's thesis is that all faculty in all types of higher education institutions need to be researchers and should be evaluated on and rewarded for the quality of their scholarship. But faculty scholarship should no longer be seen as a monolithic activity the sole objective of which is the generation and dissemination of new knowledge in the field. Although the generation of knowledge that advances a field may be a legitimate goal for some faculty at some institutions, equally legitimate goals in faculty scholarship lead to quite different kinds of faculty work. Boyer describes four kinds of scholarship that illuminate the patterns of faculty activity nationwide: the scholarship of discovery, the scholarship of integration, the scholarship of application, and the scholarship of teaching. The definitions of these four scholarship are well known today in academic circles and need not be repeated here. What is crucial from the ensuing debate is that chairs and other administrators need to refocus the faculty reward system that is in place in each institution to provide greater flexibility and greater acceptability of diverse faculty work. Within each department, and across departments, one-size evaluation and one-size reward can no longer adequately fit all.

Institutional Mission, Faculty Rewards, and the Role of the Chair

A reward system for faculty cannot be discussed without relating it to the mission and priorities of each institution. One of the key roles of chairs is to develop a mesh between the priorities of the institution, those of the department, and those of individual faculty members, whose careers are played out within the department.

Table 7.1 and Figure 7.1 illustrate the importance of the chair's role in aligning individual and institutional needs. Table 7.1 presents four parallel processes for departments and individual faculty members, and further highlights the chair's role in bringing these processes into alignment. In the area of *planning,* for example, the chair meets with each faculty member annually to ascertain the professional goals on which each faculty member wishes to work in the coming year. The chair's role is to ensure that these goals are compatible with the departmental mission statement and strategic planning outcomes, and to advise faculty where their proposed goals are not compatible (and about the possible consequences of their spending their time on incompatible goals). The chair provides encouragement and support to all faculty members to find linkages between their own goals and those of the institution and department. The chair also provides feedback to the department as a whole on the goals of the faculty in order to foster connections between individuals and among groups and to identify any gaps or opportunities for collaboration.

In the area of *formative development,* individual faculty members receive formative feedback on their performance from their chair both pre- and post-tenure. This feedback, which is designed to help individual faculty continue to grow as professionals, finds its parallel in the retreats and committee meetings that the chair orchestrates for the department as a whole in an effort to help the department grow in desirable directions.

In the area of *assessment* and evaluation, individual faculty members are reviewed annually by the chair (and perhaps by a department committee as well) and are cumulatively evaluated for promotion and tenure. The parallel assessment process for the department is the program review that the institution requires the chair to undertake periodically. Another parallel here is that individuals from outside the discipline are likely to be involved in the

Table 7.1. The Parallel Processes for Departments and Individuals: Planning, Development, Assessment, and Rewards.

Process/Purpose	Individual	Department
Planning	Personal goals	Mission statements, strategic planning
Formative development	Formative pre- and post-tenure	Retreats, committee meetings
Assessment	Annual review, promotion and tenure	Program review
Rewards	Salary increases, promotion and tenure	Departmental rewards

Source: Developed by Carla Howery, Deputy Executive Officer of the American Sociological Association, Washington, D.C., 1998.

assessment of a faculty member for tenure, promotion, or both, and in the assessment of the department's programs. As there are consequences for a negative evaluation for individuals, so too are there consequences when a department's programs are deemed unsatisfactory. In each case the chair plays a major role in remediation.

Finally, in the area of *rewards,* individual faculty earn tenure, promotion, and salary increases and the chair prepares the documentation for each reward, based on criteria that the department collectively, under the chair's leadership (or that of a previous chair, perhaps), has determined. The department as a whole may be rewarded by the institution—for example, for exceeding its goals in a given year—and the chair sets in motion the process for determining how the departmental reward is to be utilized (such as for technology, travel, research support, or clerical help).

As Figure 7.1 suggests, those faculty whose work is of high quality and is highly compatible with the mission of the institution or department (the *effective match* quadrant of the table) are the "stars" of academe who get the highest rewards the institution can provide (such as early tenure consideration, early promotion, maximum

Figure 7.1. The Match of Individual Faculty Interests and Talents with Institutional and Departmental Needs: Implications, Rewards, and Faculty Development.

Quality of Professional/Scholarly Work
(Broadly Defined, Well Measured)

		High	Low
Compatibility with Mission	High	*Effective Match* Rewards, new opportunities, success	*Unskilled Match* A plan to enhance skills
	Low	*Mismatch* Continue what is done well but set explicit expectations for new areas and rewards	*Unskilled Mismatch* More serious remediation with carrots and sticks

Source: Developed by Carla Howery, Deputy Executive Officer of the American Sociological Association, Washington, D.C., 1998.

allowable salary increases, travel funds, and other opportunities). For these faculty, the chair's role is to provide (or recommend) appropriate rewards and congratulations and, where feasible, utilize the talents of these people to assist their less successful colleagues in various ways.

Those faculty whose work is highly compatible with the institutional or departmental mission, or both, but of low quality (in scholarship or teaching, for example) fall into the *unskilled match* quadrant. The chair's role here is to work with these faculty to create a development plan for enhancing those skills that may be deficient, while encouraging faculty to continue utilizing their skills in the areas in which they have been working and have strength.

The *mismatch* quadrant represents an interesting if at times difficult group of faculty. These are the people who are doing high-quality work that is not consonant with the institutional or departmental mission. In other words, they are doing things well that the institution or department has chosen not to reward. They may be disciplinary superstars whose reputations keep them traveling and away from campus more than is appropriate; they may be publishing frequently but in fields not supported by the department's research priorities; or they may be excellent teachers who are utilizing a pedagogical approach that is not acceptable to the institution or department. The chair's role here is to help refocus the energies of these faculty by encouraging and rewarding them for what they do well and by setting explicit expectations for their future performance and providing rewards only if they meet these expectations.

Finally, the *unskilled mismatch* quadrant represents those faculty—probably a small number in any department—whose work is of low quality and not compatible with the institutional or departmental mission. With these individuals, the chair needs to work out a plan for more serious remediation—a plan with carrots, sticks, and time limits built in to ensure that these faculty take seriously the need to improve.

Faculty Evaluation and the Chair

There is probably no role that department chairs are called on to perform that is more consequential than assisting in the professional development of their faculty and evaluating each faculty member's performance and suitability for institutional rewards. Faculty development and faculty evaluation are inextricably linked. A development plan is the logical outcome of any evaluation process; evaluation is a necessary consequence of any effort to develop.

In the voluminous literature on faculty evaluation and development over the past several decades, one conclusion seems paramount: any faculty development or evaluation activity must be undertaken, at least initially, where the faculty "live"—that is, at the department level. This is why the chair's role is so crucial in both of these processes. Let us examine the chair's role in faculty evaluation first.

When the dean or chief academic officer requires a professional judgment of the value of a faculty member's work, he or she must turn to department peers—especially to the chair. Even the long-standing tradition of extramural reviews of scholarship relies on the judgment of disciplinary peers. Given the obvious expertise of department peers and of the chair in the evaluation of faculty work, why are the tenure, promotion, and salary determination processes on many campuses fraught with contentiousness? The following are some likely causes:

- Faculty need to be more effective in documenting their accomplishments in light of institutional priorities.
- The department chair or appropriate committees need to be more attentive to referencing the norms of the discipline in the evaluation of faculty work.
- The department chair and appropriate committees need to take better account of individual differences in performance or work assignments.
- The department chair and appropriate committees need to better acknowledge the nonlinear path of most faculty careers—for example, interest in teaching or research may wax or wane in cycles in a faculty career—and to embrace the opportunities for different kinds of scholarship (in the encompassing sense in which Boyer used this term in *Scholarship Reconsidered*) at different life-cycle points.
- The department chair and appropriate committees need to develop and provide for the allocation of a range of

rewards, both tangible and intangible, for faculty work, as well as for support for faculty development.

How can the evaluation process at the department level be handled more effectively? What can the chair or department committees do to ensure that judgments made at the department level are viewed as valid and trustworthy by senior administrators or university-wide committees? How can chairs avoid the disappointment and demoralization—both for the faculty member under review and for the chair who laboriously crafts the departmental recommendation for that faculty member—when the dean or others higher up in the institution fail to endorse the conclusions of the chair and overturn the recommendation? Following are some steps for enhancing the credibility of departmental recommendations.

• *Each department needs to develop a statement of faculty performance expectations for tenure, promotion in rank, and salary increases (or other forms of reward and recognition, if they exist).* These departmental documents need to be compatible with institutionwide expectations—that is, each department's mission must reflect that of the institution—but in addition the departmental documents need to include such special information as normative statements about faculty work emanating from the major disciplinary associations to which department faculty belong (see Diamond and Adam, 1995); the uniqueness of any aspect of the department's mission or priorities that may explain nontraditional faculty career patterns in that unit; the weight given to various dimensions of faculty performance in personnel decisions for faculty at different stages of their careers—whether defined in terms of the "sacred categories" of teaching, research, and service; in terms of Boyer's four scholarships model; or in terms of the various ways that faculty performance often illustrates points of intersection among the "sacred categories"; the kinds of evidence or documentation that faculty are required (or allowed) to submit for evaluation; and the criteria for early tenure or promotion, if these are possible.

• *The development of departmental performance expectation documents must involve the unit faculty as a whole so that consensus can be built and faculty can feel ownership of the documents.* Building consensus and ownership for the documents is especially important in large departments where faculty careers may take many shapes. There needs to be consensus about the kinds of work that are appropriate for faculty in this discipline, the kinds of evidence that are acceptable to document that work, the differences in performance expectations (if any) for faculty at different academic ranks, and the kinds of professional, community, or institutional service that are rewarded in the department. The essential notion here is that the department, as a unit, has goals and the faculty are expected to contribute to their realization.

- *The departmental performance expectation document must be acceptable to the dean and chief academic officer of the institution, as well as to any oversight committee that makes recommendations to the dean or chief academic officer.* Until the departmental document has been approved, in writing, by senior administrators, it cannot be used to assess performance of department faculty. The chair's role in this process is to explain and justify any controversial or unusual facets of the department document so as to make them acceptable to superiors.

- *The departmental (as well as institutional) expectations for faculty performance should be shared with all candidates for academic positions in the department, thoroughly discussed with any new (or newly hired) faculty, and reviewed by the entire department on a regular basis.* The more survival information the chair shares with applicants for faculty positions, the more these individuals are in a position to decide whether the department is in fact where they wish to be employed and the more they know about what it will take for them to be successful.

- *The chair and department promotion and tenure committee must make all personnel judgments based on these written documents.* Only by strict reliance on these written documents can the chair or appropriate committees obviate claims of favoritism, partiality, subjectivity, and the like. If these documents are explicit and thorough, the outcome of a personnel review, at least at the departmental level, should never be in doubt. A short and very helpful manual that is must reading for chairs and other faculty evaluators is Robert M. Diamond's *Serving on Promotion and Tenure Committees* (1994).

Evaluating Faculty with Special Assignments

There may be occasions when departmental faculty undertake special, time-consuming assignments, either at the request of the chair, dean, or other administrator or because of their own interest in the assignment. Such special assignments could be in teaching, research, or service, or at some intersection point of two or more of these areas. Of special importance to the chair and department personnel committee, however, is the fact that these assignments may represent nontraditional paths in the institutional (or departmental) reward system.

Examples of such nontraditional paths include not-uncommon faculty activities such as the following:

• Teaching courses outside one's own department
• Undertaking an extensive curriculum revision of the undergraduate major
• Contributing professional expertise and time to a community project
• Taking on an administrative assignment outside the department

How should the chair evaluate such special assignments during the faculty member's annual review and, more importantly, at the critical personnel junctures (tenure, promotion in rank) where faculty performance is closely scrutinized in light of departmental and institutional expectations? The answer lies in how these special assignments are approved in the first place.

Chairs in many institutions meet individually with each faculty member in the spring term to plan out that faculty member's work assignment for the following year in a way that meets the department's needs (for staffing the courses that need to be taught and handling other department obligations) and takes into account the individual faculty member's special interests in teaching, research, and service. The decisions reached (one hopes, mutually) during this meeting become the basis for the contractual work assignment for each faculty member for the following year, and that contractual work assignment is the yardstick against which the chair will subsequently evaluate the faculty member's performance.

If, in the planning meeting, the chair agrees to allow a faculty member to undertake a time-consuming special assignment, the chair needs to codify this in writing and get written approval from the dean or other senior administrators that the faculty member who undertakes this assignment in lieu of more traditional work will be evaluated and rewarded based on the quality of his or her work.

An alternative option that the chair can explore in the case of nontenured faculty is to secure written permission from senior administrators to stop the tenure clock for the period during which the faculty member is engaged in special assignments that ordinarily do not count toward tenure at that institution. Although this is not as satisfactory as a commitment to count nontraditional work for institutional rewards, it does offer some protection to the faculty member with special assignments. The bottom line is that the chair has an obligation to ensure that the institutional reward system does not discriminate against faculty who take on approved alternative nontraditional roles.

From the Department to the Next Level

Departmental reviews of faculty are often viewed with skepticism by institutional committees, deans, and other senior administrators. This skepticism may be well founded; there are countless examples of promotion or tenure documents sent up from the department that for academics or administrators from other disciplines lack credibility. The documents may read like a whitewash of the faculty member's record of performance, glossing over gaps or shortcomings in an effort to be "collegial"; or the documents may extol a performance that, to outside eyes, seems ordinary. There have also been cases in which the departmental recommendations seem overly critical or condemnatory of a faculty member's performance, leaving outsiders to wonder whether the review constitutes some kind of personal attack rather than a supposedly objective assessment of performance.

There is a need for chairs to ensure the credibility of tenure and promotion recommendations sent up from the department. Given the amount of time that chairs (and departmental committees) spend in formulating their recommendations, and given the consequences for the faculty members under review, it is imperative that the recommendations coming to the administration from the department—from the only people in the institution with the disciplinary expertise needed to assess the quality of a faculty member's performance as a teacher or scholar—be viewed as credible. This credibility will be enhanced if

- The departmental recommendations evaluate the faculty member's record in terms of the written departmental and institutional expectations for faculty performance, or in light of other written statements that approve (or fail to approve) of a faculty member's performance in nontraditional areas.
- The recommendations bolster their conclusions by citing expectations for faculty performance disseminated by the major disciplinary associations to which department faculty belong.
- The recommendations bite the bullet when it comes to making hard decisions about a colleague's performance; they make it clear to readers that the department has taken the responsibility for monitoring and assessing the quality of its own members. When departments fail to exercise this responsibility, they invite outsiders with no expertise in the discipline to usurp that role.
- The recommendations assess a faculty member's contributions fairly and consistently; they are neither whitewashes of shoddy performance nor ad hominem attacks on an unpopular colleague. They make the case for their conclusions by dealing with and evaluating the quantitative and qualitative evidence.

Deans and senior administrators look to the chair for precisely these kinds of recommendations. It is not easy for chairs to balance their role as advocate for the departmental faculty with that of evaluator of faculty performance, but unless chairs can demonstrate their ability to do this in the kinds of recommendations they send forward, there will continue to be a credibility gap, resulting in departmental recommendations being overturned at higher levels.

Faculty Development and the Role of the Chair

Yet another hat that many chairs wear is that of faculty developer. Even in institutions with centralized faculty development programs, no one is as close to the action and as aware of the needs of individual faculty members as the department chair. Faculty development is the means by which chairs ensure proper alignment between faculty interests and needs, on the one hand, and institutional and departmental priorities, on the other.

When it comes to faculty development, the chair's position is unparalleled. Chairs see the faculty in their departments with regularity; they are in the best position to identify and determine how to meet the needs of individual faculty members. They are the persons who must broker individual faculty needs and institutional demands, and align faculty roles with the reward system of the institution. They are likewise perceived by most of the faculty as the individuals to turn to for advice.

As was suggested in Table 7.1, faculty development can be the catalyst for moving all faculty into the effective match quadrant—that is, those faculty whose work is viewed as high in quality and compatible with the mission of the department or institution. How the chair motivates faculty to develop in those areas in which they are currently not being rewarded is directly related to the chair's skills in leadership.

Three approaches characterize the way chairs perceive their role as faculty developer:

1. *Laissez-faire approach.* In this model the chair takes no action. He or she assumes that faculty development is the province of each faculty member, that faculty are professionals and are capable of doing what they need to do to grow and mature in their fields. There is no need for intervention by the chair in anyone else's life.

2. *Crisis-oriented approach.* In this model, the chair feels a need to act only when something has gone wrong, when a faculty member is in trouble or experiencing difficulty in some way. For example, the chair may seek to get involved when a faculty member receives low student ratings, but is unlikely to do anything for those faculty who get high ones.

3. *Active interventionist approach.* In this model, chairs view their role as proactive. They bring information to the faculty about development opportunities; they sponsor department seminars on teaching or research; they involve themselves as much with the good teachers and good scholars as with the mediocre or poor ones. They seek to avoid crises rather than respond to them after

the fact. They do not wait to be asked for help, but offer it whenever it seems appropriate.

Clearly the third approach—active intervention—is the one that leads to the most effective faculty development. It is also this approach that yields the best alignment of faculty interests and departmental needs, and of faculty roles and institutional rewards.

Given the typically limited amount of funding available for faculty development on most campuses these days, opportunities for faculty development may themselves be viewed as part of the reward system. The chair may be in a position to dispense (or at least recommend) funding for the purchase of instructional software, travel to a pedagogical conference in the discipline, sabbatical leaves to develop new skills or areas of competence, and the like. Such opportunities can serve to enhance the effectiveness of all faculty members and to revitalize the spirits and energy of those faculty whose motivation to excel has weakened.

Chairs need to be aware of the potential conflict that may arise between their role as faculty developer and their role as faculty evaluator. The former role focuses on providing help; the latter on rendering judgments. Although effective chairs have performed successfully in both of these roles, each role requires a different kind of behavior and relationship to one's faculty members.

Final Thoughts

The need to align, or realign, faculty roles and rewards at the departmental level points to new and exciting roles for the department chair. This chapter has viewed the chair as the person who seeks to achieve alignment within the department for faculty roles and rewards. It has also viewed the chair as the mediating agent between each individual faculty member's personal goals and the needs of the department as a collective. It has considered ways of enhancing the credibility of the chair's recommendations for faculty rewards at decanal and higher institutional levels.

At a time when all segments of higher education are being forced to rethink what they do and why and how they do it, it is fitting that department chairs rethink how they can be most effective as leaders whose actions, at least as much as those of anyone else in the institution, affect the quality of faculty careers, student life, and academic programs.

References

Altman, H. B. "Rewarding Faculty Performance: What Can We Do When the Cupboard Is Almost Bare?" In *Academic Chairpersons: Selecting, Motivating, and Rewarding Faculty*. Proceedings of the Tenth Annual Conference on Academic Chairpersons. Manhattan: Kansas State University, 1994.

Altman, H. B., and Spangehl, S. D. "Faculty Merit Pay: A Framework for Making Departmental Decisions." *The Department Advisor*, 1991, 7(1), 1–5.

Boyer, E. L. *Scholarship Reconsidered: Priorities for the Professoriate*. Princeton, N.J.: Carnegie Foundation for the Advancement of Teaching, 1990.

Diamond, R. M. *Serving on Promotion and Tenure Committees: A Faculty Guide*. Bolton, Mass.: Anker, 1994.

Diamond, R. M., and Adam, B. E. (eds.). *The Disciplines Speak: Rewarding the Scholarly, Professional, and Creative Work of Faculty*. Washington, D.C.: American Association for Higher Education, 1995.

Rice, R. E. *Making a Place for the New American Scholar*. American Association for Higher Education New Pathways Working Paper no. 1. Washington, D.C.: American Association for Higher Education, 1996.

Part Three

Leading Innovative Change in Curriculum and Teaching

As department faculty continuously monitor their own functioning by paying attention to the ways in which they make decisions and handle conflicts and how they listen to, communicate with, and support each other, they become able to put aside their turf issues and make decisions that are good for the students, the faculty, and the department. They can then look at how their discipline is developing, what students should learn, how and where these things should be taught, and how their learning will be measured. These issues—outcomes assessment, integration of technology, service learning, and curriculum renewal—are discussed in the next four chapters. In the last chapter in this section, Peter M. Senge raises some highly provocative questions about the future of higher education.

Two recently published reports demonstrate additional challenges for higher education. State officials are increasingly accepting the concept that results should somehow count when allocating resources to public colleges and universities. The Public Higher Education Program of the Rockefeller Institute of Government at the State University of New York (1998) completed a survey indicating that half of the states now link some of their spending on public colleges to performance, and all but a handful appear likely to do so in the next five years.

State governors also believe that postsecondary institutions should be held "accountable for meeting state priorities and local/ regional needs" and that taxpayer support for public colleges should be tied to "specific institutional performance measures" (Education Commission of the States, 1998, p. 26). Governors from thirty-five states who responded anonymously to the poll indicated that there is a special concern about "achieving closer collaboration between policymakers and education leaders" as an important strategic policy initiative (p. 26). Other changes in postsecondary education that are required to meet critical needs of all stakeholders were strongly advocated by the governors: "Encourage lifelong learning in postsecondary education (98 percent), Allow students to receive their education anytime and any place via technology (83 percent), Require collaboration with business and industry in developing relevant curriculum (77 percent), and Integrate applied or on-the-job experience into academic programs (66 percent)" (Education Commission of the States, 1998, p. 11).

Job training and development of employment skills were rated as a critical challenge by 86 percent of the governors. Nearly all of the governors thought that it was important for states to link spending on colleges to institutions' performance, to put more emphasis on faculty productivity. Solid majorities of the governors also said they believed that states should "prod colleges to collaborate with business in developing their curricula, and should push colleges to integrate applied or on-the-job experiences into their academic programs" (Schmidt, 1998, p. A38).

Because both of these reports (Education Commission of the States, 1998; Public Higher Education Program of the Rockefeller Institute of Government at the State University of New York, 1998) conclude that resources should be allocated to universities based on measurable performance academic leaders at the highest levels in universities need to incorporate these concepts into mission statements and strategic goals. Yet although academic administrators need to set the direction, it is at the department level that these changes will take place. It is at the department level that faculty, who best understand their discipline and its potential, have impact on other areas that could not possibly be imagined by those outside that area of expertise.

As chairs and their faculty members continue to examine the

ways in which their team functions together and set in place workable structures, such as the departmental statement on promotion and tenure; as they become aware of the ways in which they operate successfully and what opportunities they have for ongoing professional development; and as a climate of trust is built, chairs and faculty can tackle some of the task functions. What are the knowledge, skills, attitudes, and values they want students to learn? How will faculty incorporate these objectives into their courses and structure relevant experiences that are meaningful for students as they also contribute to the community? How will they renew the curriculum? What will be the role of technology? How will they measure the success of what they are doing?

Major efforts are already under way throughout the country to make student learning the central focus in higher education. The rationale for this monumental shift from an emphasis on teaching to a concentration on learning, as advocated by the Education Commission of the States, has already been presented convincingly by Barr and Tagg in a 1995 *Change* article that has played a pivotal role in changing our view of education. Comparing the instruction paradigm with the learning paradigm, Barr and Tagg suggest a new role for faculty—that of "designers of learning methods and environments" (p. 17). However, because so many faculty members still feel that teaching is their responsibility and that learning is the students' business, chairs must explore with faculty new options for ensuring student learning.

Lion F. Gardiner has designed Chapter Eight "to help chairs develop a clear view of assessment research in the academic department and a vision of how they can use assessment to help lead change." He argues that "without the essential guidance provided by a well-crafted mission statement, clearly defined outcome goals and objectives, and credible evidence of the department's performance," a chair will have difficulty increasing the quality of student learning. The chapter identifies the land mines in the outcomes assessment process and demonstrates ways of avoiding them. Gardiner also provides a rich array of specialized resources to increase understanding of and monitor student learning.

In his discussion of service learning in Chapter Nine, Edward Zlotkowski demonstrates how chairs can open the internal system of the department to the external community in which students are working and will continue to be employed after graduation. Academic departments need to work with corporate education that has been expanding so rapidly that it may be the university's largest competitor in the next decade. Chairs must network with industry, government, health care, social service agencies, primary and secondary education, and the social community. Chairs need to expand the boundaries so that departments can become part of the larger system instead of maintaining an ivory tower mentality that stations higher education both apart from and above the world. Zlotkowski describes the impact that service learning has had as an important part of the learning experience for students and faculty on more than six hundred college campuses.

Once decisions are made about what students need to learn, faculty as a team need to decide how technology will be integrated into teaching and learning. In Chapter Ten, A. W. (Tony) Bates discusses how faculty can be given ownership of technological change in the department. Because bimodal distributions exist in many departments—with some faculty very advanced in their knowledge of technology while others are hesitant to engage because they do not want to expose their ignorance or do not know how much work will be involved and whether it will be worth it—it is not easy to bring everyone on board. Nonetheless, Bates concludes that faculty are not the problem. Most faculty, he feels, are anxious to use technology but lack the resources and specialist support they need. Providing skilled professionals to support faculty, though initially expensive, is cheaper and a better long-term decision.

Good teaching and learning are directly connected to whether the curriculum supports the mission of the institution and is responsive to changing societal needs. Renewing the curriculum is basic to good teaching and learning. What a chair might do to facilitate an understanding of the curriculum, to test whether it meets contemporary student needs, to encourage curriculum transformation that reflects trends in the discipline, to support the integration of new knowledge, to build interdisciplinary bridges, and to link the curriculum with new pedagogies are the questions dealt with in Chapter Eleven. In handling these questions, Ann S. Ferren and Kay Mussell discuss practical strategies that are firmly built on key questions in curriculum renewal.

Peter Senge, who has written the concluding chapter of this book, is a nationally known innovative leader, one of our most forward-looking thinkers. Looking at academe with the insights of an experienced academician yet with the objectivity of an outside expert on organizations, he writes about what a university might be like. When chairs are passionate about innovation, they need to find out who their natural partners are. Senge suggests asking faculty "what they see as significant challenges and opportunities for innovation" and goes on to say, "Asking people with passion for creating something new how you can help is one of the most effective leadership strategies." He also suggests that university administrators should work in genuine partnership with chairs and faculty, from whom many of the bold ideas needed for real change will come. Acknowledging the difficulty of transforming traditional concentrations of power and sustaining deep shifts in values, Senge addresses issues that chairs can do something about—material they will find compelling.

References

Barr, R. B., and Tagg, J. "From Teaching to Learning: A New Paradigm for Undergraduate Education." *Change*, 1995, *27*(6), 12–25.

Education Commission of the States. *Transforming Postsecondary Education for the Twenty-First Century*. Denver, Colo.: Education Commission of the States, 1998.

Public Higher Education Program of the Rockefeller Institute of Government at the State University of New York. *Current Status and Future Prospects of Performance Funding and Performance Budgeting for Higher Education: The Second Survey*. Albany: Nelson A. Rockefeller Institute of Government, State University of New York, 1998.

Schmidt, P. "Governors Want Fundamental Changes in Colleges, Question Place of Tenure." *Chronicle of Higher Education*, June 19, 1998, p. A38.

Chapter Eight

Monitoring and Improving Educational Quality in the Academic Department

Lion F. Gardiner

To provide effective leadership for educational change in an academic department, a chair needs to understand clearly the department's purpose or mission, the specific results or student learning outcomes the department intends to produce, and the extent to which and specifically how the department produces its results. Without the essential guidance provided by a well-crafted mission statement, clearly defined outcome goals and objectives, and credible evidence of the department's performance, a chair will have difficulty leading toward specific changes in student learning.

Well used, the mission statement, intended outcomes, and information on performance permit clear thinking about the quality of a department's performance on the part of everyone concerned: chair, faculty, staff, and students. Without these elements, confusion may reign about purpose, desired and actual results, and the need for change. Evidence of student learning produced by assessment research can be thought of as the department's academic bottom line. Without such evidence, the chair cannot lead others to change the quality of student learning.

This chapter is designed to help chairs develop a clear view of assessment research in the academic department and a vision of how they can use assessment to help lead change. It shows how a department can define the student learning outcomes it desires to

165

produce, and use assessment to monitor and improve the quality of students' learning. It introduces basic concepts and principles and it identifies pitfalls and suggests ways of avoiding them. A concluding section suggests specialized resources that can assist chairs in understanding student learning and in carrying out the crucial tasks of defining and monitoring this learning.

The Societal Context for Assessment in the Department

Since the mid-1980s, an enormous amount of energy has been devoted to assessment in colleges and universities. Much of this assessment has focused on the outcomes of student learning and has been motivated by the needs of stakeholders external to colleges and universities. State departments of higher education and regional and disciplinary accrediting agencies have asked institutions to provide credible evidence of their graduates' level of development. These external demands for evidence of results will almost certainly continue to grow in the years ahead.

Effective leadership inside the institution also requires high-quality information about the functioning of the academic department. In other words, administrators and faculty members should be using effective professional methods at every point to understand their organizations and to produce the highest quality results for their various clients, regardless of any formal mandates from external bodies to do so.

Society is asking higher education to educate all of its students to a much higher level than ever before. Institutions are often expected to achieve these results with fewer resources and with a growing level of dissatisfaction on the part of their stakeholders with the quality of graduates' knowledge, skills, and values. As the limited learning of many graduates of colleges and universities becomes increasingly apparent, institutions are seeking ways in which they can significantly raise their standards for their graduates and improve their effectiveness in producing high-quality student learning.

The Central Role of the Department in Academic Change

The academic department, as the primary educational enterprise on campus, is responsible for providing most of an institution's instruction. Therefore, the department must play a key role in improving the quality of students' educational experiences. The mantle of frontline leadership for this change falls on the shoulders of the department chair and faculty.

If a department is to serve its student clients at the high level society now requires and successfully compete for students with the new commercial and Web-based providers of higher education services, the chair and faculty must thoroughly understand their students and the students' development, and how to use skillfully the best research-based methods to facilitate this development in the most economical fashion. Understanding students and departments requires careful and continuous monitoring of conditions through assessment research.

Assessment fits naturally within a department's research-oriented academic culture. It involves developing interesting and important questions about the department's work to which faculty members and administrators want answers, designing a research program that can provide these answers, and using the results of the research to improve continuously the quality of a department's educational activities in order to enhance the quality of students' learning.

Planning, managing, and improving the educational processes of an academic department is demanding work. Students and their learning and development are inherently complex. For students to develop the knowledge and higher-order cognitive skills that institutions value and that they and society require is difficult. Producing this development reliably necessitates carefully organizing and coordinating the efforts of many people and monitoring their work and results, even in small departments.

Further complicating efforts to help students learn at a high level is students' often relatively low level of preparation for rigorous academic work and their failure in many cases to devote the time and effort required for deep learning (Gardiner, 1996). In addition, because most new department chairs lack formal preparation for their professional work as teachers, managers, and leaders, many of the daily activities and tasks they face may pose significant challenges. Fortunately, today we have thirty years of accumulated research on student learning and development and educational processes to draw on. In many cases, this research has led to the development of practical methods that can substantially improve the quality of a department's work and produce significant gains in students' learning.

Planning and Monitoring Education

The complexity of student learning and development requires careful planning and monitoring of a department's diverse educational processes so that everyone can thoroughly understand and continually improve them. Wise stewardship of resources, particularly student and faculty time, and ensuring that all graduates are well educated require diligence.

Two steps are central to effective planning and monitoring: first, defining the educational outcomes or results the department *intends* to produce, and second, determining the outcomes it actually *does* produce. The focus at every point is on results. All educational activities are guided by specific intentions—what the faculty believe students should know and be able to do when they leave the institution, including important values they believe students should develop. These intended outcomes are the basis for the design, implementation, and assessment of curricula and instruction, academic advising, and cocurricular activities, and the development and management of the campus climate and culture. These deliberately predetermined aims should control departmental behavior.

Departments as Systems

The academic department can be thought of as a system. The departmental system includes all of the resources, or *inputs,* that are available to the department to support its work: buildings and equipment, students, faculty members, and office and technical staff. The specific knowledge, skills, and values each person brings to the work of the department are also inputs. The educational activities the department engages in are its *processes*: curricula, courses, academic advising, student clubs, seminars, and field trips. *Outcomes* are the results produced by the system's educational processes. Student outcomes may involve *cognitive* development, *affective* development—having to do with interests, appreciations, attitudes, and values (Krathwohl, Bloom, and Masia, 1964)—or *motor* skill development.

Each educational process—an individual course, the advising program, a student organization—can itself also be thought of as a system with its own inputs and outcomes. For example, students with particular characteristics (inputs) enroll in a course, engage in certain study behaviors (processes), and as a result possess new skills (outcomes).

The chair and faculty should always distinguish clearly among these three organizational components. They should focus on results: what they *should* be and what they *are*. One of the important causes of the relatively low level of learning that characterizes many or most college students may be the common tendency of departments to focus on inputs and processes and give relatively little attention to their intended and actual outcomes. Departments often focus on seeking additional fiscal support for their activities and more and "better" students (inputs), and on developing new programs (processes), rather than stopping to reflect on what they are trying to accomplish, their intended outcomes, and carefully monitoring the outcomes they actually produce. *Good planning starts with purpose (the mission) and desired results and formulates these intended outcomes in terms of written outcome goals and objectives.* These carefully worded statements form a solid foundation for all educational planning, implementation, assessment, and quality improvement. Assessment reveals goal achievement and thus requires goals.

Desired inputs and processes can also be articulated in terms of input or process goals and objectives. This ordinarily happens in strategic planning, in which desired institutional change is being addressed (Gardiner, 1989).

Planning: Mission Statements, Goals, and Objectives

All planning begins with the *mission statement*. Mission statements describe the purpose or mission of the department, curriculum, or course. They should be carefully constructed and systematically used to inform practice. The department mission statement should be consistent with the college mission statement and derived from it (Gardiner, 1989). Formal, written *goals* and *objectives* that define a department's desired student learning translate the mission statement's necessarily broad language into more specific and practical operational language. Goals and objectives direct decision making and action on a daily basis.

Among their other virtues, clearly stated and effectively used statements of outcomes can provide a department with the following:

- A coherent outline of complex types of student development that is consistent with research-based student development theory. This framework can constitute a sound blueprint for developing curriculum and instruction and for designing assessments that can produce valid information useful for decision making.
- Concrete targets for everyone to aim for and monitor as the department seeks to serve its students more effectively.
- A means for gaining commitment on the part of both faculty members and students to develop important but difficult student competencies.
- A device for focusing everyone's attention and scarce resources on what is most important for the department's students and thus for reducing waste.
- A vehicle for communicating departmental aims clearly to various audiences both inside and outside the institution so that they can understand and support efforts to change.
- Evidence of leadership and sound management practice in the department for all of the department's stakeholders.

Often driven by the demands of external bodies rather than internal needs, departments all too frequently have rushed headlong into assessment without stopping to reflect adequately on what they were assessing and to ensure that they have carefully articulated their desired outcomes, the achievement of which they would assess. Thus, in many cases assessment may be inadequately aligned with a college's or department's mission and therefore be unable to produce the most useful information for a department.

Writing Effective Goals and Objectives

Outcome statements should communicate unambiguously to all of their users, including students, what a department is trying to achieve. There are a number of key principles to observe when defining outcomes that will enhance the clarity and utility of these statements. Chairs and department faculty need to develop the requisite knowledge and skills to recognize and construct effective goals and objectives. Without these abilities, outcome statements are often vague, leading to conceptual confusion. Poorly constructed outcome statements cannot be assessed. (See this chapter's resources section for sources of detailed instruction.)

Curricular goals and objectives are ideally formulated prior to developing the goals and objectives of the courses within the curriculum. The desired higher-level curricular outcomes guide the faculty as they write goals and objectives for courses.

While determining cognitive outcomes, which are the most common outcomes in higher education, in addition to ensuring that the right *disciplinary content* is included in a goal or objective, the *intellectual* or *cognitive level* necessary for students to perform an outcome behavior should be set at the appropriate level. A guide is required to do this reliably. The most commonly used standard for controlling cognitive level when developing outcome statements at both the curricular and course levels is the Taxonomy of Educational Objectives, or Bloom's Taxonomy (Bloom, 1956). This taxonomy has six cognitive levels ranging from the lowest, requiring only recall of memorized information, through comprehension and application of concepts to the problem-solving behaviors of analysis, synthesis, and evaluation.

Although a department will have disciplinary outcomes for its various majors, certain of the college's general education outcomes, such as those having to do with higher-order cognitive skill development, will need to be integrated into courses for majors as well as those of the general education curriculum. These important outcomes are often difficult to produce, and many or most of the college's courses will have to contribute to producing the synergistic effect necessary for these types of development to occur reliably and effectively.

Using Goals and Objectives

The department's outcome goals and objectives express its educational mission or purpose in detail, and its mission is its raison d'être. However, *even the best structured statements of outcomes are useful only if they are used,* and they should be used on a daily and weekly basis for communicating with students about their development, for developing and revising courses and cocurricular programs, for designing assessments of various sorts, for program evaluation, and for communicating about the department's work with administrators, trustees, parents, prospective students and state higher education officials.

Few sets of goals and objectives are perfect. Regardless of how carefully they have been developed, as they are used for practical purposes in the department, ways will emerge for improving them. Knowledge changes, and students' and society's needs change with time. Therefore, the department's outcome statements should be improved periodically. They should not, however, be changed on a whim or the spur of the moment. The department's five-year program evaluation is a reasonable point at which to review the goals and objectives to determine if they are all current and continue to meet needs.

Monitoring the Department's Performance

Being clear about what the department should be doing is only a first step in the process of education. The department should achieve its outcome goals and objectives through activities that research shows can produce these outcomes with the department's students. Understanding the students and monitoring the activity of the department and the results it produces is essential to knowing how well the desired outcomes are being produced and why. This information is necessary for departmental effectiveness and efficiency and therefore for the exercise of leadership.

Assessment Versus Evaluation

Assessment and subsequent evaluation provide essential leadership tools for the department chair. Leadership toward specific needed changes is inconceivable without these tools. The rich array of information about the department produced by the various types of assessment in a well-crafted assessment program can provide a chair with numerous opportunities for creative leadership for change.

The term *assessment* as used in this chapter refers to a process of discovering what is—for example, determining the characteristics of the students or faculty (inputs), the nature of a department's educational processes, and the actual outcomes the department produces. *Evaluation*, conversely, generally involves making value judgments about the quality or acceptability of conditions in the department as revealed by assessment. Is the quality of the student outcomes being produced by the department sufficiently high? Are the department's educational processes consistent with research-based best practice?

Assessment, therefore, produces the data or evidence required to consider the current quality of what a department is doing. It provides a basis for modifying the department's educational processes to improve the quality of its student outcomes. Assessment provides evidence that can serve as a foundation for a department's *continuous quality improvement* process. Improving quality depends on evaluation and evaluation depends on assessment.

Interpretation of assessment results involves translating *data*—for example, the results of a pencil-and-paper test—into *information*: determining what the data mean. Evaluation places a *value judgment* on the assessment information: To what degree are the conditions revealed by assessment acceptable when judged against a previously set standard?

Two types of evaluation serve very different purposes. *Formative evaluation* permits judgment of the adequacy of an educational process while it is under way. For example, four weeks into the semester a teacher in a course can judge how well students are learning by referring to their test results (outcomes). The teacher can also give students a questionnaire inquiring, for example, about how they are experiencing the course and what they like most and least, and asking for suggestions they have for improvement. (These perceptions, together with learning, are also outcomes of the educational process.) The teacher then considers all the assessment information, as well as his or her own observations, and may make changes in the educational process that will improve learning.

Summative evaluation, in contrast, occurs at the end of a learning process, for example, a course or curriculum. Students may take a final examination that will demonstrate the amount they have learned. A student questionnaire may inquire about satisfaction with the course or the college experience. Both types of evaluation, formative and summative, are essential to understanding and improving the educational process and therefore student learning.

Using Assessment Research to Enable Leadership

Assessment research can provide a department chair with the tools and information required to support leadership for change in many ways. It can do the following:

- Identify entering students' abilities and needs, determine the learning and development achieved by graduates, and develop a richly detailed picture of students' educational experiences
- Enable the chair, faculty members, and students themselves to monitor the progress of each student individually and all students collectively
- Raise the level of urgency for change by helping overcome the negative impact of tradition, inertia, and self-interested political maneuvering by developing teamwork and persuading members of the faculty that change in the department's educational processes is necessary
- Convince students that change in their learning methods may be required
- Enable the chair and faculty to monitor the impact of change efforts and adjust these efforts as they progress
- Build a department culture that trusts, respects, and pervasively uses evidence for decision making
- Enable senior administrators to understand the unit's contribution to accomplishing the institution's mission, to provide the unit with necessary resources, and to track its performance so they can guide it
- Provide evidence to communicate more broadly to parents of prospective students and the public the department's capacity to educate its students

Technical Aspects of Assessment

Department chairs need to be alert to certain technical aspects of assessment. The quality of the evidence that a department's assessments are able to produce depends heavily on the care given to their design. The detection of various types of cognitive and motor performances, of internal affective states, and of institutional phenomena each requires appropriate methods. Failure to ensure high-quality design can invalidate the results of assessments, making them useless or misleading for decision making. Both chairs and faculty members need to develop the knowledge and skills necessary to plan, implement, interpret, and use the results of assessment effectively in their departments. Chairs can provide the leadership necessary to develop these important professional abilities. (See the resources section of this chapter for sources of detailed instruction.)

Types of Assessment

Each type of assessment provides department chairs with a tool for examining and understanding a different aspect of their department. Just as there are three types of goals and objectives—outcome, input, and process—so there are three types of assessment. *Outcome assessment* provides evidence about the results of students' learning. *Process assessment* provides information about the characteristics of the students' educational experiences—for example, in orientation, academic advising, courses, and residence halls. *Input assessment* provides evidence about resources such as faculty and student characteristics.

All three types of assessment are necessary for understanding the department and guiding its behavior so that it can produce high-quality student learning outcomes, *and their use should be carefully integrated.*

Assessing Outcomes

Although students' perceptions of their level of learning and their satisfaction with their college experience are important outcome variables to monitor, they are not *learning* outcomes. These too must be assessed. Continuous assessment of the results produced by each curriculum and course is necessary if resources such as faculty and student time, tuition, tax revenues, and gifts are to be used effectively to produce the maximum possible amount of student learning.

- *Assessment of curricula.* The whole should be greater than the sum of its parts. The outcomes of the curriculum—all of its courses taken together—must be assessed. The effect of a single course, important as it can be, is far smaller than the cumulative impact of all of a student's courses and cocurricular experiences. The department needs to know what that impact is. To what extent has the curriculum in the major advanced the development of important general education outcomes such as critical thinking skills and dispositions? Have all of the students acquired essential disciplinary knowledge, skills, and values? What contribution have cocurricular activities made to achieving the department's goals and objectives?

- *Whose standards of performance?* Much evaluation today, such as that provided by standardized tests, is *norm-referenced*; it employs as its standard the performance of populations of students—norm populations—on other campuses used in the development of commercial instruments. Such norms provide no information about the degree to which students have achieved a department's own intended outcomes unless the faculty have closely compared the tests' specifications with their own objectives and identified specific areas of coverage. The standard of performance of such tests depends on test takers elsewhere with possibly unknown characteristics, not standards predetermined by the faculty in the department.

Criterion-referenced evaluation, conversely, compares the department's students' outcomes with the absolute standards of performance provided by the faculty's own carefully developed outcome objectives (the criteria of comparison). Criterion-referenced evaluation generally permits a closer alignment of specific indicators of performance with the department's curriculum than is possible with norm-referenced indicators.

- *Value-added assessment.* A department that finds that its graduates demonstrate high-level competence cannot automatically claim credit for this positive state. Students bring many abilities with them to college. To determine its contribution to its students— the value it has added—a department needs to remove its students' baseline input abilities from their assessed outcome levels. This is a methodologically complex matter and should be planned carefully (Anderson, Ball, Murphy, and Associates, 1975; Astin, 1991;

Light, Singer, and Willett, 1990; Pascarella and Terenzini, 1991; see index entries *change* and *value-added*).

• *Assessment in courses: Teacher-made classroom tests.* Teacher-designed outcome assessments provide essential evidence of learning in courses—for individual students, their instructors, and anyone else who needs to know the outcomes produced by a course. These assessments can be of many types, such as traditional paper-and-pencil tests, projects, or performances. Classroom assessments, at least those that assess cognitive functioning, are every bit mental measurements as are professionally constructed commercial instruments that purport to assess, for example, skill in critical thinking or moral judgment. Therefore, faculty members should exercise great care in constructing such assessments.

Research that has examined teacher-made classroom tests has consistently revealed instruments that primarily assess the lowest levels of cognitive functioning on the Taxonomy of Educational Objectives (Milton, 1982). This research suggests that rather than assessing higher-order cognitive skills, our faculty-made tests most frequently ask for memorized facts and low-level conceptual learning. How valuable can these results and the grades derived from them be as a basis for decision making about student learning and development?

Most college and university faculty members are still unprepared for their work as educators, their graduate training in most cases being limited to learning and practicing an academic discipline or professional field. They require careful preparation for their work as assessors. The department chair should provide leadership to ensure that faculty develop the skills required to plan and execute assessment competently.

• *Determining the cognitive demand of assessments: Ensuring high expectations.* Ensuring that the intellectual demands made on students are high in both the learning process and assessment is essential. A simple and inexpensive way to determine the intellectual demands of assessments, including classroom assessments, is to evaluate them using the Taxonomy of Educational Objectives. This exercise may also spark interest in and early faculty commitment to assessment research. As such it can be a powerful leadership tool for raising the level of urgency for change in the department.

1. Collect the most recent set of final examinations from all courses in the major, or in the department more broadly, or sets from more than one semester.
2. Have two people who can competently use the taxonomy independently rate the cognitive demand of every test item or assessment component. In some cases, they may need to consult with faculty members teaching the courses to determine specifically how the material an item assesses was taught. Student experiences when learning can influence the cognitive level of an assessment item.
3. Have the two readers compare their ratings for items and resolve any disagreements, or in cases of disagreement, have a third person rate disputed items.
4. Finally, to determine the cognitive demand being made on students by each course, calculate the mean ratings of the items, or percentage of items or components at each level on the taxonomy, for the assessments in each course. Similarly, the overall cognitive demand of the curriculum as a whole can be determined by combining the results for the curriculum's courses. In each case, determine whether the cognitive level of the assessments matches the levels set in the course and curricular objectives. If they do not match, assessment should be adjusted up to the appropriate level. What is the overall intellectual demand being made by the institution on its students? Is this demand high enough?

The learning activities in each course should be appropriate for the cognitive levels specified in its objectives and in the objectives of the curricula of which it is a part. The Taxonomy of Educational Objectives is helpful for determining the cognitive demands of classroom activities and homework assignments.

The suggestions for assessment made here are only examples. Like any other research, assessment research requires a coherent, well-thought-out design, and the quality of the design and its implementation will go far toward determining the usefulness of the assessment results for leadership and decision making.

• *Grades.* Chairs need to understand the profound limitations of grades as indicators of learning outcomes. The common basis of grades in scores from classroom tests of uncertain validity and reliability, the frequent inclusion in grades of class attendance and participation and other variables that are not learning outcomes, and markedly different standards that may be used within single classes and from class to class, all of which are usually unknown to the users of grades, conspire together to limit the value of grades in determining what students know and are able to do. Far more satisfactory are the results of high-quality assessments of specific outcomes and standards of performance articulated in objectives.

Assessing Student Inputs

A department needs to have many kinds of information about its students besides their high school and transfer college grades and their placement scores on writing and mathematical tests conducted by the college. Among these types of information are various aspects of students' cognitive development, their attitudes toward self and schooling, and their learning approaches and skills. These and other variables that interest the faculty should be systematically assessed to provide information for academic advisers and students, for teachers in courses, and as a baseline for longitudinal monitoring of students' development.

Assessing Educational Processes

Having identified inadequacies in the student learning and development outcomes that a department is trying to produce, a common finding of outcome assessment, a faculty will attempt to discover ways of improving the effectiveness of its educational processes. Developing assessments that can illuminate the current condition is a natural step to take.

If one or more student outcomes as assessed are not at the level previously determined by the faculty to be acceptable and articulated in the department's curricular objectives, specific action must be taken to close the department's performance gap. This is where a close coupling of outcome and process assessment can be important. Process assessment research can help pinpoint weaknesses in students' educational experiences so that the department can respond more effectively to its students' needs.

A department should examine the educational processes that have the greatest impact on students' learning. These may include courses, academic advising, and other out-of-class contacts between students and the faculty and other students. In each case, consulting the higher education literature will reveal the specific qualities of each process that researchers suggest have the most powerful impact on student learning (Astin, 1993; Gardiner, 1996; Pascarella and Terenzini, 1991). One might determine for each course the consonance of its outcome goals and instructional objectives with the outcome goals and objectives of the curricula it serves. Are the assessments used in each course valid with respect to assessing the specific behaviors articulated in its instructional objectives? How have students been performing on these assessments and on their individual items?

Approaches to Assessment Research: Design Considerations

There are a number of important considerations chairs should keep in mind when beginning to structure a program of assessment. Each consideration requires careful thought if the assessment research to be embarked on is to provide the most trustworthy and useful results for the least investment in student and staff time and money.

• *Single versus multiple methods.* Generally, employing multiple methods of assessment to examine a variable of interest will provide a fuller picture of reality than using a single method.

• *Quantitative versus qualitative methods.* Quantitative methods such as standardized test scores, counts of students retained after their first year, and mean time to graduation have the advantage of producing numerical data that can be statistically manipulated to make comparisons and reveal patterns not otherwise detectable. However, quantitative data may lack the richness of detail that can be captured by qualitative methods such as student writing, interviews, focus groups, or ethnographic research. Both quantitative and qualitative methods are important; both should be considered for their individual strengths when designing assessment research.

• *Paper-and-pencil tests versus other methods.* Testing is not synonymous with assessment. Paper-and-pencil tests constitute only one class of assessment devices. Today, many other methods exist, each with its own strengths and weaknesses. One should use the methods best suited to the task at hand.

• *Commercial versus locally designed instruments.* Commercial tests have the advantages of professional psychometric design, convenient processing, comparison of local data with norm populations, and low cost in faculty time. They may not, however, provide more than one or a few numerical scores or be criterion-referenced and assess a department's intended outcomes as articulated in its goals and objectives (Nichols, 1995a, b, c). Before a commercial instrument is used, its purposes should be closely compared with the department's intended outcomes.

Ethical Considerations in Assessment

Assessment has significant implications for people's lives. Therefore, the department chair as leader needs to be sensitive to the ethical considerations involved.

- Assessment should be aimed at creating increased value for the department's clients—first and foremost its students.
- The department chair should ensure that all students experience a high-quality educational process and are educated so that they are able to perform at a high level when assessed.
- The purposes of all assessment should be plain and the processes should be transparent to everyone concerned: faculty members, students, parents, senior administrators, trustees, journalists.
- The department chair should ensure that each step in the goal-setting and assessment processes moves ahead only when everyone involved is ready, when everyone is trained and competent for the task at hand, and when previous steps have been properly executed.
- Assessment costs money and consumes student and staff time. It should be carefully planned and executed and the results should be used seriously to improve quality.
- Results that reflect unfavorably on the department should be confronted honestly and acted on with dispatch, not swept under the bureaucratic carpet. Such results present a chair with a test of moral leadership. Revelation of problems is one of the most important purposes of assessment. Such results are potentially much more valuable than those that make good advertising copy for the public information office. Deliberately searching for problems—and then promptly

fixing them—is one of the most powerful ways of improving quality in an organization.

The Process: Defining Outcomes and Planning Assessment Research

Defining outcomes for a curriculum or course is always an intellectual challenge. Doing it well takes time—ordinarily several months for a curriculum. Doing it poorly takes more time in the long run, and rather than clarifying meaning it can lead to confusion and wrangling. Defining outcomes and designing a plan for assessment are key opportunities for leading change. Here are several important practical steps chairs can take when leading a department effort to define outcomes and plan assessment research.

• *Provide high-quality training for everyone involved.* Most academicians have never developed formal outcome statements of the type described here and they lack the knowledge and skills required to do it well. In addition, they may initially view the process as needlessly bureaucratic and as merely one more administrative fad, soon to be forgotten. Faculty are busy people, and their time should be used with care. Therefore, the rationale for defining outcomes with specificity should be carefully explained, and everyone should clearly understand the many benefits of having a high-quality set of outcome goals and objectives to guide their professional practice.

Campus experts or off-campus consultants should conduct appropriate training for everyone involved. Consultants can be essential for getting things started and for ensuring a high-quality process. For the long run, however, the campus and department should develop their own talent to a high level.

• *Appoint a writing team.* A committee or possibly the faculty as a whole, if the department is small, can supervise the overall outcome definition process. However, the actual writing is an intense task and large committees are unwieldy. A subcommittee or writing task group of two people is often ideal. The larger steering committee lays out the task, frames the content of the goals and objectives, and supervises progress. The writing team works over the ideas and partial statements from the larger committee and completes, cleans, and polishes them for cyclical review by the committee until they effectively reflect the faculty's meaning.

• *Set up a cyclical process for reviewing goals and objectives as they are developed.* If a college is developing outcomes for all of its departments, a central review mechanism may work well. If development is within a single department, those with the most expertise may do the reviewing. The purpose of the review, say, at the college level, is not to judge the quality of content; that is for the disciplinary experts to decide. The reviewers examine the clarity and effectiveness of the statements and possibly their uniformity across departments. Statements from diverse disciplines that are presented in a common format and couched in similar language may be easier for users to understand. This sort of uniformity should not, however, violate the integrity of the disciplinary content of the statements.

• *Develop a reasonable time line.* Like Rome, goals and objectives cannot be defined and assessment research cannot be designed in a day. A department should allow sufficient time for people to develop commitment to the process, learn the skills necessary to the task, and engage in a thoughtful iterative process that can produce high-quality results. Still, the department should establish a firm time line and hold people to it, or the process may extend forever.

• *Ensure that there is broad involvement in the process.* A key step in leading for change is for the chair to ensure that everyone is involved in the change process. Experience shows that involving people in the process of defining outcomes produces better results than if the department chair or a committee alone writes them. Involvement in designing the assessment plan has a similar effect. Actively involving people at many points can provide an opportunity to develop a sense of community, empowerment, and leadership throughout the department (Tichy, 1997).

Involving everyone appropriately in the process will go far toward ensuring faculty commitment to using the goals and objectives as well as student willingness to participate in assessment and do their best. Although it may seem more efficient for the chair to write the department's outcome statements, excluding others from the process may lead to mere bureaucratic compliance with management dictate to use these statements. Furthermore, being involved in constructing the statements helps everyone more deeply understand the department and its educational processes. And because writing outcome statements is a challenging task, broad involvement enables many hands to make lighter work.

Designing assessment research is similarly intellectually challenging and as demanding of time commitment as defining outcomes. The suggestions made for the earlier phase of the work apply to assessment as well.

Involving Faculty: Reducing Resistance to Assessment

In departments where department-wide assessment is a new concept, the chair should help everyone to understand the purposes of assessment and the substantial benefits that clearly defined outcomes and their assessment can bestow on the department in the form of significantly enhanced student learning and organizational effectiveness. The best way to ensure understanding is to involve every faculty member in the process. There are a number of specific ways in which broad involvement in goal setting and assessment may help a leader reduce possible faculty resistance to change. Everyone is busy, and most people probably avoid additional tasks that they may view as needless bureaucratic activity. Also, in some cases, where the purpose of assessment has not been fully explained, faculty have confused assessing the outcomes of student learning with faculty evaluation and thus have felt threatened by the process. Finally, some members of the faculty may suspect that the results will confirm their worst fears about their students' learning. In each of these cases, involving people early and continuously can lead to greater understanding of and personal commitment to the purpose and process.

Involving Students

Chairs should ensure that students, as the subjects of much of assessment and the ultimate beneficiaries of most, are intimately involved at various points in the process of assessment. The reasons for involving students include, first, that assessment is necessary for effective learning. Learners require frequent feedback on the effectiveness of their work. In most courses, students need much more, and more timely, feedback on their learning than they get. Much of the assessment they receive is designed to produce grades for the purpose of sorting people, not for the purpose of learning. Midterm and final examinations generally cannot provide timely feedback; in addition, in many cases students never learn which items they answered correctly or incorrectly or what the correct responses are.

Second, the need for assessment of learning is clear and the pressure from external stakeholders for credible evidence of high-level learning is escalating. In addition, there is a growing critical consumer awareness on the part of students. It would seem prudent for a department to ensure that all students are fully informed and understand and support the role of assessment in producing evidence of outcomes.

Third, student motivation to try hard during assessment is a significant concern for departments. If students do not value the assessment process because they do not understand its purpose or, like the faculty, see it as merely an annoying bureaucratic exercise rather than as an essential component of their learning and a means of ensuring the quality of the department's program, they may expend only desultory effort or actively resist the process. *A less than maximum effort on the part of students can invalidate the results of assessment.* The results are not trustworthy evidence of students' abilities because these abilities were not exerted.

Ensuring that assessment is an integral part of the educational process of the department is a first step toward increasing its value for everyone and convincing faculty and students alike that they should take it very seriously. Informing students about the role of assessment in the institution and its departments should begin early, and the message should be repeated often. Students should hear about the important role of assessment in learning when they first apply for admission and by integrating assessment into orientation to the institution and the department, into academic advising, and into every course. These steps will go far toward ensuring that every student understands the process and how it can help him or her monitor his or her learning and development.

Showing students how all general education and major curricular goals and objectives and those at the course level are integrated and how assessments are carefully designed to help them and their teachers monitor their learning and development and their achievement of these outcomes can help gain students' enthusiastic support for the assessment process. *Assessment becomes an integral part of student development and the college experience.*

A deeper level of involvement may be possible as well by asking students to identify problems with the outcome definition and assessment process, to contribute creative ideas, and to help with various phases of the work to be done. Learning about the material to be assessed and the design, administration, and interpretation of assessment and how the results are used to improve the educational process is real academic learning, too.

Using Assessment Results: An Opportunity for Leadership

The findings of assessment research and the time, money, energy, and emotion that will have been devoted to the process improve student learning and create value for taxpayers, donors, and society *only if the findings are used to improve the quality of the educational process.* Yet more than a few institutions and departments stumble here. The point of assessment is to understand the department more deeply and improve its capacity to help its students learn. Like mission statements, goals, and objectives, however, *assessment results must be actively used to be useful.* A skillful chair can use the fruits of assessment as a powerful tool to lead for change.

Faculty and Staff Development

Over the last twenty to thirty years, the role of college educator has been transformed into a technically complex profession with the impedimenta of other mature professions: an empirical research base, a body of accepted best practice, theoretical and applied scholarly journals, diverse professional associations, conferences, and doctoral training. Most college and university educators, however, were traditionally educated solely in an academic discipline or field and lack professional training as educators. Therefore, we have much to learn if we are to be able to employ the best research-based modern methods to help our students learn. Fortunately, today there are many high-quality resources to assist us in our work.

Developing the knowledge and skills required to design, implement, and interpret the results of assessment research necessitates study and practice. Using these results effectively to improve student learning and development requires understanding the sequence of stages through which students develop various societally important abilities, and being able to use skillfully the methods known to foster this development.

When assessment results for an intended outcome are unacceptable, the professional literature of higher education and research-based best practice are the appropriate guides for redesigning educational processes.

Leadership and Management of the Process

Effective goal setting and monitoring of results require leadership; they need strong advocates or champions for timely and successful execution. The department chair should take the lead in helping everyone understand the importance of defining and assessing learning outcomes, developing commitment to the process, and ensuring that everyone is appropriately involved.

The chair should ensure that people have the necessary resources to do the job well and that the process is efficiently managed: that there is an appropriate time line, that the steps in the process are carried out with dispatch, that people have the training they require to do the job well, and that a means of cyclical review is in place to ensure that high-quality outcome statements and assessments result.

It is impossible to overemphasize the importance of making the effort to develop an effective set of outcome goals and objectives for curricula before moving ahead to assessment. In addition to their importance as the foundation for program evaluation, these statements are necessary precursors to defining outcomes for a curriculum's courses. Although the task is challenging and initially time-consuming, this investment will redound to the benefit of the department and its students and can lead to significant improvement in program quality and learning for years to come.

Resources

This chapter has provided an overview of how chairs and faculty can define outcomes and use assessment research to monitor an academic department's capacity to produce learning and development in its students. Chairs and their colleagues will have to study the professional literature relevant to their work as educators and develop the personal and professional knowledge and skills necessary to carry out effectively these complex tasks. There are many resources that can help. Some particularly useful ones are described here.

Local Resources

First, the department should identify resources that may exist on campus. Significant amounts of data may be available from assessments conducted by the department, the dean's office, student affairs, or institutional research. There may also be people on campus with valuable technical skills who can help the department. These people are often found in offices of institutional research or assessment, schools or departments of education, social science departments, and faculty-instructional development, learning resources, and career development centers.

General Resources

The American Association for Higher Education (AAHE) has published what is perhaps the most comprehensive guide to assessment-related resources in higher education, *Learning Through Assessment: A Resource Guide for Higher Education* (Gardiner, Anderson, and Cambridge, 1997). This book provides background to the current assessment movement in the United States and reprints the nine AAHE Principles of Good Practice for Assessing Student Learning. It describes serial publications in the areas of assessment, measurement, and evaluation as well as institutional research, planning, and professional research in higher education. It includes an annotated assessment library with abstracts of more than three hundred books, monographs, and other publications on assessment, and provides descriptions of associations and organizations, assessment instruments, and Internet, multimedia, and technological resources for assessment.

To take stock of developments in assessment and keep up-to-date on assessment activities on other campuses around the country, possibly the best source is *Assessment Update: Progress, Trends, and Practices in Higher Education,* a bimonthly newsletter published by Jossey-Bass (www.josseybass.com). It contains articles, regular columns by experts, and information about instruments, conferences, and publications, among other topics.

For detailed accounts of assessment experiences on specific campuses around the United States, consult the books by Trudy Banta and Associates (1993); by Banta, Jon Lund, Karen Black, and Frances Oblander (1996); and by James Nichols (1996b).

Clarifying Mission Statements and Defining Outcomes

A department needs to know what it is trying to accomplish before it develops educational programs or attempts to assess its effectiveness. The starting point for the whole process of monitoring departmental performance should be the department's mission statement. First, it should conform to the college mission statement. It should be properly constructed such that it can do the work required of it. Gardiner (1989) and Nichols (1995a) provide guidance for writing a new mission statement or reviewing an existing one.

Specific ideas for outcomes the department may wish to articulate as goals and objectives can come from many sources. Literature research can help a department avoid reinventing the wheel. Publications on specific types of abilities such as critical thinking, highly valued by faculty everywhere, can suggest component skills and dispositions that, when achieved, together constitute the overarching behavior known as critical thinking (Facione, 1990; Paul, 1995; Erwin, 1998).

Because the literature on student development is very large, however, compendia of research and accepted practice may be the best place to start. These resources can orient readers to the area of student development, suggest numerous possibilities for desirable departmental outcomes and interesting questions for assessment research, and provide references to numerous additional specialized resources.

In *How Colleges Affect Students: Findings and Insights from Twenty Years of Research,* Pascarella and Terenzini (1991) review 2,600 studies of student development and college's effects on students conducted since 1968. They summarize and critique these studies and provide suggestions for practical application of the findings of this research in colleges and universities.

Redesigning Higher Education: Producing Dramatic Gains in Student Learning (Gardiner, 1996) provides a more compact review and synthesis of research related to key abilities that society requires, how these abilities develop, the effectiveness of current practices, the learning potential of students today, and recommendations of researchers for best practice.

What Matters in College: Four Critical Years Revisited (Astin, 1993) describes a study that considered 146 input variables, 192 student environmental-educational process variables, and 82 outcome variables. Astin's findings can illuminate the interactions among students' characteristics when they arrive on campus, what a department does with them, and the outcomes these activities may be expected to produce.

For a practical handbook for understanding and writing goals and objectives of all types, consult Gardiner (1989). Ideas for outcomes appear in the goals and objectives of other departments and institutions and in compendia in the literature. Bowen (1977) presents a "catalogue of goals," and Gardiner (1989) and Lenning (1977) present lists of outcomes from various institutions.

Assessment: General Resources

There are several resources that can serve as textbooks for assessment. Anderson, Ball, Murphy, and Associates (1975) and Linn (1993) provide general treatises on assessment, measurement, and evaluation. For the details of assessment design, standard textbooks on testing and measurement in education and psychology are helpful (see, for example, Carey, 1994; and Cronbach, 1984). Textbooks written specifically for assessment in higher education

include Angelo and Cross (1993); Astin (1991); Cross and Steadman (1996); Dressell (1976): Erwin (1991); Jacobs and Chase
(1992); Light, Singer, and Willett (1990); Nichols (1995a, b); and
Palomba and Banta (1999). Nichols (1995c) has also written a
guide for academic departments.

The annual June assessment conference presented by the
American Association for Higher Education (www.aahe.org) is an
excellent place to learn how assessment is being used to improve
student learning.

There are many electronic resources for assessment. ASSESS-L
(ASSESS.LSV.UKY.EDU) is a helpful listserv for higher education
assessment issues of all types. Subscribers are an excellent source
of information. To subscribe, send the following message on one
line to the address just presented: *subscribe assess <your first name>
<your last name>*.

A Web site with detailed information about the skills and dispositions of critical thinking, problem solving, and writing, and instruments for assessing them, is http://nces.ed.gov/evaltests/
default.asp.

For information about other assessment conferences, electronic resources, and instruments, consult Gardiner, Anderson,
and Cambridge (1997).

Assessing Major Field Outcomes

Publications that specifically discuss issues of and methods for
assessing the major, including descriptions of experiences on
diverse campuses, are Adelman (1988, 1989); Applebaum (1987);
Banta and Associates (1993); Banta, Lund, Black, and Oblander
(1996); Farmer (1988); Fong (1988); and Nichols (1995a, b, c).

Using the Findings of Assessment Research to Improve Student Learning

The references by Astin (1993), Gardiner (1996), and Pascarella
and Terenzini (1991) just described contain large amounts of
information on how students learn and develop and on experiences known to produce various types of development in students.

Faculty Professional Development

The Professional and Organizational Development (P.O.D.) Network in Higher Education is the primary professional association for faculty and staff members, administrators, and others involved in the professional development of faculty members as educators. Consult the P.O.D. Web site (www.podnetwork.org) for information about faculty development and P.O.D.

Searching the Professional Literature

Convenient searches of the enormous literature on higher education, including works on student learning and development and on the specification of outcomes, assessment, and academic departments, can be conducted easily through the ERIC database located at <http://ericir.syr.edu/Eric/>. This database includes entries from the inception of the ERIC system in 1966 up to within a few months of the present.

References

Adelman, C. (ed.). *Performance and Judgment: Essays on Principles and Practice in the Assessment of College Student Learning.* Office of Educational Research and Improvement Publication OR88–514. Washington, D.C.: U.S. Department of Education, 1988.

Adelman, C. (ed.). *Signs and Traces: Model Indicators of College Student Learning in the Disciplines.* Office of Educational Research and Improvement Publication OR89–538. Washington, D.C.: U.S. Department of Education, 1989.

Anderson, S. B., Ball, S., Murphy, R. T., and Associates. *Encyclopedia of Educational Evaluation.* San Francisco: Jossey-Bass, 1975.

Angelo, T. A., and Cross, K. P. *Classroom Assessment Techniques: A Handbook for College Teachers.* (2nd. ed.) San Francisco: Jossey-Bass, 1993.

Applebaum, M. I. "Assessment Through the Major." In C. Adelman (ed.), *Performance and Judgment: Essays on Principles and Practice in the Assessment of College Student Learning.* Washington, D.C.: U.S. Department of Education, Office of Educational Research and Improvement, 1988.

Astin, A. W. *Assessment for Excellence: The Philosophy and Practice of Assessment and Evaluation in Higher Education.* Phoenix: Oryx Press, 1991.

Astin, A. W. *What Matters in College? Four Critical Years Revisited.* San Francisco: Jossey-Bass, 1993.

Banta, T., and Associates. *Making a Difference: Outcomes of a Decade of Assessment in Higher Education.* San Francisco: Jossey-Bass, 1993.

Banta, T. W., Lund, J. P., Black, K. E., and Oblander, F. W. *Assessment in Practice: Putting Principles to Work on College Campuses.* San Francisco: Jossey-Bass, 1996.

Bloom, B. S. (ed.). *Taxonomy of Educational Objectives: The Classification of Educational Goals. Handbook One: Cognitive Domain.* New York: Longman, 1956.

Bowen, H. R. *Investment in Learning: The Individual and Social Value of American Higher Education.* San Francisco: Jossey-Bass, 1977.

Carey, L. M. *Measuring and Evaluating School Learning.* Needham Heights, Mass.: Allyn & Bacon, 1994.

Cronbach, L. J. *Essentials of Psychological Testing.* New York: HarperCollins, 1984.

Cross, K. P., and Steadman, M. H. *Classroom Research: Implementing the Scholarship of Teaching.* San Francisco: Jossey-Bass, 1996.

Dressell, P. L. *Handbook of Academic Evaluation.* San Francisco: Jossey-Bass, 1976.

Erwin, D. I. *Assessing Student Learning and Development: A Guide to the Principles, Goals, and Methods of Determining College Outcomes.* San Francisco: Jossey-Bass, 1991.

Erwin, T. D., for the Council for the National Postsecondary Education Cooperative Working Group on Student Outcomes, Panel on Cognitive Outcomes. *Definitions and Assessment Methods for Critical Thinking, Problem, Solving, and Writing.* Washington, D.C.: U.S. Department of Education, National Center for Education Statistics, 1998. (http://nces.ed.gov/npec/evaltests/default.asp)

Facione, P. A. "Critical Thinking: A Statement of Expert Consensus for the Purposes of Educational Assessment and Instruction." Unpublished manuscript, 1990. (ED 315 423)

Farmer, D. W. *Enhancing Student Learning: Emphasizing Essential Competencies in Academic Programs.* Wilkes Barre, Pa.: King's College, 1988.

Fong, B. "Assessing the Departmental Major." In J. H. McMillan (ed.), *Assessing Students' Learning.* San Francisco: Jossey-Bass, 1988.

Gardiner, L. F. *Planning for Assessment: Mission Statements, Goals, and Objectives.* Trenton: New Jersey Department of Higher Education, 1989. (ED 403 809)

Gardiner, L. F. *Redesigning Higher Education: Producing Dramatic Gains in Student Learning.* ASHE-ERIC Higher Education Report, vol. 23, no.

7. Washington, D.C.: Graduate School of Education and Human Development, George Washington University, 1996.

Gardiner, L. F., Anderson, C., and Cambridge, B. L. (eds.). *Learning Through Assessment: A Resource Guide for Higher Education.* Washington, D.C.: American Association for Higher Education, Assessment Forum, 1997.

Jacobs, L. C., and Chase, C. I. *Developing and Using Tests Effectively: A Guide for Faculty.* San Francisco: Jossey-Bass, 1992.

Krathwohl, D. R., Bloom, B. S., and Masia, B. B. *Taxonomy of Educational Objectives: The Classification of Educational Goals. Handbook Two: Affective Domain.* New York: Longman, 1964.

Lenning, O. T. *Previous Attempts to Structure Educational Outcomes and Outcome-Related Concepts: A Compilation and Review of the Literature.* Boulder, Colo.: National Center for Higher Education Management Systems, 1977. (ED 272 109)

Light, R. J., Singer, J. D., and Willett, J. B. *By Design: Planning Research in Higher Education.* Cambridge, Mass.: Harvard University Press, 1990.

Linn, R. L. *Educational Measurement.* Phoenix: Oryx Press, 1993.

Milton, O. *Will That Be on the Final?* Springfield, Ill.: Thomas, 1982.

Nichols, J. O. *A Practitioner's Handbook for Institutional Effectiveness and Student Outcomes Assessment Implementation.* (3rd. ed.) New York: Agathon Press, 1995a.

Nichols, J. O. *Assessment Case Studies: Common Issues in Implementation with Various Campus Approaches to Resolution.* New York: Agathon Press, 1995b.

Nichols, J. O. *The Departmental Guide and Record Book for Student Outcomes Assessment and Institutional Effectiveness.* (2nd ed.). New York: Agathon Press, 1995c.

Palomba, C. A., and Banta, T. W. *Assessment Essentials: Planning, Implementing, and Improving Assessment in Higher Education.* San Francisco: Jossey-Bass, 1999.

Pascarella, E. T., and Terenzini, P. T. *How College Affects Students: Findings and Insights from Twenty Years of Research.* San Francisco: Jossey-Bass, 1991.

Paul, R. W. *Critical Thinking: How to Prepare Students for a Rapidly Changing World.* Santa Rosa, Calif.: Foundation for Critical Thinking, 1995.

Tichy, N. M. *The Leadership Engine: How Winning Companies Build Leaders at Every Level.* New York: HarperCollins, 1997.

Chapter Nine

Service Learning and the Engaged Department

A Strategy with Many Uses

Edward Zlotkowski

On the first day of class they shuffle in and stake out seats in the last row, as close to the door as they can get. They are long and lean, but by the time they have finished sliding down into their seats they are all but invisible. We make little or no eye contact: their interests and conversation are emphatically self-contained. When I finally do manage to get them to join the class in giving me their attention, the expressions on their faces read like an indulgent, bemused challenge: "Teach us if you dare!"

It is the rare faculty member who has not encountered a situation of this kind. Regardless of institutional type, participant age and background, and the specific course being taught, the students' attention spans, their willingness to engage, and their patience with abstractions and intellectual complexity often seem in short supply. And when students, instructor, and course material fail to establish more than forced, formal contact, the possibility of a truly satisfying—let alone transformative—learning experience becomes remote.

Such a problem, however real, may at first seem to lie outside the purview of the department chair. What can a chair do to address a problem that is pandemic in scope? Besides, with so many other responsibilities calling for attention, why should he or she even try? In the pages that follow, I explore one especially hopeful approach to instructional design—namely, our ability to renew student interest and engagement while at the same time boosting faculty morale and creativity through partnerships with off-campus communities, especially communities that have not been adequately served by our market economy.

Over the past decade, this partnering strategy—most frequently referred to as *service learning*—has emerged as one of the most exciting and potentially valuable educational innovations available to faculty and the departments within which they work. Indeed, higher education as we know it may well need innovations like this to survive—politically, intellectually, even financially— because only such directly engaged forms of knowledge production and dissemination can address our postindustrial, postmodern society's full range of educational and civic needs. As John Abbott (1996), leader of an international effort to link experts across the disciplines "in a search for new learning strategies," has suggested, "today, people worldwide need a whole series of new competencies—the ability to conceptualize and solve problems that entails *abstraction . . . systems thinking . . . experimentation,* and *collaboration . . .* but I doubt such abilities can be taught solely in the classroom, or be developed solely by teachers. Higher-order thinking and problem-solving skills grow out of direct experience, not simply teaching; they require more than a classroom activity. They develop through active involvement and real-life experiences in workplaces and in the community" (pp. 3–4; emphasis in original). Department chairs will play a pivotal role in determining whether the academy can, in fact, meet these needs, because innovative strategies will be created, if they are created at all, at the department level.

Service Learning Defined

One frequently cited definition of service learning reads as follows:

> We view service learning as a credit-bearing educational experience in which students participate in an organized service activity that meets identified community needs and reflect on the service activity in such a way as to gain further understanding of the course content, a broader appreciation of the discipline, and an enhanced

sense of civic responsibility. Unlike extracurricular voluntary service, service learning is a course-based service experience that produces the best outcomes when meaningful service activities are related to course material through reflection activities such as directed writings, small group discussions, and class presentations. Unlike practica and internships, the experiential activity in a service learning course is not necessarily skill-based within the context of professional education [Bringle and Hatcher, 1996, p. 222].

The value of this formulation lies not only in its specification of key service-learning features but also in its differentiation between service learning and both volunteerism and traditional practica and internships. A clear awareness of these distinctions is essential if one is to understand service learning's potential to shape the academic-civic dialogue and to facilitate higher education's ability to deliver enhanced social and educational value.

Among the key service-learning features referred to here, the very first is contained in the phrase "a credit-bearing educational experience." As an educational experience, service learning is no different than a textual analysis, a problem set, a case study, or a laboratory experiment; that is, it represents an activity whose rationale is fundamentally related to its ability to promote learning. From this perspective, the service is merely a vehicle of the learning. However, unlike more traditional educational vehicles, the kind of learning that service learning promotes is deliberately multifaceted and includes "course content, a broader appreciation of the discipline, and an enhanced sense of civic responsibility." To accomplish these complex objectives, service-learning employs a variety of reflection strategies, and hence reflection must be considered another key feature. When engaged in service learning, students not only act in a way that has real-world consequences, but they also learn to process their actions carefully, deliberately, and analytically, thereby becoming what the late Donald Schön (1983, 1987, 1995) called "reflective practitioners."

Learning, however, is only one of service learning's two primary concepts; just as important is the concept of service. To be sure, service in this context is marked by distinctive characteristics. It is, in fact, every bit as multifaceted as the learning it promotes. However, unlike most of that learning, it finds its ultimate logic not in student growth but in community benefit. Thus we arrive at a third key feature: service learning seeks to establish academy-community relationships that are fully *reciprocal*—that is, reciprocal in both sides' willingness to learn and serve, reciprocal in both sides' willingness to balance benefits with responsibilities. The phrase "identified community needs" in Bringle and Hatcher's definition points to this reciprocity in that it suggests that the community needs that are to be met must be clearly identified and agreed to by all parties. In this way, service learning differs from some other, more traditional kinds of fieldwork in which the community's needs are clearly subordinated to the academy's educational objectives—where in fact the community becomes merely a means to an academic end.

But an emphasis on reciprocity is not the only factor that helps distinguish service learning from other, more traditional forms of experiential education. As Bringle and Hatcher note, service learning is not necessarily organized around the development of professional skills. While typically the only students who do practica or internships are those concentrating in the disciplinary area in which the field experience is offered—for example, only nursing students do nursing practica and only journalism students do journalism internships—service-learning experiences are open to all students. In addition to providing service-learning capstone courses that do indeed resemble the traditional internship in many respects, departments also can and do offer service projects across the entire range of their offerings, including introductory courses, electives, and even courses for nonmajors. In this way, service learning can be viewed as a valuable complement and supplement to the traditional practicum and internship experience. Because students can become involved in such work at an earlier point in their academic careers, that work can serve both to introduce them to real-world applications and to provide hands-on learning opportunities for a much larger number of students.

Perhaps in part because this approach does provide so many opportunities for students to appreciate a discipline's concrete relevance, its growth as a *discipline-specific undertaking* has been especially apparent. New books and monographs, special editions of established journals, and the inclusion of service learning in the programming of national and regional associations help paint the picture of a movement building an ever stronger discipline-specific base.

Leadership in a Period of Major Change

Summarizing concepts identified by key authors in the field, Ann Lucas (1994) distinguishes between two kinds of leadership: "Transformational leaders create a shared vision, energize others by communicating that vision at many levels, stimulate others to think in different ways and to excel, give individual consideration to others, and provide an organizational climate that helps others to accomplish activities of value and feel appreciated. In contrast, transactional leaders are managers who plan, organize, lead, staff, and control or monitor programs toward organizational goals" (p. 47). She goes on to argue that "it is important that a chair be a transformational leader, since that is precisely the kind of leader who can perform these essential tasks: revitalize faculty and improve professional development, act as a catalyst to improve the departmental culture, use the untapped talents of faculty, help faculty formulate departmental goals identifying new directions, and create a quality curriculum responsive to major changes in the discipline" (p. 49). Lucas's call for chairs who can respond proactively to departmental needs by encouraging innovation and fostering individual growth resonates especially well in today's culture of widespread academic change. Although individual faculty members may deny the necessity of such change, responsible chairs cannot afford to do so. Failure to recognize what is at stake in our need to adjust to new cultural circumstances may well result in a loss of majors, a loss of institutional leverage, and ultimately a loss of jobs.

No one has described the implications of today's educational realignment better than R. Eugene Rice, director of the American Association for Higher Education's (AAHE) Forum on Faculty Roles and Rewards. In a highly influential essay entitled *Making a Place for the New American Scholar* (1996, p. 8ff), Rice identifies several pivotal points in what he refers to as the "assumptive world of the academic professional"—that is, that "complex of basic assumptions" that have come to dominate and structure the work of faculty. These pivotal points include a privileging of research above all other forms of scholarly activity, of pure research above applications, of specialization above connections and context, and of the internal values and priorities of the academy above the needs and concerns of non-members. It is these assumptions, Rice argues, that have shaped the professional socialization of "the large number of older senior faculty who now head departments and influence tenure and promotion decisions."

However, even as this assumptive world pulls the academy in one direction, "institutional developments . . . pull it in another" (Rice, 1996, p. 9). Primary among these developments is pressure to pay more serious attention to undergraduate education and to the needs of the larger community:

> As we moved into the 1990s . . . [the] priorities that had been central to the assumptive world of the academic professional began to be not necessarily challenged and rejected but added to. The junior faculty interviewed for the "Heeding New Voices" inquiry report that, in one sense, it is a new day on campus. . . . Extensive peer review of one's publications continues to be what is valued most; but in addition to thorough student evaluation, one's teaching also has to be peer reviewed in multiple ways. While new faculty are, on the local level, being encouraged to engage in the very gratifying work of curricular development and reaching out to the broader community through newly initiated service-learning programs, they are being told that their more cosmopolitan responsibilities to professional associations and their guild colleagues are to be their first priority.
>
> Some of the best new faculty are being attracted to a new set of priorities focused on the essential missions of our institutions. On the other hand, the old priorities—the assumptive world of the academic professional—remain intact [Rice, 1996, p. 10].

What all this suggests for chairs is both the necessity and the difficulty of seeing the bigger picture, of being able to maneuver effectively in a context far more challenging than even that which existed only ten years ago. As Rice suggests, on the surface many of the old assumptions remain in place. Many, if not most, faculty whose academic values and attitudes were formed during the 1960s, 1970s, and early 1980s continue to see excellence in terms of traditional research published in peer-reviewed journals and continue to regard the traditional lecture-discussion as the most effective way to teach. A minority, however, no longer subscribes to these priorities. Following the lead of thinkers like Ernest Boyer (1990) and Ernest Lynton (1995), they regard traditional research as only one legitimate form of scholarship, as only one way of demonstrating excellence. They also have serious reservations about the efficacy of the traditional lecture-discussion approach in reaching an ever more diverse student population and in helping students develop both the skills and the will to become active, lifelong learners.

At the very least, such a situation demands that chairs make every effort to inform themselves about the new forms of teaching and scholarship that are emerging. In the present context, this means, above all, making a serious effort to understand the new, more engaged forms of scholarly activity so as to make room for them in the department's efforts to stay abreast of disciplinary developments and institutional priorities. A chair who cannot distinguish between service learning and traditional community service can hardly judge the appropriateness of student or junior faculty interest in this area. A chair who thinks that the department already has a strong outreach program because it offers internships may be puzzled, or even insulted, by a dean's observation that the department needs to do more to get behind the institution's new civic agenda.

Identifying Excellence

Aside from understanding clearly what service learning is and how it complements but differs from other forms of experiential learning, perhaps the major task facing chairs is recognizing and rewarding excellence. Because I have already described elsewhere (Zlotkowski, 1998) a four-part matrix for identifying areas of faculty responsibility, the most useful strategy here may be to develop an analogous four-part schema for chairs. What do chairs have a right to expect from service-learning faculty? Basically they should focus their attention on four factors: (1) faculty ability to design and implement a course-specific service activity; (2) faculty ability to design and implement multilevel reflection activities; (3) faculty ability to document, evaluate, and communicate the significance of the service activity; and (4) faculty familiarity with the community partner.

Course-Specific Service Activities

Nothing is more fundamental to the departmental and disciplinary value of a service project than a faculty member's ability to recognize the most appropriate way to frame that project within the overall objectives of the sponsoring course. Constructing a theory, testing a theory, strengthening problem-framing and problem-solving skills, implementing a procedure, providing real-world relevance, broadening and deepening students' powers of imagination, and sympathetic identification represent different but equally legitimate ways to frame the service experience from an academic perspective. Not infrequently chairs encounter department members whose enthusiasm for community-based work exceeds their expertise. Unless chairs understand that service-learning projects not only can be but should be course-specific—that is, they should be carefully and productively linked to course content—they may be tempted to let faculty go their own way while at the same time harboring misgivings that are only allowed to surface later in the context of an important evaluation. Chairs have a right to expect, from the very beginning, that faculty who wish to sponsor service projects will understand precisely how such work contributes to students' course-related learning.

Still another key area in which chairs have a right to expect careful pedagogical decision making is the way in which the service assignment has been formally integrated into the structure of a course. Should it, for example, be mandatory or elective, short-term or long-term, individual or group? How carefully has a faculty member taken into account his or her students' availability and level of expertise as well as his or her own experience and ability to guide such work? How well has that work—whether a major or minor, mandatory or elective component of the course—been integrated into the course's overall workload? If the service component is significant and mandatory, has sufficient thought been given to its effect on other course assignments? Unless faculty understand how service projects themselves can be effective vehicles of course content, they may be tempted simply to tack those projects onto everything already in place. Chairs can then look forward to a stream of student complaints about "unreasonable expectations."

Reflection Activities

Perhaps no aspect of service learning more seriously challenges traditional faculty competence than the ability to design and implement effective reflection activities. On the one hand, many faculty in technical and preprofessional disciplinary areas feel uncomfortable promoting exploratory, open-ended processing of any kind. On the other hand, even faculty in the social sciences and the humanities frequently lack experience in linking course-related topics to broader questions of civic responsibility and contemporary societal need. In terms of Bringle and Hatcher's (1996, p. 222) definition, they facilitate reflection "in such a way as to gain further understanding of the course content" and even "a broader appreciation of the discipline," but they stall when it comes to reflection that seeks to promote "an enhanced sense of civic responsibility." Why, they may ask, should they even learn to do so if they are not teaching (and often even if they are teaching) political science? Is not such a concern extraneous to their course's primary concerns and their own professional training?

Indeed, it may at first seem that what service learning demands in this quarter flies directly in the face of the course-specific criteria discussed earlier. But the contradiction is more apparent than real— or at least it is real only if one insists that education in a democracy does not necessarily have a public dimension. Once one concedes that the very design of the American system rests squarely on a decentralized sense of responsibility whereby citizens themselves help address public problems, the seeming contradiction between discipline-based expertise and the public uses of that expertise disappears. Far from being extraneous or irrelevant, reflective exercises that lead students to consider the social implications of their discipline-specific work as well as the social responsibilities that attach to expert knowledge in a democracy become a natural extension of traditional course content. Indeed, multilevel reflection is the catalyst that ultimately makes possible successful combining of community-based fieldwork and traditional academic classwork.

Documentation, Evaluation, and Communication

Although the identification of discipline-specific service projects and the design of multilevel reflection activities make academically rigorous, departmentally relevant service learning possible, it is only this third area that allows chairs to sustain support for service learning and hence make it an essential part of a department's strategic vision. Unfortunately, it is precisely here, in this area, that even many skillful service-learning practitioners fall short, choosing to put their energy almost exclusively into project implementation. By adopting such an "unscholarly" stance—by default if not by design—these individuals inadvertently reinforce the very doubts that make progressive academic change so difficult.

Chairs have a right to demand that all service-learning activities fully conform to the scholarly (in the broad, Boyer-defined sense of the word) norms of their department. Such norms may include providing detailed, fully developed syllabi as well as evaluations and impact measures, working on course-related presentations and publications, and developing research projects, for both student and faculty, related to community-academy collaborations. In other words, service learning must never be viewed as a substitute for scholarly expectations and values but rather as an extension of them (Zlotkowski, 1995, 1996). Just as Rice's (1996) analysis of today's academic culture suggests that traditional assumptions continue to hold sway even as new ones are developed, so chairs have a right to ask those committed to new forms of teaching and scholarship to demonstrate their value—*even as they ask those committed to traditional practices to make room for new forms to develop.* Hence the chair's role calls not just for understanding but also for the will and skill to ensure that standards are applied in an even-handed manner. This applies both within the department and in representing the work of faculty in other academic forums.

Direct Experience and Personal Commitment

The final dimension of service-learning work with which chairs need to be concerned is the strength of the faculty-community connection. Although it is possible to design and implement academically successful service-learning projects by developing the competencies discussed in the sections on service activities and reflection activities, community-based work is far more likely to be successful, and far more likely to provide a base on which to develop departmental resources, if the faculty involved have themselves had firsthand experience with the community. Such experience can be conceived of as having two dimensions: a functional dimension and a more extended dimension.

By *functional* dimension I mean sufficient contact to ensure clarity of communication, shared objectives and priorities, adequate student supervision, and agreement in regard to activities, deadlines, and evaluation. Collaborations that result in significant benefits on both sides usually begin long before the first day of class and sometimes extend over the course of many semesters. In this way, placements turn into partnerships as both academy and community participants become accustomed to otherwise unavailable resources. Student learning takes on a whole new dimension even as the community finds itself with capabilities otherwise beyond its scope (Morton, 1995).

But even when this happens, faculty may still not have developed, and still may not choose to develop, an *extended* personal commitment to such work. By this I mean that they may not have allowed a course-based partnership to affect other aspects of their professional lives. Thus they may have little interest in exploring the potential of their community connection to support their own research interests or some other form of professional outreach. Similarly, they may not feel called to serve on a community advisory board or an agency's board of trustees. From a chair's perspective, extended commitments of this kind are unnecessary. As long as faculty have enough experience and commitment to represent the department, and the institution, in a professionally responsible way, they can frame their personal commitment as broadly or as narrowly as they wish.

Using Service Learning to Full Advantage

Earlier in this chapter I suggested that the pervasive atmosphere of change we are currently experiencing in higher education is fundamentally linked to demands for closer community-academy ties and to an expectation of more direct social and educational benefits. If this is true, then chairs, departments, and faculty in general will have increasingly little choice as to whether or not to abandon the academy's traditional sense of itself as standing apart. The primary question will be not *whether* but *how*. By making room for forms of engaged scholarship such as service learning, departments can address these new demands without sacrificing academic rigor or scholarly integrity. In this section, I add to this general argument by briefly identifying some of the specific benefits that service learning can make available to the department chair.

Faculty Renewal

Over the past few years I have visited perhaps a hundred campuses to work with faculty on service-learning issues. I have been on campuses when faculty were not at all pleased to be returning in the second week of August, when my visit was scheduled for a Friday afternoon before spring break, when the provost or dean preceded me by announcing that there would once again be no merit pay increases. On not one of these occasions did I encounter faculty unwilling to respond with both enthusiasm and creativity to working together.

Although I and other service-learning advocates know of countless individual faculty members whose careers have been redefined by service learning, whose productivity and creativity have been tapped for the first time in their academic lives, whose professional sense of purpose has been recovered for the first time since graduate school, it is not this possibility of individual renewal I want to stress here. What strikes me forcefully almost every time I get together with faculty around this kind of work is their pleasure in experiencing themselves as a community—a community of scholars with special skills and a unique calling. Beyond the cynicism born of countless hours of bureaucratic obligation, the burnout that results from efforts marginally understood and even less appreciated, there remains a core of idealism that service learning almost always fans into flame. It is almost as if this coming back in from the cold of traditional academic isolation reassures us that being a teacher-scholar is after all a noble way to spend one's life, that what we as academics do really does matter, can matter, if only we choose to let it.

Enhanced Academic Coherence

Because service learning necessarily includes a public dimension, it also has the power to bring together otherwise discrete professional interests. The fact that community-based projects tend by their very nature to be cross-functional and results-oriented allows them to provide a natural platform on which faculty can talk across disciplinary and subdisciplinary areas of specialization. In some instances this can lead to department- or programwide partnerships that allow many classes with many instructors to link their work (Firmage and Cole, forthcoming). In other instances, it can provide an excellent opportunity to develop learning communities with members of other departments. Faculty members and students can reap the advantages of being involved in a multidisciplinary project without sacrificing the strengths that come from disciplinary and departmental affiliation.

There is finally one other way in which service learning helps promote academic coherence. As James Votruba (1996), former vice provost for outreach at Michigan State, has noted, "Traditionally, we have treated the academic trilogy of teaching, research, and service as if they were separate and conceptually distinct forms of professional activity. In times of limited resources, it is assumed that any attempt to strengthen one part of the trilogy must be done at the expense of the others. If outreach is to become a primary and fully integrated dimension of the overall academic mission, this 'zero sum' mentality must be overcome" (p. 30). By linking teaching directly to professional outreach activities—thereby providing opportunities for what Boyer (1990) has called the scholarships of application, integration, and teaching—service learning helps faculty transcend traditionally discrete or even conflicting demands. In doing so, it conserves faculty energy and concentrates departmental resources.

Student Interest and Motivation

As the scenario at the beginning of this chapter reminds us, lack of student intellectual engagement poses for many faculty a recurrent, troubling concern. Hence, few aspects of service learning more quickly catch faculty attention than its ability to open new avenues to student interest. A little over a year and a half ago I was participating in a service-learning colloquium sponsored by an accounting department. Approximately twenty full-time faculty members were present, and the presenter, a full professor in the department, was reporting on the results of his findings vis-à-vis student reactions to service learning in an intermediate accounting course he had taught. Of the twenty-five students enrolled, twenty-three concluded that a service assignment should be either an optional or even a mandatory feature of the course. When asked why, they replied that such an assignment made accounting more concrete and hence more enjoyable.

Two years earlier I had been asked to speak at a prestigious liberal arts college where the chair of the chemistry department confided to me that she planned to introduce service learning into the department because it seemed to be the most promising way to demonstrate to minority students that chemistry was indeed related to their other interests. Indeed, a growing body of research supports the wisdom of her decision. For example, Richard Fox and Shirley Ronkowski (1997) recently looked at the preferred learning styles of political science students. They conclude that "in lower level introductory courses, a greater emphasis should be placed on activities that provide concrete and active experiences for students, since lower division students indicated a greater preference for these styles than upperclass students. If one of the aims of lower division classes is to interest as many students as possible, particularly women and traditionally underrepresented students, in choosing political science as a major . . . then this strategy could be beneficial toward meeting this goal" (p. 736). But other studies suggest that it may not be only "women and traditionally underrepresented students" who find "concrete and active experiences" attractive and academically motivating. Charles Schroeder (1993), vice chancellor for student affairs at the University of Missouri-Columbia, found that "approximately 60 percent of entering students prefer the sensing mode of perceiving compared to 40 percent who prefer the intuitive mode. The learning styles of those who prefer sensing are characterized by a preference for direct, concrete experiences; moderate to high degrees of structure; linear, sequential learning; and, often, a need to know why before doing something. In general students who prefer sensing learning patterns prefer the concrete, the practical, and the immediate" (p. 22).

Schroeder makes at least two other observations that are of interest here: (1) unlike the majority of students, most faculty evince learning characteristics indicative of intuitive learners; and (2) "approximately 75 percent of the general population has been estimated to prefer the sensing learning pattern" (p. 24). Thus it would seem as if the traditional faculty approach to learning is not only at odds with that of most students, but it is also at odds with a large majority of the general population! If one characteristic of the current academic readjustment is an ever greater rapprochement between the academy and society, those departments that are able to find ways to bridge the interests and preferences of the two groups are more likely to have long-term success. As a bridge between the concrete and practical, on the one hand, and the abstract and theoretical, on the other, service learning has few equivalents.

Resources and Recommendations

It is not uncommon for faculty to view themselves as *professors,* as masters of content, rather than as *educators,* concerned with the ways in which that content is packaged and delivered. Hence it would follow that whatever adjustments higher education needs to make, it will undoubtedly make them in and through those individuals whose job it is to think about the packaging and delivery of the educational product. Former Stanford University president Donald Kennedy sees the situation differently. In a 1995 article entitled "Another Century's End, Another Revolution for Higher Education," he first suggests that the current period of educational readjustment may well prove to be as revolutionary as the late nineteenth-century change that brought us the graduate school. Then he suggests that this second revolution—however deep, however pervasive—is not likely to be led by central administrations "because the action [in our institutions] is all peripheral: it takes place at the level of department faculties" (p. 3). If Kennedy is correct both in his assessment of the significance of what is now happening and in his assessment of how this transformation will take place, the role of department chairs will perforce acquire an unprecedented level of importance. How much skill and vision chairs bring to their job—their ability to assume the functions of Lucas's (1994) *transformational* leaders—may well determine just how successful higher education will be in adapting to the needs of the twenty-first century. Given this set of circumstances, it seems only appropriate to conclude this chapter with a brief review of some of the resources of which chairs can begin to avail themselves if they choose to exercise the leadership we need.

With regard to service learning and the national movement to create more effective academy-community partnerships, the single most important development is the recent concentration of attention on disciplinary issues. I refer, first and foremost, to the AAHE series *Service-Learning in the Disciplines,* which not only explores course and program models but also includes more general, theoretical pieces on the circumstances that define this kind of work. By the end of 1999, eighteen volumes will have appeared, including volumes on composition, political science, teacher education, nursing, psychology, accounting, sociology, environmental studies, medical studies, Spanish, philosophy, peace studies, communication, engineering, history, biology, management, and women's studies. Volumes in other areas may be added at a later date or may be developed in other venues.

Indeed, as I indicated earlier, many of the national disciplinary societies are already developing resources of their own. These include special workshops, study groups, and sessions for chairs at national conferences. They also include more and more service-learning-related articles in disciplinary journals and in-house publications. Special publications and journal issues are being planned or considered in anthropology, gerontology, chemistry, mathematics, economics, religious studies, public administration, and the arts. More formal sources of information would include the national offices of Campus Compact, the National Society for Experiential Education, and AAHE, all of which maintain discipline-coded databases of service-learning faculty and projects. Recently, the Corporation for National Service in Washington announced that its K-12 service-learning clearinghouse (located at the University of Minnesota [http://www.nicsl.coled.umn.edu/otherweb.html]) is being expanded to encompass higher education. By the time this chapter appears in print, the higher education section of the clearinghouse should be fully operational.

National discipline-related resources represent one of the most important sources of information and assistance available to chairs. A second, equally important source of support are offices located within individual institutions. Over the past five years, the number of colleges and universities that have established special programs to support faculty interested in developing community-based projects and assignments has grown enormously. Campus Compact, the country's only national organization devoted exclusively to developing community-academy partnerships, now has almost six hundred members, the vast majority of whom support centralized service-learning programs. But the Compact's list is by no means inclusive of all higher education programs, and I would estimate, on the basis of my own experience, that one-quarter to one-third of the country's colleges and universities provide some kind of formal support. Even in those cases where no formal program exists, extracurricular community service programs most certainly do, and the staff of such programs are almost always very willing to share their contacts and resources.

To conclude this chapter, I offer five suggestions that I hope will make it possible for all chairs, regardless of their personal interest in community-based work, to help their departments profit as much as possible from whatever service learning their institution, their faculty members, or even their students express an interest in seeing provided.

1. Make sure that everyone in the department knows what service learning is and what it is not; that is, it is not volunteerism or just another word for internships. (Unfortunately, I have seen too many faculty take public stands before they knew what they were talking about!)

2. Insist on the same level of excellence in service learning as in any comparable departmental undertaking. Service learning is neither an alternative to traditional academic rigor nor something that needs to pass additional tests just to prove its worth.

3. Find out what kind of support your institution is able to provide to faculty working in this area. Ask someone in your office to compile a brief disciplinary resource list that includes publications

and articles, national association programming, course descriptions and syllabi from other schools, and the names, e-mail addresses, and phone numbers of successful practitioners elsewhere.

4. Defuse defensiveness. The fact that service learning is useful and appealing to some does not mean that everyone has to do it or that it implies a devaluing of more traditional forms of scholarship and teaching. The great advantage of sponsoring service learning is that it allows a department to extend the kinds of learning opportunities it offers and provide additional avenues for demonstrating excellence.

5. Consider developing service learning as a departmental resource: Are there particular community agencies or nonprofit groups, government offices, or K–12 schools that could regularly provide an opportunity for faculty and students to test-apply theory, develop new skills, and link their teaching and learning to real-world practice? If so, it may be worthwhile to cultivate a departmental partnership that extends beyond the individual course or one-time project.

Conclusion

Shortly before he died, Boyer maintained, in a keynote address to the National Association for Physical Education, that "service is going to emerge with greater vitality than we have seen it in the last 100 years, simply because the university must be engaged if it hopes to survive. The social imperative for service has become so urgent that the university cannot ignore it" (1996, p. 138). Service learning offers institutions of higher education an opportunity to link that service to the core responsibilities of generating and disseminating knowledge. Chairs who understand the educational as well as the social potential of this approach will not let that potential escape them.

As for those long, lean, disinterested students with whom I began, their story has a happy ending. Thanks to their involvement with disadvantaged high school students through a discipline-specific project, several of them found a new, more personal way to relate to the course texts. For two of them, that engagement in turn led to two of the finest analytical essays I received that semester.

References

Abbott, J. "The Search for Next-Century Learning." *AAHE Bulletin,* 1996, *48*(7), 3–6.

Boyer, E. L. *Scholarship Reconsidered: Priorities for the Professoriate.* Princeton, N.J.: Carnegie Foundation for the Advancement of Teaching, 1990.

Boyer, E. L. "From *Scholarship Reconsidered* to *Scholarship Assessed.*" *Quest,* 1996, *48*(2), 129–139.

Bringle, R. G., and Hatcher, J. A. "Implementing Service Learning in Higher Education." *Journal of Higher Education,* 1996, *67*(2), 221–239.

Firmage, D. H., and Cole, F. R. "The Challenges of Integrating Service-Learning in the Biology–Environmental Science Curriculum at Colby College." In H. Ward (ed.), *Acting Locally: Concepts and Models for Service-Learning in Environmental Studies.* Washington, D.C.: American Association for Higher Education, 1999.

Fox, R. L., and Ronkowski, S. A. "Learning Styles of Political Science Students." *PS: Political Science & Politics,* 1997, *30*(4), 732–737.

Kennedy, D. "Another Century's End, Another Revolution for Higher Education." *Change,* 1995, *27*(3), 8–15.

Lucas, A. F. *Strengthening Departmental Leadership: A Team-Building Guide for Chairs in Colleges and Universities.* San Francisco: Jossey-Bass, 1994.

Lynton, E. A. *Making the Case for Professional Service.* Washington, D.C.: American Association for Higher Education, 1995.

Morton, K. "The Irony of Service: Charity, Project and Social Change in Service Learning." *Michigan Journal of Community Service Learning,* 1995, *2*(1), 19–32.

Rice, R. E. *Making a Place for the New American Scholar.* American Association for Higher Education New Pathways Working Paper no. 1. Washington, D.C.: American Association for Higher Education, 1996.

Schön, D. A. *The Reflective Practitioner.* New York: Basic Books, 1983.

Schön, D. A. *Educating the Reflective Practitioner.* San Francisco: Jossey-Bass, 1987.

Schön, D. A. "The New Scholarship Requires a New Epistemology." Change, 1995, *27*(6), 27–34.

Schroeder, C. C. "New Students—New Learning Styles." *Change,* 1993, *25*(5), 21–26.

Votruba, J. C. "Strengthening the University's Alignment with Society: Challenges and Strategies." *Journal of Public Service and Outreach,* 1996, *1*(1), 29–36.

Zlotkowski, E. "Does Service-Learning Have a Future?" *Michigan Journal of Community Service Learning,* 1995, *2,* 123–133.

Zlotkowski, E. "A New Voice at the Table? Linking Service-Learning and the Academy." *Change,* 1996, *28*(1), 20–27.

Zlotkowski, E. "A Service Learning Approach to Faculty Development." In J. P. Howard and R. Rhodes (eds.), *Service Learning Pedagogy and Research.* San Francisco: Jossey-Bass, 1998.

Chapter Ten

Giving Faculty Ownership of Technological Change in the Department

A. W. (Tony) Bates

Of all the challenges facing chairs of departments, perhaps the most difficult is the impact of technology on teaching and learning.

The basic university teaching paradigm for most subjects has not changed a great deal for seven hundred years. Where technology has been introduced in the past, in the form of overhead projectors, slide shows, film, and videotapes, presentational qualities have been enhanced and students have seen better examples and illustrations, but the basic method of instruction is still unchanged. Rightly such technology has been termed *audiovisual aids,* an enhancement to but not a replacement for the basic classroom method.

All that is now changing. The new technologies of the Internet and multimedia are not just enhancing the teaching and learning environment; they are fundamentally changing it. These new technologies are having as profound an impact on education as the invention of the printing press did.

In this chapter I explore the nature of these changes and the implications for chairs of departments. The good news is that chairs do not need to be experts in the use of technology for teaching,

I am grateful to Jossey-Bass for permission to include material from my book *Managing Technological Change: Strategies for Academic Leaders* (Jossey-Bass, 2000).

although a good understanding of the relationship between technology and teaching will be immensely helpful. It is important, however, that chairs have strategies for dealing with the impact of new technologies on teaching, and this chapter sets out what some of these strategies might be.

How Technology Is Changing Teaching

New technologies have some of the following advantages over traditional classroom teaching:

- Learners are now increasingly able to access high quality teaching and learning at any time, at any place.
- Much of the information previously accessible only through a professor or instructor is now readily accessible on demand through computers and the Internet.
- Well-designed multimedia learning materials can be more effective than traditional classroom methods; students can learn more easily and more quickly through the use of integrated illustration and animation, through different structuring of materials, and through increased control of and interaction with learning materials.
- New technologies can be designed to develop and facilitate higher-order learning skills, such as problem solving, decision making, and critical thinking.
- Interaction with teachers can be structured and managed through on-line communications to provide greater access and flexibility for both students and teachers.
- Computer-mediated communication facilitates team teaching, the use of guest faculty from other institutions, and multicultural and international classes.

As a result, new technologies are leading to major structural changes in the management and organization of teaching. These developments are increasingly being referred to in the United States and Canada as *distributed learning,* in the United Kingdom as *networked learning,* and in Australia as *flexible learning.* The Institute for Academic Technology at the University of North Carolina has provided a useful definition of distributed learning:

A distributed learning environment is a learner-centered approach to education, which integrates a number of technologies to enable opportunities for activities and interaction in both asynchronous and real-time modes. The model is based on blending a choice of appropriate technologies with aspects of campus-based delivery, open learning systems and distance education. The approach gives instructors the flexibility to customize learning environments to meet the needs of diverse student populations, while providing both high quality and cost-effective learning [DEOS-L list serve, March 1995].

Thus, these new technologies have the potential not only to enrich existing classrooms but, equally importantly, to allow institutions to reach out to new target groups, such as lifelong learners, people in the workforce, and the physically disabled.

In practical terms, we are seeing the following developments:

- An increase in off-campus teaching, not just for "full" distance learners who cannot access the campus at all, but also for many on-campus students who find it more convenient and cheaper to study at least partly from home or the workplace
- Substitution, in part, of real laboratory experiments and techniques with computer simulations
- New kinds of courses, such as certificate and diploma programs, for those already graduated but needing professional updating
- Customized courses for specific clients, such as private sector organizations, and multiple use of materials to serve different client groups, such as undergraduate students, lifelong learners, and employers
- The development of partnerships and consortia that share courses and materials, to achieve economies of scale and the necessary investment to develop high-quality learning materials; examples are the Western Governors' initiative and the Southern Regional Electronic Campus in the United States
- Increased competition, not only from other public institutions enlarging their reach beyond state or national boundaries, but also from new private sector organizations, such as the University of Phoenix on-line programs, and corporate universities

It is thus important to realize that the use of technology for teaching is not just a technical issue. It also raises fundamental questions about target groups, methods of teaching, priorities for funding, and above all, the overall goals and purpose of the department. Therefore, decisions about technology need to be embedded in and subordinated to educational goals, while at the same time being sensitive to the potential and opportunities that new technologies can offer. This is why the challenge of technology is so important and so difficult.

Why Use Technology?

In order to develop appropriate strategies, it is important to understand the different rationales for using technology and to identify which rationale is the most important to the department.

To Increase Access and Flexibility for Students

Higher costs to students (fees, living expenses, travel) and fear of ending their studies with a large personal debt has led to a rapid increase in the number of students who are working part-time. With the best will in the world, it is often difficult for such students to avoid lecture times clashing with job obligations; but without the opportunity for part-time work, many students will be denied the opportunity of higher education.

The rapid rate of change in the workplace is also requiring all graduates to continue to be lifelong learners. In many professions it is now essential to update knowledge and skills on a continual basis. However, the requirements of this target group are very different from those of students entering college directly from high school and committed to full-time or even part-time studies. Since lifelong learners are already in the workforce, it is impractical for them to attend a campus on a regular and frequent basis. They often need not full degree programs but short courses, certificates or diplomas, or even "just-in-time" training in small modules. Furthermore, the more specialized the subject area is, the less likely professionals are to find the provision of such teaching locally. Also, this target group is often able and willing to pay the full cost of such programs, thus bringing in much needed revenues to a department. The flexible delivery of courses and programs through new technologies has many advantages for this target group.

To Improve the Quality of Teaching

It is my experience that in large research universities, improving the quality of teaching is the major reason for using new technologies. Level or reduced public funding combined with increasing enrollments and higher operating costs as faculty become older and receive salary increments have forced most universities and colleges to increase class sizes to balance budgets. Also, in order to protect research time, increasing use has been made of untrained and often inexperienced teaching assistants.

Increased teacher-to-student ratios, increased teaching loads, use of inexperienced or predoctoral teaching assistants, and the lack of interaction and reduced contact between tenured faculty and students at an undergraduate level are leading to growing dissatisfaction with the current classroom teaching environment. The use of technology is seen as one way of easing or alleviating some of these problems.

To Reduce Costs

Reducing costs is a rationale more likely to come from politicians, the business community, government officials, and senior managers than from faculty or department heads. It is also, for me, the least convincing of the rationales for using technology.

The introduction of technology is likely to lead to increased rather than reduced costs, at least in the short term. There are several reasons for this. First, there is a high cost of investment in both technological infrastructure (networks, computers, technical support staff) and staff development. There is a steep learning curve that demands a heavy investment of time from all staff, a point that is addressed in more detail later in this chapter. Furthermore, technology is changing rapidly. The average life of a computer is often less than four years. In particular, software that facilitates the development of course materials, such as WebCT, Toolbook, and Director, is constantly being introduced, updated, and improved. Even when faculty become skilled in using technology, they need constantly to update and improve their skills.

Although technology can replace some aspects of teaching and can enhance or facilitate communication between teachers and students, good quality teaching in higher education still requires high levels of teacher-student interaction if creative, critical, and analytical thinking and good communication skills are to be achieved. Higher education is therefore likely to remain people-intensive. In a knowledge-based society, there is no point in merely reducing cost if it also leads to lower-quality graduates.

To Improve Cost-Effectiveness

Although technology is unlikely to reduce absolute costs, it can improve the cost-effectiveness of operations in higher education in several ways:

- By enabling institutions to reach out to more and different students
- By using technology to reduce or eliminate those activities currently carried out by instructors that are best done by technology, thus freeing faculty for more productive use of their time
- By using technology to improve the quality of learning, either by enabling new skills and learning outcomes to be achieved or by enabling students to achieve existing learning goals more easily or more quickly.

We shall see, however, that increased cost-effectiveness in higher education requires more than just investment in new technologies; it also requires radical changes in teaching methods and organization. In particular, if technology is to be used cost-effectively, we need to ask what activities it is replacing.

Technology and Teaching

As mentioned in the introduction to this chapter, there are basically two different approaches to the use of technology for teaching. The first is to use technology as a classroom aid; the second is to use it for distributed learning. These approaches should be seen as two points on a continuum rather than as necessarily discrete approaches.

Classroom Aids

E-Mail

Perhaps the most pervasive current use of technology in higher education is the use of e-mail to supplement regular classroom teaching. Thus e-mail is used not only for administrative purposes but also increasingly for communication between teachers and students.

Many faculty are replacing office hours, which require a set time and place for students to contact them, with a bulletin board or e-mail service. A bulletin board enables announcements to be made by an instructor to all students in a class; e-mail allows for individual communication between an instructor and a student, or between individual students.

Some instructors have gone even further and established listservs, which enable all students and the instructor to have on-line discussions about relevant or contemporary issues associated with the course. An on-line "chat" facility allows instructor and students to communicate in real time. Some instructors are also allowing students to submit assignments by e-mail.

In all cases, these technologies tend to be supplements to classroom teaching, although their use may well replace some other activities, such as office hours or the physical delivery and collection of assignments. In general, however, most instructors report that this use of e-mail tends to increase rather than reduce the amount of time they spend in contact with students, which may be good for the students but can lead to work overload for instructors. Also, student expectations of instructors' availability and speed of response may become unreasonable. It is a good idea to set down standards, which give students some idea of when they can expect a response and protect instructors from constant harassment for immediate responses.

Lastly, a point I shall return to later, the use of e-mail requires both instructors and students to have access to e-mail through computers and an Internet account. Without explicit policies regarding networking of instructors and students, some students may be severely disadvantaged by lack of e-mail access, as indeed may some instructors.

Presentational Software

The use of presentational software such as Microsoft's PowerPoint is another pervasive use of computer technology to enhance classroom teaching. PowerPoint is a relatively easy piece of software to learn, although the skill level needed for the incorporation of graphics, animation, charts, and video and audio clips can escalate rapidly. Furthermore, design skills in the choice of fonts, the layout of the screen, and the use of illustration make a big difference to the quality of the presentation. Preparation for the use of presentational software requires a little more time than the preparation of a chalk-and-talk lecture, but it may in fact lead to savings in time where complex overheads or slides were previously used.

The major requirements are adequate training in the use of the software, a personal portable computer for the instructor, and the provision in lecture theaters of data projectors that can be quickly and easily hooked up to the instructor's portable computer. These technologies require substantial capital investment, some training, and a limited amount of technical support. Although the benefits often appear obvious, they are in fact difficult to quantify.

Videoconferencing

Videoconferencing is used primarily to increase access and to spread limited subject expertise over a wider area. It is particularly popular in multicampus organizations, such as state university systems in the United States. For instance, a small rural campus may have only two or three students who want to register for a particular course. These students can be linked to a larger class in a major urban center without the need to hire an additional instructor.

The use of videoconferencing for the regular delivery of teaching requires a substantial investment in capital (not so much for the equipment as for room reconstruction and adaptation), in networks to carry the videoconferencing signals, and if several campuses are linked, in leasing or buying switching equipment. There are several different budgeting arrangements for videoconferencing. Sometimes departments are charged for use; other times the service is considered free, because infrastructure costs are often paid for on a statewide or institutional basis. Nevertheless, the local equipment, technical support, and preparation time of instructors are all direct costs for an institution, and the money for infrastructure comes out of the system somewhere.

The major attraction of videoconferencing to faculty is that there is relatively little change in their normal teaching methods, although videoconferences generally result in more time being spent in preparation. Videoconferencing also tends to be quite stressful, particularly if the instructor tries to use interactive techniques to include remote as well as local students. Class size also increases, so the amount of interactivity for an individual student tends to diminish.

Although videoconferencing may enable additional students to have access to courses in their more immediate neighborhood, it also increases instructors' workloads and adds overall cost to the system, and the marginal cost for each additional student served is high (Bates, 1995).

The World Wide Web

Many instructors are now using the World Wide Web both as a presentational tool in lectures and as a means of making lecture notes conveniently available to students at other times. The Web has the additional advantage that through Internet links instructors can access other Web sites from around the world and bring materials from these sites into the lecture. Another use of the Web is to create databases of slides, photographs, and illustrations that can be drawn on for a lecture or made available to students on-line.

The disadvantage of using the Web is that it requires the use of a special if simple computer language (HTML) to create Web pages, and the maintenance of a Web server (host computer) for the site. The Web is therefore time-consuming and requires either substantial technical skill and preparation time from an instructor or significant technical support, often provided by graduate students funded by small teaching grants who convert lecture notes into Web pages. Also, the Web works best when the host site is on a UNIX-based server. This requires a department to have a specially dedicated computer and technical staff support, both of which have capital and operating cost implications.

Furthermore, as we shall see, using the Web only for lectures fails to exploit many of its unique features.

Multimedia and CD-ROM

A relatively small number of instructors (less than 10 percent in the United States and Canada) are using multimedia or CD-ROM technology to support classroom teaching. Language laboratories, computer-aided design in architecture, simulated science experiments, and large research databases containing multimedia resources such as graphics, compressed video, and audio are examples of the main uses of multimedia and CD-ROMs to support classroom teaching.

Multimedia and CD-ROMs are usually used in computer laboratories (where desktop personal computers may be networked to a local server) or with stand-alone computers that have a CD-ROM drive. (Currently, multimedia materials with video and audio clips generally require too much bandwidth for convenient delivery over public Internet systems.)

Some faculty are beginning to use multimedia to develop problem-solving and decision-making tools based on expert systems. An experienced subject expert enters various data and criteria necessary for problem solving and decision making into the computer database, which also contains a large database of facts and information. The subject expert, usually working with a computer programmer, also enters decision rules or chain decisions to certain outcomes. There may also be numerical calculations predicting, for instance, the probability of different outcomes. Students explore the computer environment thus created and try solutions to problems and make decisions, and the computer program "predicts" the likely outcomes of their decisions based on the underlying expert system provided by the subject expert.

The development of such uses of multimedia generally requires a combination of subject expertise, computer programming, and graphics and computer interface design skills. It also requires investment in sophisticated and high-cost multimedia hardware and software both for development and for student use, a high level of teaching skill, and a high level of computer expertise.

As a consequence, good-quality multimedia learning materials are extremely expensive and time-consuming to produce (in the order of $100,000 to $500,000 per CD-ROM, toward the higher end if subject-expert time is included). To justify the high level of expenditure, extensive use of the material is required with large numbers of students, or clients able and willing to pay high prices for sophisticated learning materials must be found. To cover the high cost of development and to ensure widespread use of the developed materials, consortia of universities may need to get together to develop materials for joint use, or it may be necessary to form partnerships with private sector organizations, such as publishers, to share the risk.

Consequently, although the number of commercial CD-ROMs suitable for application in higher education is increasing, it is still often difficult to find the right kind of material that will meet a particular instructor's needs. Furthermore the relatively few instructors willing to use off-the-shelf CD-ROMs generally prefer to customize or select materials for their own use rather than use the CD-ROM as a substitute for classroom teaching. As a consequence, the use of multimedia to support classroom teaching is still relatively low in higher education.

Some Issues in the Use of Classroom Aids

One reason for the rapid take-up of newer technologies such as videoconferencing and the Web is that these have been easily integrated with traditional classroom teaching methods. No major rethinking of traditional teaching methods has been necessary. However, without changes in teaching methods, the use of technology merely adds to both the workload of faculty and the study load of students. We are adding more cost for relatively small additional benefits.

Thus, it can be seen that for financial reasons the more sophisticated one becomes in using technologies, the more it becomes essential to replace other activities with technology to justify the investment. In particular, once information and learning activities are codified in a technological format, some thought needs to be given to the rationale for the teacher being present at the same time as the students. The highest cost in the use of technology for teaching and learning is instructor or subject-expert time. Can some of that time be redeemed by replacing or more likely by reducing traditional activities such as lectures, wet laboratories, or seminars? Can face-to-face teaching time be concentrated on those aspects of teacher-student communication that is best done in a face-to-face mode? If so, what are those aspects, and what is the best way to organize for this? These questions lead us into a discussion of distributed learning.

Distributed Learning

Distributed learning can also be seen as a continuum. At one end is the use of technology to supplement face-to-face teaching but with significant elements of the learning conducted independently by learners through technology and a much-reduced requirement for students to be regularly in class. At the other end of the continuum is delivery of courses and programs totally at a distance from the campus (distance learning).

One of the key elements of distributed learning is the use of communications technology as part of the teaching and learning experience. Students do not so much interact *with* the technology, as *through* the technology with teachers and other learners. This approach can be particularly useful where the subject matter requires students to apply concepts or principles to their own context. On-line communication is also useful for areas of knowledge in which there are ambiguities or in which different values and interpretations are considered legitimate, and particularly for the development of collaborative learning, by which students often remote from one another can work together on common tasks.

The main value, though, of distributive learning is its flexibility and the opportunity to widen access, allowing teaching and learning to extend well beyond the university campus. For instance, in my own university we are offering postgraduate courses over the Internet that are available not only to our on-campus master's degree students but also to students registered with the Monterrey Institute of Technology in Mexico and with the Simon Rodriguez Experimental University in Venezuela. We also offer the same courses to participants from all other parts of the world registered with the University of British Columbia for continuing professional development. The courses are delivered using a combination of the Web, printed textbooks and articles, and video-conferences. The same course material, assignments, and marking schemes are used for all the students, although the Monterrey Institute of Technology is responsible for marking and accrediting its own students.

These courses are not only very popular, with between two hundred and three hundred enrollments per course worldwide, but they also make a reasonable profit for the university after all costs have been met. Such courses, however, require approaches that are radically different from those of the traditional classroom model. Courses are developed by teams of subject experts, instructional designers, and computer and graphics specialists. Learners access a great deal of the information required from the Internet. The main role of the course instructors is to research and select appropriate content, to develop a Web-based course study guide, to provide discussion topics, to encourage and moderate widespread and high-quality student participation in on-line discussions, to mark assignments, and to provide feedback and guidance to learners.

Student support and administrative services also become critical when students are scattered around the world. Simple issues such as ordering textbooks and paying fees become much more complex when students are based in another country (see Bates and Escamilla, 1997, for a fuller discussion of these issues).

This approach is not suitable for all courses. International competition for courses over the Internet is now fierce and widespread. An institution wanting to go global with its teaching must have strong competitive advantages in terms of the reputation of its teachers or its overall excellence, and the quality and reliability of service it provides to students, wherever they are. Not all subject areas or learning goals are suitable for technology delivery, although technology is more able to meet learning goals effectively than most traditional teachers believe.

Defining the Role of the Department Chair in Technology Decision Making

Key tasks, then, for a department chair are to help a department

- Define priority subject and topic areas for the use of technology.

- Identify new target groups that could be reached through the use of technology.
- Identify areas of support available elsewhere in and outside the institution, and determine the organizational and support staffing for technology-based teaching that needs to be provided by the department.
- Identify the role of and priorities for face-to-face teaching in an increasingly sophisticated technology-based learning environment.
- Decide on key areas of investment and resource allocation for technology-based teaching.

The remainder of this chapter sets out some strategies for meeting these requirements.

Developing a Teaching Plan

The most critical strategy is to develop a three-to-five-year teaching plan for the department that covers all forms of teaching, including regular face-to-face teaching, technology-based teaching, extrasessional studies, and pure distance education. In other words, all the teaching needs of the department should be addressed in an integrated way. This means relating teaching methods to the needs of different target groups, to the interests and areas of expertise of the faculty, and to the resources likely to be available over a three-to-five-year period. In developing such a plan, it is also important to be aware of the potential for new revenue generation by using new methods and reaching new target groups.

Note that this is not specifically a technology plan. The use of technology needs to be embedded within the overall teaching plan. Technology is a means to an end, not an end in itself. The teaching plan I am suggesting is also different from (but might be integrated with) a plan for curriculum development and renewal. A teaching plan focuses not so much on *what* to teach but on *how*. Following are some possible steps to developing such a plan.

A Strategy for Inclusion and Buy-In

No plan will work without the support of faculty and students. It will be essential, then, to explain to staff and students the reason that a plan needs to be developed, and to seek their maximum participation in the process.

This is not likely to be an easy task, especially in a research university. It may be seen as just another exercise by the bureaucracy to reduce expenditure or resources, it may be seen as diverting staff from current teaching and research activities, or it may be seen as extra work, especially for key participants. There may be fears that even if developed, the plan will not be implemented.

There are, however, counterbalancing arguments for maximum participation. The plan is likely to have an impact on every faculty member, so it is in the interest of each faculty member to participate. A well-designed plan could in fact relieve current major areas of concern or avoid difficulties for faculty and students in the future. Teaching is a critical part of the work of the department and needs to be organized in the most effective way. Staff and students will be able to identify their needs and influence priorities for the department.

Some way should be found, through departmental meetings, subcommittees, task forces, and so forth, to involve every faculty and staff member in the department, including administrative support staff, such as secretaries, and a wide range of students. Spreading the load can make each individual's commitment to the planning process more manageable in terms of time.

Scanning the Environment

In developing a teaching plan, staff and students will need to address some of the fundamental issues facing higher education today and how these are likely to affect their day-to-day work over the next five years.

A task group should be established to identify the external and internal environments in which the department is likely to work over the next five years. The task group should identify, among other things:

- The likely financial scenario over the next three to five years
- Expectations on enrollments from both the public and the university or college administration
- New trends in subject matter and teaching, including the impact of technology on teaching, and different approaches

to teaching and learning the key subject areas within
the department
- Interdisciplinary developments
- The activities of potential competitors
- The department's current strengths and weaknesses
- Future opportunities and threats for the department

These elements can be identified in a variety of ways, including by brainstorming, by having a small group research and write a report, by inviting external speakers, and so forth. It is important, however, that it is done before the main planning activity starts. The environmental scan should also be done quickly, because the main trends should be relatively clear, and honestly, so that major problems or difficulties are not swept under the carpet.

Developing a Vision for Teaching

Because I live on the West Coast of Canada I often notice quizzical looks from colleagues when I start discussing the importance of developing a vision for teaching. The assumption is that I am talking about something vague or idealistic.

Nothing could be further from my mind. I am influenced by the work of Robert Fritz (1989), who defines a vision as a set of concrete scenarios reflecting exactly what we would really like to be doing in the future. Applying this view to teaching and the use of technology, the aim is to develop, through a group process, detailed descriptions of how the department will be teaching in five years. The scenarios should reflect what it would be like then to be a faculty member, what it would be like for a variety of different kinds of students to be learning, and even what ideal student support services would look like. The scenarios would also include a description of how technology would be being used in teaching and learning.

It is important that such scenarios identify ideals in concrete terms and take into account the possibilities now available through technological and other means. This vision has to reflect what we really want, not some compromise to meet existing limitations. The aim is to develop scenarios that almost everyone in the department really wants, through a process not of compromise or bargaining but of brainstorming and creativity.

One value of such a group exercise is to clarify in practical terms what colleagues mean when they talk about improving teaching and learning, or being learner-centered, or developing research skills, and so forth. Another value of the process is that it should provide some clear goals and targets to drive the planning process. The defined vision is in fact unlikely ever to be realized and will change over time. It is primarily a process for getting staff to think seriously about and discuss teaching methods in concrete terms, and for getting them to think beyond current limitations and reality so that quite different goals and objectives can be identified.

The process could involve input from specialists from outside the department, such as innovative faculty from another institution, a vice president responsible for external relations, and specialists in educational technology, distance education, or faculty development. The main purpose of such external input is to bring in new ideas or perspectives that may challenge the status quo and offer alternative approaches.

Discussions about technology must be a key part of such a visioning process, because technology can change the whole nature of the teaching-learning context. The visioning process is a way to explore the many opportunities and challenges that can be met through the intelligent use of technology. Visioning also provides a process and context for involving a critical mass of people within the department in discussing the advantages and limitations of different technologies for teaching. The debate that occurs through the visioning process makes it easier to identify priorities for the use of technology and provides a basis for making difficult decisions about technology that are nevertheless likely to be supported throughout the department.

Setting Goals and Priorities for the Next Five Years

Once a strong and detailed vision statement has been developed, the process becomes more like a traditional strategic planning exercise. Having set a vision for the next three to five years, what are the key actions that the department needs to take to move toward these goals? What are the likely constraints, and what resources can be found to move in these directions? What current activities could be changed or abandoned in order to meet the stated goals? It is in this context that a subplan for the use of technology for teaching within the department can be developed.

The need for an overall teaching strategy in order to decide on appropriate uses of technology cannot be too highly stressed. Far too often the use of technology is influenced by the latest technological developments, whether or not they are appropriate to the department's teaching or learning goals. Technology choice is often influenced by individual faculty enthusiasms, resulting in a lack of technical support at a level needed to attain and sustain high-quality learning, and duplication of effort and facilities. A lack of a departmental strategy for technology can result in students being unsure about the importance of technology, purchasing inappropriate equipment, having to change computers from course to course, or feeling frustrated by the lack of professionalism in a department's teaching.

Student Access to Computing

A critical part of any teaching plan must be a clear policy regarding student access to computers. Several different approaches may be taken.

Laissez-Faire Policy

A laissez-faire policy is common and probably the worst approach. In a laissez-faire policy, each instructor is left to make his or her own decision about the use of technology and whether a student needs to use a computer. There are many problems with this approach. Students taking different courses within the same department may purchase a computer for one course then find it unsuitable for another. A student may have to make a substantial financial commitment for computer purchase and Internet access, only to find that the use of a computer is not essential for the course or that subsequent courses do not require computer use. Students may have to learn specific computer skills or software for one course then find in another course that the same functions require different software or skills.

If the department provides access to computers through a computer lab and different machines and software are specified for different courses, technical support costs rapidly escalate. Institutions should no more tolerate a laissez-faire approach to student computer access than they would tolerate open access to any classroom at any time for any instructor; the result is chaos.

Student Computer Laboratories

Another common strategy is to have departmental or facultywide computer laboratories where students can access the Internet and teaching software. The computer lab can enable some standardization of equipment and teaching approaches and removes the responsibility from students to provide their own computers.

However, there are major disadvantages to this approach. One is the very high cost of installing and maintaining computer laboratories. When the use of computing for teaching and learning is marginal and student use is low, the cost of computer laboratories is not such an issue. When such uses become widespread, however, and most courses and students require some use of computing, an enormous investment has to be made in space, machines, software, and technical support. Furthermore, given rapid technological change in hardware, software, and networks, the maintenance and replacement costs for laboratories are also very high.

Another limitation is that the requirement to use laboratories reduces access and flexibility. Students still have to come on campus and may have to reserve computer time if use of the laboratories is extensive.

Students Provide Their Own Computers

In many universities in the United States and Canada, a majority of students will already have their own computers upon entering college. At my own university, 70 percent of new students not only have their own computers but also have Internet access.

Furthermore, each cohort of students brings a new generation of computers with them, allowing the teaching to adapt to the increasing multimedia and communications functionality of computers. Students who have their own computers and Internet access have much more flexibility and opportunity to study.

There is always likely to be a need for computer laboratories in specialist areas such as computer-aided design or for advanced computer courses, and a need to provide financial support and assistance to students who may have real difficulties in providing their own machine. There is also a need for students with their own machines to have easily accessible ports and power points on campus where they can plug in their machines. Nevertheless, it is likely to be a better investment to ensure that students can easily access the university or college networks on-line through modems and high-speed networks, using their own computers, rather than to depend on extensive and very expensive hardware installations on campus.

Academic Computing Policies

Whatever the preferred policy for student access to computers, it will still be critical for departments to have a clear academic policy regarding the use of computers for teaching and learning. The teaching plan should clearly indicate for each program or set of courses what the expectations are regarding student use of computers, and these policies need to be consistent across disciplines.

This does not mean that every course should require a computer. If a computer is required, however, a clear statement should indicate

- What kind of computer is required (for example, Pentium or Macintosh PowerBook, with Netscape Communicator and Internet access), including peripherals (for example a CD-ROM player) and network access
- Why a computer is needed (the teaching purpose or the value added to the teaching through the use of the computer)
- Any specialist computer skills (for example, the use of attachments to send assignments or the ability to create Excel spreadsheets) that the student may need to take the course, and opportunities for developing those skills outside the course.

In general, the simpler and more basic the standard is, the more manageable the policy will be. For instance, for all our distance education courses at the University of British Columbia, we require students to be able to access and operate Netscape 3.0, and they must be able to send documents in Rich Text Format; that is our only technical standard. For students on campus, higher standards could be set, but this would then limit access and the potential target groups for courses.

You can be sure that different faculty will demand different standards. Those who want to go outside the generally agreed-upon departmental standards should have to bear the cost of providing specialist laboratories and software from within their own disciplinary budgets.

Developing this kind of policy can be a major source of dissension within a department. Chairs of departments have a critical role to play in getting faculty to develop policies for the use of computing for teaching that are consistent and student-focused. They also have a critical role in influencing institutionwide decision making about technology infrastructure so that campus infrastructure and technology services strengthen rather than work against the teaching goals of the department.

A departmental teaching plan based on a strong visioning process makes it much easier to reach agreement on common standards and to provide guidance to chairs on university-wide policy requirements for academic computing. However, setting three-to-five-year goals for teaching, and choosing technologies to support such strategies, while essential, are not sufficient. The department should also deal with the issue of how the technologies will be managed.

Managing Technology-Based Teaching

In most countries, faculty have considerable autonomy with regard to teaching. Consequently, the most common approach to encouraging the use of technology, at least in universities in the United States and Canada, has been through earmarked grants to individual faculty, with general infrastructure support for networks and desktop equipment funded centrally.

Some universities have also invested in central multimedia production services or training facilities, but this is more the exception than the rule. A study in the Australian Graduate School of Management (1996) found that centralized technology-teaching support units were more common in smaller and newer Australian universities, but uncommon in the large, divisional research universities.

Consequently the main approach to the use of new technologies in higher education has been to provide individual faculty members with small grants that provide for funding of a part-time graduate student and some equipment. This is what I have called the "Lone Ranger" approach (Bates, 2000).

The Value and Limits of Lone Rangers

There are several advantages of using small grants to encourage faculty to use technology: It can get a wide range of faculty started on using new technologies for the first time. It provides opportunity for experimentation and the development of faculty skills in using technologies. It avoids having to make difficult decisions about long-term investment in technologies that may prove ephemeral. It allows graduate students to develop computer skills that can be applied to their area of subject expertise. Finally, it maintains the autonomy of faculty to decide on the teaching method that best suits them.

However, on most university and college campuses, the Lone Ranger approach means that amateurism rules in the use of technology. Standard classroom methods, such as lecture notes, may be carried across to a Web site, failing to adapt to the requirements of the medium and, more importantly, failing to exploit the many unique features of the technology.

A characteristic of many Lone Ranger projects is that often there is not a final product that can be used on a regular basis in a teaching context. This is because the project drags on, being constantly upgraded or improved, or it has to be redesigned as a result of inappropriate technology decisions in the early stages of development. The initial funding is often inadequate to complete the job, and much effort is spent seeking additional funding to continue the project.

Often the graphics and the interface are poor compared with those of commercial products with which students are familiar, and the potential for high-quality learner interaction with the multimedia materials and other students is often missed. Products, when finished, have limited applicability because they are not of a high-enough standard in terms of graphics and interface, or sufficient in volume, to become a commercial product.

In other words, Lone Ranger materials usually lack quality in the final product. There are several components of quality in technology-based educational materials. The first is the quality of the *content,* which is where the status and research capability of an institution becomes critical. Is this a unique or valuable teaching material for which there is a need or demand? This is not usually an issue in most research universities, but it may be an issue for some two-year colleges. Do they have the staff or reputation to compete with the local research university that may also be offering similar courses over the Web? If so, why not use the university's courses and free faculty for other activities that can best be done locally on a face-to-face basis?

The second component of quality is the standard of *media production.* Are the graphics clear? Are the screens easy to read? Are the sound and video easy to hear and see? Are the unique features of each medium (video, audio, text, computing) fully exploited? Is the material well assembled? Is the screen designed in such a way that students intuitively understand the range of activities open to them and how to accomplish them (interface design)? Can they navigate their way through the materials easily?

The third component of quality is *instructional design.* Are the learning objectives clear? Does the material result in the desired learning outcomes? Does it have the appropriate mix of media to achieve the learning outcomes in the most efficient manner? What is the quality of the interaction between student and learning materials? What is the role of the tutor or instructor relative to the technology-based learning? Is the material well structured and well organized?

The fourth important factor is the quality of *delivery.* Are the materials easy for the student to access? Can learners ask questions or discuss materials with other students? Who gives feedback? What happens if students have technical problems? At what times is help available?

Fifth, there is the issue of *project management.* Time lines and budgets need to be established; teams need to be created; meetings need to be organized; materials need to be produced, distributed, and maintained; and deadlines need to be met.

Last, and perhaps most critical, there is the question of *resourcing and priority.* Are there enough resources to do a proper job?

Does the instructor have enough time, through the reduction of other activities, and enough help from other professionals, such as graphics designers, to produce a good quality set of materials? Is the project considered of sufficient priority to get the support needed for the job to be done well?

Too often, technology-based projects are treated as research and development (R&D). There is a big difference, however, between R&D and regular teaching activities. The technology has to be reliable so that wherever a student may be in the program, it performs the way it was intended. The multimedia material has to be accurate, comprehensive, and related to clear learning outcomes. The multimedia material has to be designed so that it fits into an overall course structure. Budgets and time lines must be maintained or students will not get the material in time.

All of these factors contribute to quality in technology-based teaching and learning materials. New technologies, then, are likely to remain marginal, despite high levels of capital investment, and will merely add costs to the system if we do not implement procedures and methods to ensure the professional management of technology-based teaching.

Project Management

It has already been argued that there is a great deal to be learned about how to exploit fully the new technologies for teaching and learning. The challenge is to encourage instructors to be innovative while at the same time maintaining quality control and cost-effectiveness in the delivery of teaching.

Although new technologies require new educational applications, a great deal is already known about the process of producing high-quality, cost-effective multimedia learning materials. This knowledge has been developed both in the large, autonomous distance-teaching universities and in private sector multimedia companies in areas such as computer games, advertising, and film and television production.

The process is known as project management. Each course or teaching module is established as a project, with the following elements:

- A fully costed proposal that

  Identifies the number and type of learners to be targeted
  (and in particular their likely access to technology)
  Clearly defines learning goals or outcomes
  Indicates the choice of technologies
  Presents a carefully estimated budget (including staff
  time, copyright clearance, and use of media production
  resources, as well as cash)

- A team approach that involves (depending on the design
  of the project) a combination of the following:

  Subject-experts and academics
  A project manager
  An instructional designer
  A graphics designer
  A computer interface designer
  A text editor
  An Internet specialist
  A media producer

- An unambiguous definition of intellectual property rights
  and a clear agreement on revenue sharing between the
  university and the design team
- A plan for integration with or substitution for face-to-face
  teaching
- A production schedule with clearly defined milestones or
  deadlines, and a targeted start date
- A process for project evaluation and course revision and
  maintenance
- A defined length of project before redesign or withdrawal
  of the course

Project management is still the exception rather than the rule
in most universities and colleges, especially for Web-based courses.
The Center for Distributed Learning for the California State University system (www.cdl.edu) is one of the few higher education organizations that is extensively following a project development model.
However, its approach is to develop self-contained multimedia

modules that instructors can integrate into their own courses rather than develop whole courses through the project management model.

In the distance education and technology (DET) unit at the University of British Columbia, we operate a five-stage approach to project definition. This process could easily be adapted for use on a departmental or faculty basis. Individual professors or discipline areas are invited once a year to submit a short proposal (usually two to four pages) requesting funds or assistance. We provide a short questionnaire to help the process at this stage.

One of our senior managers (an experienced instructional designer with project management training) then works with the lead academic to develop a fully costed proposal. This is a critical stage of the process, during which objectives are clarified, alternative modes of delivery are explored, and resources are identified.

The project proposal then goes, in competition with all the others, to a committee of academics for adjudication. A set of criteria for selection has been developed, including the number of students to be served, strategic positioning in terms of the faculty plan and technology innovation, potential for revenue generation, and so forth.

Following allocation of funds, a detailed letter of agreement is drawn up between the academic department and the DET unit that clearly sets out responsibilities on both sides and ties down production schedules, intellectual property, and sharing of revenues.

Once the project is funded, DET managers track progress, schedules are rearranged to take account of changing circumstances, budgets are sometimes changed (but more likely rearranged) as a result—all by mutual agreement.

Project management is not necessarily limited to the use of technology for teaching. Indeed, there is a logic to treating all courses or programs as projects, whatever the balance between technology-based and face-to-face teaching.

However, a project management approach has major implications for how funding is handled in a department. If all courses are considered projects, they should be resourced accordingly. Resources include both cash and staff allocations. Thus each year a department's total teaching resources would be allocated across a range of projects that would constitute the department's teaching program each year, but the department would ensure that adequate resources would be carried forward or committed for future years to continue and maintain the courses. Project leaders would be expected to work within the resource allocations and deadlines assigned to each project.

The differences between the Lone Ranger and project management approaches are really a matter of timing and purpose. To encourage staff who are novices in using technology, and to encourage research and development in the use of new technologies, a weak criteria approach to funding and the encouragement of Lone Rangers may be best. Instructors with little experience in using technology usually prefer the privacy and control of the Lone Ranger approach.

However, as a department moves to regular teaching with new technologies, as more experience is gained by instructors, and as students become more experienced in using the technology for learning, the more important it becomes to move to a project management model, to achieve high-quality materials and teaching, and to ensure that deadlines and budget targets are met.

Centralization Versus Decentralization

The project management model requires a team approach that includes not only subject experts but also technology specialists and instructional designers. Where should such critical support staff be located and how will they be paid for?

Whether support staff are located centrally (serving the university as a whole), departmentally (serving all disciplines), or within a specific school or subject area will depend on a number of factors, in particular on the size of the institution. The larger the organization is, the greater will be the opportunity to decentralize even specialist activities.

However, even in cities with a well-established high-tech industry, there are probably no more than a handful of interface designers with expertise in designing high-quality educational computer interfaces. These designers need to be hired on a contract basis as and when needed for high-priority and well-funded projects.

Graphics designers are more common than interface designers, but it is still difficult to find such people with good experience in using technology for education. These individuals could be employed centrally on a permanent basis to work with different departments and faculties to establish the overall look and feel for their projects and to design specific templates for Web-based courses that can be used as a model for detailed course design. Certainly with the growth of technology-based teaching, most faculties in large research universities could justify employing their own instructional designer or faculty development officer or both.

Finally, there is probably a need for every faculty (at least in large universities and colleges) to have at least one general technology support person who can do basic work such as Web design and who can provide technical support for networks and computer laboratories, and so forth. However, this person should also be able to draw on other units and departments for more specialist help.

The extent to which a department needs to staff up with technological support people should be determined in the light of the department's teaching plan, which would establish goals and priorities for the use of technology. Project management allows for the establishment of temporary teams that can be reconstituted at different times on a flexible basis, and such arrangements can accommodate a variety of organizational arrangements. Chairs need to work with other department chairs to identify resources that can be shared, and with their deans to identify university-wide support requirements for both faculty development and course production and delivery.

Some difficult decisions will have to be made, however, about the balance of teaching and support staff. In general, priority tends to be given to academic staffing. As a consequence, one now hears complaints from faculty in universities and colleges across the continent about the lack of technical support staff.

Furthermore, there is a severe shortage of good-quality technology-support people. They can usually earn considerably more in the private sector. To recruit and maintain good-quality technology-support staff, higher education institutions need to offer such staff regular positions and a good management framework that determines priorities for their work and ensures reasonable workloads. Although there are short-term advantages in using graduate students as helpers, the practice may do these students no good in the subsequent job market. Although work experience is valuable, it is no substitute for proper training.

To use technology successfully it will be essential to find ways to provide adequate technology-support staff, and in times of limited resources this may mean reducing some areas of teaching to ensure high quality in others.

Faculty Development and Buy-In

I have deliberately left this issue until last. It is not uncommon to see the effective use of technology as an issue of faculty development. I would agree that if technology is to be used successfully, there need to be fundamental changes in the way instructors work. Professional development activities may be required if attitudes are to change and if the benefits and limitations of using technology are to be fully appreciated.

However, the issue is usually framed differently. It is usually assumed that faculty need to learn how to develop technology-based materials themselves. I believe that this is a big mistake. It suggests that faculty are the problem and that they need to be trained out of the problem. It encourages the Lone Ranger approach and results in highly paid subject-experts doing work that could be done more cheaply by someone else. I see the problem quite differently. I see more and more faculty anxious to use technology but desperately frustrated by lack of resources and in particular by lack of technological and specialist support.

I would prefer to see faculty working in teams, respecting the professional input of other professionals, such as graphics and instructional designers, but concentrating on academic policy, research, subject matter content, and overall teaching methods. Although a working knowledge of different technologies is always an advantage for an instructor, faculty need to communicate their ideas and needs to the other professionals in the team, and they need to trust in their expertise to create collectively learning materials that not only meet the expectations of faculty but surpass them.

While the provision of skilled professionals from other fields to support faculty may appear to be an expensive policy, it is a lot cheaper than diverting highly qualified research and subject matter experts into technical fiddling and fixing.

Conclusions

You may have decided by this point that the use of technology for teaching has too many difficulties associated with it, too many uncertainties, and certainly too much stress. This is a pretty fair assessment. The problem is that the issue is not going to go away.

Students from high schools who are currently entering our universities and colleges are the first generation that has been brought up all the way from early childhood with computers in their home or at school. Also, more and more students are having to pay their way through university and college. They are going to become more critical and more demanding, and they will expect technology to be used appropriately for teaching. In addition, employers are looking for students who combine information technology skills with subject expertise. I find it hard to imagine even an English literature graduate who would be considered adequately educated these days without some knowledge of how to use the Internet to further his or her studies or interest in literature, if only to be able to order books on-line. Finally, there are many competitors, private as well as public, who are more than willing to use technology to recruit students to their courses from under our noses.

The task of a department chair is to ensure that these realities are fully understood within the department and to provide strategies and support for helping faculty develop appropriate policies and practices for the use of technology in teaching. This cannot be done in isolation from the curriculum and teaching approach of the department and of disciplines as a whole. It will also require some very difficult resource reallocation decisions to provide the necessary support, at either a central or the departmental level.

However, more and more instructors are themselves ready to increase their use of technology. There are genuine educational benefits to be gained by its intelligent use, and the use of technology can provide a strong platform for faculty development and renewal.

References

Australian Graduate School of Management, Fujitsu Center. *Managing the Introduction of Technology in the Delivery and Administration of Higher Education,* Canberra, Australia: Government of Australia Department of Employment, Education, Training and Youth Affairs, 1996.

Bates, A. W. *Technology, Open Learning and Distance Education.* New York: Routledge, 1995.

Bates, A. W. *Managing Technological Change: Strategies for College and University Leaders.* San Francisco: Jossey-Bass, 2000.

Bates, A. W. "Restructuring the University for Technological Change." In Huber, M. (ed.), *What Kind of University?* Menlo Park, Calif.: Carnegie Foundation for the Advancement of Teaching, 1999.

Bates, A. W., and Escamilla, J. "Crossing Boundaries: Making Global Distance Education Work." *Journal of Distance Education,* 1997, 12(1/2), 49–66.

Fritz, R. *The Path of Least Resistance.* New York: Columbine, 1989.

Other Useful Readings

American Association for Higher Education. "Great Expectations: What Technology Really Means for Teaching and Learning." *Change,* 1995, 27(2).

Dolence, M. G., and Norris, D. M. *Transforming Higher Education: A Vision for Learning in the Twenty-First Century.* Ann Arbor, Mich.: Society for College and University Planning, 1995.

Kaufman, R., and Herman, J. "Strategic Planning, Schooling, and the Curriculum for Tomorrow." In S. Dijkstra and others, *Instructional Design: International Perspectives.* Hillsdale, N.J.: Erlbaum, 1997.

Oblinger, D., and Rush, S. *The Future Compatible Campus.* Bolton, Mass.: Anker, 1998.

Ross, D. "Project Management in the Development of Instructional Material for Distance Education: An Australian Overview." *American Journal of Distance Education,* 1991, 5(2), 24–30.

Rowley, D. J., Lujan, H. D. and Dolence, M. *Strategic Choices for the Academy.* San Francisco: Jossey-Bass, 1998.

Chapter Eleven

Leading Curriculum Renewal

Ann S. Ferren
Kay Mussell

Recently, an adult student approached the registrar's office at a public university about returning to full-time study after a twenty-year gap. Somewhat skeptical about just how her work taken at the institution so many years earlier might apply, the registrar entered her courses into the computerized degree-audit program and found that not only were the twenty-year-old course numbers and titles the same as the current curriculum, but the general education and major requirements matched up as well. In short, it appeared that she could continue her program of study in psychology as though she had not been away. Interestingly, the department chair had been the chair when she was first enrolled at the institution long ago!

This may well be an isolated instance, yet one could conclude from this scenario that the curriculum is stable and that department chairs need not be concerned with change. In reality, however, even if the basic structures of courses, credits, and program requirements do not change a great deal, content and pedagogy are always evolving. Department chairs are inevitably at the center of this process as they respond to both internal and external pressures, communicate between the department and the rest of the institution, and set the context for faculty discussion of change in all aspects of curriculum—general education, the major, and electives. To provide leadership, inspiration, and guidance for curriculum renewal, the department chair must understand the purposes of the curriculum, how curriculum change takes place, what prompts resistance to change, and the crucial nature of their own role in the process.

Change and Continuity in the Curriculum

To a great extent, the foundation of the college curriculum is the disciplines. Academic specialties emerged in American higher education in the nineteenth century as colleges and universities, led by Harvard, Johns Hopkins, and the University of Virginia, reorganized into departments to support a more specialized curriculum (Graff, 1988; Brubacher and Rudy, 1997). Departments represented their interests to the rest of the institution and frequently acted to protect their turf. Inevitably, then, departments sought to cover the field by including a sufficient number of specialists to teach all aspects of the discipline. Because each specialist had a specific role to play in the department's offerings, faculty members were essentially free agents whose judgment about the content of their courses was rarely questioned.

Gerald Graff (1988) argues that individual faculty ownership of the pieces of the curriculum does students a disservice because there is no mechanism for systematic integration of learning and because any controversies that arise are resolved among faculty members rather than becoming the subject of classroom inquiry. Under the specialist and coverage principles, as change occurs in the discipline at large, individual departments respond by hiring faculty with new specialties while eliminating outdated fields and methods as faculty members retire. Thus, curriculum at the department level has traditionally changed one course at a time in response to individual faculty interests.

In addition to those factors that are unique to disciplines, external considerations also raise curricular issues that test the leadership skills of department chairs. Revision of general education requirements, changes in student interest or demand, evolution of institutional values, change in administration, shifts in employment opportunities, or new legislative mandates or accreditation standards can require faculty to rethink their assumptions about the curriculum. All of these considerations have shaped the recent history of curriculum reform in American higher education.

The 1970s was a period of erratic and intense curriculum reform stimulated by student unrest, claims of lack of relevance, and a more diverse new professoriate joining colleges and universities. The results were dramatic. Many colleges dropped formerly structured requirements, developed new courses and interdisciplinary or multidisciplinary majors in women's and ethnic studies, and experimented with different models of instruction, such as experiential learning and independent study. What had once been the province of the department became an institutional issue, and faculty supported and resisted the changes based on deeply held values about what and how to teach.

By the mid-1980s, a different kind of pressure for reform emerged, stimulated by national reports lamenting the loss of traditional curricula and noting the incoherence and ineffectiveness of the baccalaureate (Bennett, 1984; Association of American Colleges, 1985; National Institute of Education, 1984). College curriculum, heretofore only a campus issue, became a public concern when critics of the changes begun in the 1970s made charges that were fiery enough to make their books bestsellers (Bloom, 1987; d'Souza, 1991; Hirsch, 1987). Colleges responded with widespread discussion of the role of requirements in a liberal education, and many reinstated general education requirements in new formats. Faculty interest in the renewal of the curriculum was widespread and passionate. As campuses struggled to embrace new perspectives on race, class, and gender; changed requirements to include courses on ethics, the environment, and international perspectives; and created more professional majors such as mass communication, defenders of the status quo such as the National Association of Scholars mobilized to protect what they believed to be the intellectual heritage of a democratic society. Seventy-five percent of all colleges and universities reported that they were engaged in curriculum change (American Council on Education, 1988), and new language, such as *political correctness* and *culture wars,* emerged to chart the controversies.

Although the 1990s have been characterized by a calmer change process, the results demonstrate the new power of economic and political interests in shaping the curriculum. No longer ivory towers protected from outside interests, universities are expected, and often urged, to address societal needs directly. Curricular changes include the integration of technology, the development of new majors to match employment and economic development needs, experimentation with accelerated study such as three-year programs and combined bachelor's and master's programs, and responses to mandates from state legislatures or governing boards. To respond to questions from a highly critical public about cost and value, institutions must demonstrate a renewed commitment to the quality of undergraduate teaching; shift resources from administration, research, and graduate education to serve additional undergraduates; develop more engaging teaching strategies; and consider how best to assess student learning. Department chairs have been expected to interpret, guide, and implement these changes at the unit level.

Each of these reforms creates tension over competing conceptions of what students should know, and inevitably raises questions about what self-governance means in an environment of competing demands. Faculty steeped in the culture of academic specialization often identify change as a struggle for the control of the campus, and see accountability as a threat to autonomy. They particularly question the right of boards, employers, parents, and legislators to critique the curriculum and its purposes and to require documentation of outcomes. As a result, campuses have been less responsive than expected.

A twenty-year review of student transcripts shows the continuity of the curriculum, with distributions across all fields remaining much the same except for the addition of internationally focused courses and new fields such as computer science and media studies (Adelman, 1995). Although faculty have been reworking the content and pedagogy of undergraduate education over several decades, the undergraduate curriculum as measured by course enrollments remains fundamentally the same as it was a quarter century ago and, indeed, remarkably similar across campuses. Students take roughly one-third of their course work in general education and one-third in a major, assuring both breadth and depth to their study. General education programs continue to be designed around basic skills and distribution requirements across the arts, humanities, social sciences, and natural sciences. Majors continue to be designed around introductory courses surveying the field, followed by more specialized topics courses, and increasingly topped off by a capstone experience.

What is not captured by national reports and trend analysis is the dynamic of the curriculum on a single campus. For department chairs, the challenge is to understand their programs in the institutional and national context and proactively address the eternal question: What should students know? In addition, a chair needs to create an environment that promotes faculty responsiveness and self-determination and reduces adversarial reactions to the interests of other stakeholders.

To begin the process, the chair might engage colleagues around some key questions in order to focus the issues and open up discussion of the diverse perspectives that members of the department hold:

- What are the goals and objectives of the departmental curriculum?
- How does the curriculum of the department support the mission of the institution and produce the expected student outcomes?
- Is the curriculum responsive to changing societal needs?
- Do changes in course-taking patterns reveal changing student intellectual and career interests?

The Curriculum Change Process

The curriculum represents both a collective view of what students should study at a particular institution and how individual courses should be designed. Although boards of trustees and administrators may ultimately be responsible for the quality of education on campus, they are far removed from the development of academic programs. The internal governance processes of the campus grant almost unassailable authority to faculty, departments, and colleges through a variety of curriculum committees.

Although the approval process is designed to ensure that colleagues agree that each new course and program change meets quality standards for the campus, in reality there are few challenges to individual courses or changes in major courses of study once the proposal leaves the department. The traditional process, relying on an unspoken agreement that department experts know best, may even discourage a comprehensive look at the curriculum. Few poets would dare question the addition of a new language to the computer science major, and it is the rare department chair who suggests balancing this compartmentalized perspective with consideration of intra-institutional concerns.

At times, both department and college curriculum committees function as watchdogs for resources and protectors of the status quo. By requiring excessive paperwork and taking months to review a proposal, a committee can dampen enthusiasm for change. A politically astute chair will use informal communication to build support for the proposal long before it comes to the committee.

When a campus does decide to undertake significant reform across department lines, turf battles, resistance, and adversarial stances can swamp the rational curriculum-approval process. Even faculty committed to improving education are reluctant to support innovation if they are unsure of the impact it will have on enrollments in their department or on their relative status as a department. Observers of such reform note that considerable misunderstanding and argument stem from the differing nature of disciplines and educational values, a matter often masked within departments that need worry about the structure and norms of a single discipline only when considering change (Stark and Lattuca, 1997).

This decentralized curriculum change process can result in incoherence and catalog bloat. With the responsibility for curriculum left to departments—indeed, often devolved to individual faculty—it is easy to add courses without reviewing proposals for overlap, redundancy, or fragmentation. It is not surprising to find a research methods course in every social science program that is little more than the statistics course offered in a traditional department. As disciplines change, as new specialty areas develop, and as new faculty are hired, curriculum committees approve courses to match these special interests. Year after year, more courses are added to the catalog than are deleted. Even in institutions that require elimination of a course that has not been taught for a certain period, a department may resist dropping such a course on the grounds that they might want to offer it in the future. The resulting curriculum has been characterized as the "collective auto-biography of the faculty" (Knefelkamp, 1990, p. 10), or more neg-atively, as a "junkyard" (Levine and Green, 1985, p. 128). The chair who wants to find resources for innovation may well be able to self-fund the new program through internal reallocation by stream-lining current course offerings.

Another dilemma for chairs under the current change process is the difficulty of managing competing interests. Mandates for change can come from many sources. Students acting as con-sumers may request courses on particular topics, whether these subjects play a role in a specific program of study or not and regardless of faculty resources or even expertise. Other depart-ments on campus may request changes in courses to better meet the needs of their students. Changes in the requirements of other departments can have a ripple effect; many economics depart-ments, for example, have watched their enrollments decline when faculty have declared that macroeconomics is "too hard" for their students and taken it off the required list for that major without consulting the economics department. Cross-campus reform movements may significantly alter the pattern of course offerings in departments, requiring that resources previously devoted to courses for specialists be reallocated to new courses for non-majors. Legislatures, accrediting agencies, or other institutional review boards may mandate changes, such as reinstating the U.S. history requirement, while job market realities may require cur-ricular flexibility to accommodate knowledge and skill develop-ment in new areas.

Disciplines experience these pressures in different ways. An information systems program, on the one hand, may face contin-uous demand to incorporate new software technologies for majors, to provide introductory courses for the campus at large, and to retool to match fast-paced industry standards to ensure that employers can hire graduates with up-to-date skills. A philosophy department, on the other hand, may experience tension from within as faculty struggle with the pressure to incorporate new per-spectives from feminist and non-Western philosophies into the tra-ditional curriculum or to rethink ethics courses in light of changing societal values. To lead a department effectively in this new environment, a department chair must mediate among all these constituencies and competing imperatives. To do so requires understanding the issues, maintaining open communication, and solving problems collaboratively.

Academic accounting practices may impede collaboration. Interdisciplinary courses can founder on such "turf" issues as which department gets credit for enrollments or whose turn it is to provide faculty to teach them. A department chair with good institutional contacts and an understanding of the context for academic collaboration can lead department members and others to more innovative and positive results.

A final aspect of the curricular change process is that the traditional structures—colleges, departments, disciplines, and majors—continue to organize the curriculum even though many would agree that the structures are rigid; knowledge is constructed, not organic; and few problems can be addressed through a single perspective. These structures may work against cooperation, collaboration, and the development of interdisciplinary and multidisciplinary courses and programs. One wry observer has noted that if you had an aerial view of most campuses, the landscape would reveal the fixed center in stone or brick buildings, with many small houses around the periphery for new curricula (Minnich, 1995). Departments of history, English, and biology are neatly ensconced in these solid structures, with administrative offices nearby, while new interdisciplinary programs in ethnic studies, women's studies, or environmental studies are placed in small, decrepit, university-owned houses on the edges of the campus—homey, separate, and vulnerable. True transformation of the curriculum requires giving up the place and space of the old in order to create something wholly new.

Given this history and practice of piecemeal and uncoordinated curriculum development, the department chair needs to encourage curriculum transformation that reflects trends in the disciplines, to support the integration of new knowledge, to build interdisciplinary bridges, and to link the curriculum with appropriate pedagogies. Through ongoing discussion, chairs can foster the introduction of new knowledge in an atmosphere that recognizes that change need not lead to culture wars, increased specialization, or fragmentation of the curriculum, but rather to a wholly new perspective. Including students in the curriculum development process enables faculty to test their conception of a good education against student interests. Focusing on student questions and student learning to shape the classroom experience will help faculty shift from delivery of information to engagement and interaction.

Department chairs can create this atmosphere for curricular change through a facilitative rather than managerial role (Lucas, 1994). They need to be prepared to give release time or graduate assistance to curriculum projects. They need to encourage collaboration through meetings that focus on active listening, not just debate. To shift a department's perspective requires that the leader demonstrate openness to all points of view in order to involve faculty in the process of changing the culture. Useful questions for shaping the discussion include the following:

- What does it mean to prepare students for the future and for lifelong learning?
- How might the department undertake proactive curricular review?
- How can faculty interests be balanced with the interests of other stakeholders?

Supporting the Role of General Education

The foundation of the undergraduate degree is the liberal arts curriculum, variously described as general education, liberal learning, or the core curriculum. Although there are perennial questions about the nature of the general education curriculum, most programs continue to be structured as distribution requirements drawing on a variety of disciplines, with the goal of covering basic skills, fundamental knowledge, and different methods of inquiry. Accounting for a significant proportion of a department's total student credit hours, these courses often subsidize small upper-level courses or graduate programs. All departments in the arts and sciences provide significant portions of this course work and must find resources to staff them along with those courses that meet the major requirements. The department chair must be fully engaged with the purposes of general education in order to lead a department's thoughtful consideration and appreciation of its role in the program. This means confronting the difficult questions of class size, course load, and rewards for teaching nonmajors.

Although professional programs may have a course or two included in the general education distribution requirements, their concerns usually have less to do with resources and staffing than with the program's effectiveness in meeting external accrediting guidelines. In recent years, changes in the standards of the National Council for Accreditation of Teacher Education (NCATE), the International Association for Management Education, the American Assembly of Collegiate Schools of Business (AACSB), and the Accrediting Council on Education in Journalism and Mass Communications (ACEJMC), to name just a few, have increasingly emphasized the importance of liberal arts courses and have decreased the overall number of credits in the professional program required for the degree. The effect is to export students from such programs as education, business, and communication into liberal arts courses. The receiving department chairs face a significant challenge if the resources to meet these new demands do not follow, and thus need good resource allocation skills as well as an appreciation for how their courses support the other majors.

Intentional and well-meaning efforts to rethink general education are not fruitful if they disregard resource needs. Many a curriculum task force, after hours of conscientious deliberation and planning, has seen its innovative proposal for reform die in the faculty senate when costed out. Faculty can quickly calculate that the introduction of a required computer literacy course for a thousand new freshmen would result in a need for three or four new faculty positions. At the same time, they can resist the claims of departments arguing for the expansion or reinstitution of a requirement if they perceive that the claims are motivated more by an interest in bolstering enrollments, maintaining tenure lines, and keeping the budget than by concerns about the intellectual integrity of the general education program. In both instances, the chair will be held accountable by department members for articulating their position and for balancing self-interest and institutional interest.

Assurance of the continuing integrity of any general education program relies on the department chair, who must take responsibility for monitoring the relevance of department courses to the overall program. If the institution has carefully articulated and broadly agreed-upon goals for general education courses, the role of the department chair is somewhat easier because guidelines are in place. Although such guidelines may be abstract, they provide a basis for discussion within departments, and they offer a department chair some leverage in dealing with faculty members whose individual sections do not match the priorities. Many chairs regularly review syllabi for multisection general education courses, and frequently a timely reminder of the stated course goals is all that is required, because curricular "drift" may be more a matter of faculty inattention than of deliberate design.

To ensure appropriate content and coverage as well as to measure student achievement, some institutions employ common examinations or assessment measures for students in large, required multisection courses such as writing or mathematics and have them graded by faculty other than the student's own. Other strategies include portfolios that are evaluated by department faculty, and spot-checking of grading patterns. To facilitate such assessment and quality control, the chair must be able to articulate the importance of the general education program to ward off claims of individual autonomy taking precedence over institutional goals. Institutionwide discussion of general education must be backed up by discussion at the department level. Chairs must engage their department colleagues in discussion of quality and coherence so that they support broader purposes than their own department-based perspective. The following questions should stimulate such a discussion:

- What types of courses are appropriate for general education?
- What makes a course a general education course?
- How should courses be staffed and multiple sections be monitored for congruence with program goals and approved syllabi without violating faculty autonomy?

Designing the Major

The curricular structure of the major is traditionally within the province of the department and subject to only the loosest institutional guidelines and academic policies, such as a required number of credits, a prerequisite system, and definitions of levels of courses from introductory to advanced. These conventions, however, often do more than structure the curriculum for easy management and ensure a coherent program of study. They also take on symbolic meaning and communicate the structure of knowledge in a field.

Some disciplines are sequential and require mastery of simpler material before introduction of more complex knowledge. These majors, notably the sciences and mathematics, share general notions of the content of a course while sections taught by individual faculty members may differ on the margins. For example, a course in calculus or organic chemistry will probably be comparable in almost every institution and rely on a single comprehensive text, although the rate of progress and the coverage will differ depending on the institution and the quality and previous experience of the students. Chairs in these departments may play only a minimal monitoring role if there is little change in the content of the major course sequence, yet leadership for significant rethinking and renewal is also possible. Ideally, courses of study will periodically be reshaped and new texts will be selected to reflect changes in the discipline. The department chair may focus on teaching methods for required science and mathematics courses and thus help shape the curriculum. Given the high failure rate in certain introductory courses, the chair may consider investing in increasing the success rate to ensure that there will be students who eventually pursue the major.

Potential interventions that lead to increased success rates may differ from one discipline to another. In mathematics, for example, establishing a tutoring lab staffed by graduate assistants can reinforce student learning in basic courses. Many campuses have opened writing centers to support both students in composition courses and the writing needs of other students, including graduate students and ESL students. Supplemental instruction by undergraduate or graduate students often works in large classes that have historically high failure and attrition rates. Appropriate strategies will emerge from disciplinary and institutional contexts and will depend heavily on the resources available, but many department chairs will find these efforts well worth the planning time and resource allocation required.

In contrast, nonsequential disciplines may be fraught with persistent disagreements about the relative importance of various subjects in the curriculum. Particularly in those disciplines where the culture wars have been most dramatic, department chairs need to manage curricular disagreements so that they do not create factions. Calls to include elective courses on women, African Americans, the Third World, and other "new" areas have altered both English and history majors, for example. Inclusion of nonfiction texts, creative writing, and film studies in the English curriculum, or statistics, computer databases, and anthropological theory in the history curriculum, has left some faculty with the belief that important content, such as Shakespeare or the Civil War, has been marginalized in favor of trendy new topics. Faculty in other departments may question the English professor applying psychoanalytic theory or the historian using sociological methods of analysis. Department chairs must be conversant with changes in the disciplines and with new methodologies in order to mediate these disputes and guide discussion of the structure and meaning of the major.

To underscore the importance of appropriate curricular revision and to discourage the notion that new courses can be offered on a faculty whim, chairs can employ a variety of strategies. They can offer travel funds for faculty attendance at curriculum or teaching conferences to learn about national trends in the field and to return with ideas to share with colleagues. Modest course development resources can be offered to faculty with promising ideas. Some departments take advantage of institutional vehicles for experimentation to test a course before adding it to the permanent curriculum. Such special-topics courses can also be used to offer a narrow and specialized course celebrating a faculty member's recent publication, to respond to student requests for specific subject offerings, or to teach timely courses that may never be repeated. Some departments have "rubric" courses with changing or rotating topics (such as topics in American history or culture area analysis). These permanent courses have a designated role in the curriculum, yet they are flexible enough that content and subject matter can change according to faculty availability and interest.

When departments have reached agreement on the role of particular courses in the major, the department chair then has the responsibility of ensuring that the courses fulfill their objectives. For example, syllabus review may reveal that a faculty member is not covering agreed-upon material in a survey course. If discussion with the faculty member yields no results, the chair can raise the issue of the role of such courses in a department meeting, putting all the issues on the table, including the question of whether the department wants to continue teaching them at all. A wise faculty member will then be bound by the department's renewed commitment.

Increasingly, studies of the major reveal that to students the major is little more than a collection of courses and not the carefully structured learning experience that faculty envision (Association of American Colleges, 1991). To counter some of the randomness that students experience when they take courses in the order that suits their busy schedules or when they transfer and collect courses from several institutions, many departments are adding a capstone or integrative experience to the major as the last step to help bring together the range of courses. Determining whether a senior seminar, internship, thesis, undergraduate research experience, or performance is relevant and what will be given up to make space for it requires a skilled discussion leader who also has an understanding of student intellectual development and assessment of learning outcomes.

The greatest curricular challenge is faced by chairs of professional programs. Changing content, forms of practice, and external licensing criteria can affect programs such as nursing, education, or clinical psychology overnight. Faced with requirements for licensure exams or accreditation standards, the department chair must stay aware of developments in the field, monitor legislation, and remain in contact with state agencies and licensing boards. A decline in the passing rate on the nursing boards, for example, would call for a curricular review to see where the deficiencies can be remedied. One state recently limited licensure in a field to students with sixty hours, thus rendering a thirty–credit masters degree obsolete. The department chair needs not only to assess the needed changes in the program but also to reallocate resources carefully to fund the program without resorting to stripping resources from the undergraduate programs to support the graduate programs. Any discussion of the major begins with several questions:

- What is the structure of knowledge in the field?
- What is the purpose of the major?
- How are students best introduced to the modes of inquiry in the field and then given opportunities to create knowledge on their own?

Providing Skills Courses and Electives

In addition to offering general education courses and the major, some departments also offer such skills development courses as writing, mathematics, critical reading, and introduction to computers, as well as popular electives such as personal finance and women's health. Because these courses are often highly enrolled and may subsidize other departmental offerings, department chairs need to give them special attention. Frequently, the demands of merely managing such a course—hiring faculty, scheduling, order books—overshadows the equally important areas of faculty development and improving content and delivery. Such courses are also of great interest to faculty and administrators outside the department, who count on them to provide students with basic skills and knowledge that support further study. It is the role of the department chair to keep mutual interests in mind and to foster communication with other departments.

Because chairs represent the department at many campus meetings, opportunities regularly arise to remind both those outside the department and faculty members within it of the goals of these courses. When complaints occur ("What are you teaching in freshman composition anyway?" "My students can't even read a demand curve."), chairs can seize the opportunity to explain what can and cannot be expected of students who have taken the course. For example, faculty who are concerned about student writing skills frequently assume that the English department is not doing its job, even though recent research shows that writing is a recursive process that must be reinforced in many courses in many disciplines. The chair's effectiveness in representing the department in the institution can be an important factor in its success.

But a chair who is truly concerned about quality will take the further step of raising these same issues with the faculty who teach the course, thus fostering a climate of continuous discussion of how quality can be improved. Communicating concerns to the faculty responsible for these *service* courses also helps to keep them aware of their external reputation as well as the goals of what they are doing. Chairs can keep the issues alive by introducing regular discussion of the department's content, methods, and goals in department meetings. And occasionally an external complaint will expose problems that need departmental attention, for example, when a composition course intended to prepare students for college-level writing has drifted toward "creative" expression and literary analysis. Despite the sensitivities that such inquiries can create, a tactful department chair can convert this external perspective to good use.

Chairs can also lead their departments to see responsiveness to outside concerns as within their own self-interest. If, for example, other departments believe that their students are not learning to use statistics as they are employed in their discipline, they may decide to teach their own discipline-specific statistical methods courses. Because enrollments in service courses are often the basis for a department's share of the resource pool, it is particularly important that chairs systematically seek outside assessment of these courses and not allow them to languish. Chairs should continually foster discussion of how well faculty teach service courses, how these courses might be renewed to avoid faculty burnout, and how to shift the focus away from faculty teaching "performance" and toward classroom interaction and student learning.

Similar issues arise for elective courses that have the potential to serve students seeking to broaden their attractiveness to future employers. The outside pressures on these elective courses are less dramatic and intense; therefore, the issue of drift or adherence to priorities may be easier to overlook. Department chairs can play an important role here as well, by helping the department to see its role in campuswide curriculum offerings. To foster change, a chair must be adept at understanding the student demand for minors and career-related courses of study, and assisting faculty in shaping courses that are responsive.

A special dilemma for chairs occurs when one of the department's elective courses becomes popular with students and produces tension about whether to deploy full-time faculty to teach the course or rely on a cadre of adjuncts. Typical courses that students seek out as electives include courses in human sexuality, women's health, and photography. At a time of budget constraints on campuses, there is a temptation to teach such courses in large sections at the lowest possible unit cost using graduate students and part-time faculty. Department chairs have a responsibility to seek the same quality standards for these courses as for the major course of study and to review regularly the role of these courses in the overall education of undergraduates. Discussion of these issues can be guided by some fundamental questions:

- What role should electives play in a student's program?
- What balance might there be between elective courses that serve departmental interests and those that meet the needs of students in other fields?
- How can faculty be brought into the curriculum planning process beyond the scheduling of their own courses?

New Understanding About Student Learning

A class session, a course, or a program of study is a plan for learning. Although faculty may differ in sophistication and appreciation of the purposes and processes of their academic planning, at some point they ask two questions: What do I want to teach? and How should it be taught? In the last decade, a critical question has been added: How will we know that students have learned? This convergence of interest in student-centered learning, active pedagogies, and assessment provides a rich context in which a department chair can enhance the understanding of faculty about the role of their courses in the personal, social, and intellectual development of the students. This task is particularly important because few doctoral programs prepare faculty for teaching, emphasizing instead specialized knowledge and research skills.

Background in the research on student learning is now essential for faculty as increased access to higher education has filled classrooms with diverse learners with different backgrounds, intentions, and styles of learning. A rich literature on student social and intellectual development is available to guide faculty in adapting their courses and programs to this diversity (Pascarella and Terenzini, 1991; Astin, 1993). Particular attention is being paid to the needs of first-year students, adult students, and first-generation students. Research has revealed significant differences between males and females in their ways of knowing and their expectations for structure and feedback (Belenky, Clinchy, Goldberger, and Tarule, 1986; Baxter-Magolda, 1992). One theme that is common in all the literature is the way in which sequence, links, and integration enhance learning; for example, taking courses at random is not as powerful as taking them in a designed learning experience that begins in the freshman year and includes nonacademic elements. Student affairs professionals have created increasingly strong partnerships with academic affairs divisions to create freshmen seminar programs based on community service, living-learning programs, and theme-oriented learning communities all aimed at integrating the total undergraduate experience in order to produce greater learning (Erickson and Strommer 1991; Gardiner, 1994). Department chairs must not only encourage faculty to participate in such programs but also ensure that they get credit and rewards for doing so.

In addition to facilitating greater faculty understanding of the factors affecting the contemporary student's ability to learn, department chairs need also to help faculty understand the challenges of the complex work world for which they are preparing students. Department chairs can sponsor conversations with potential employers, encourage faculty to integrate applied learning projects into their courses, and arrange for faculty to have brief internships of their own. Increasingly, employers downplay the importance of a particular major and seek students with good communication skills, the ability to work with others, the capacity for self-motivation, and the ability to continue learning on their own. Consequently, faculty need to review their courses for opportunities to promote collaboration skills, team building, and computer-supported learning. The impact of changing demands and new technologies is reflected throughout the curriculum as well as in new program efforts using guided study, distance learning, weekend formats, courses on the Web, and problem-based learning. As faculty embrace new strategies such as group projects, service learning, or technology, they often feel overloaded. Because there are so many opportunities for innovation, the department chair must aid faculty in preparing a systematic and sustainable plan for responding to these varied opportunities, or risk faculty resources becoming spread too thin.

Finally, increased diversity on college campuses has led faculty and administrators to encourage development of courses and teaching strategies that are more attuned to the needs of special populations. While all students benefit from attention to developmental needs, students from different backgrounds may respond in different ways. Returning adult students, for example, may need the time and opportunity to brush up on their academic skills in an atmosphere that recognizes and accommodates their insecurities. Small classes with personal attention and the opportunity to work with others in their situation can ease their transition into the classroom. Honors students may learn best in an interactive classroom that challenges them to express and defend their views and empowers them to become independent learners. Learning-disabled and physically disabled students require special accommodations and adaptive equipment to ensure access to courses and majors. Minority and international students need to see the curriculum as affirming of different cultural values and perspectives.

A chair who understands the institution's demographic profile and how it affects classroom instruction can in turn assist faculty in meeting varied student needs. To respond to the challenge of meeting student needs, the chair can reflect on several questions:

- What should faculty know about learning styles?
- What institutional resources (such as teaching center, technological services, the library, student services, and so on) are available to support a better understanding of student learning styles?
- How might faculty assess the nonacademic and affective skills needed by students?

Creating Resources to Support Curricular Change

To a great extent, the last two decades have been a difficult time to consider curricular change because support for higher education, whether through tuition dollars or state appropriation, has been unpredictable and constrained. Some campuses have suffered such severe cutbacks, in both funding and programs, that enthusiasm for curriculum development is hard to kindle. Although the data on the costs of instruction show a dramatic increase, the campus reality is that at the department level there is little risk capital. When revenues decline, senior administrators are forced to cut costs and often have neither sufficient notice nor knowledge to make selective cuts. Many cost-containment strategies directly affect the number of faculty, library materials, salaries, and equipment; and such budget reductions nearly always decrease morale. Thus the department chair who wants to keep a committed and vital faculty that also pursues change will need to be skilled at reallocating resources as institutional conditions change, or risk inviting micromanagement from the dean's office.

Finding resources for innovation is particularly daunting in the new environment for public institutions, where boards, state councils, and legislators mandate restructuring and demand increased quality at less cost. Frustrated by the slow pace of academics, they increasingly demand immediate change, granting faculty little time to discuss or review their recommendations. The leisurely decision-making pace of the campus is often preempted by *rapid response groups* populated by representatives from business, government, and higher education and charged with identifying new program needs, program overlap, and administrative reductions. Not all administrators are reluctant to set aside shared governance in favor of centralized decision making. Institutions fighting for survival believe that bold and aggressive action is called for, see their curriculum as a product to be marketed aggressively, and measure their competition in student enrollments (Kanter, Gamzon, and London, 1997).

New chairs may not anticipate that cost containment, marketing, curriculum management, and resource allocation will require as much or more of their time as hiring, tenure, or promotion. After all, as long as all faculty members are teaching their specialties and the required courses are covered, what's to manage? But faced with a dean's request for the following year's schedule of classes in a climate of shrinking resources, a chair may wonder where to begin. In an era of competing imperatives and financial stress, the competing factors that go into organizing the schedule can be staggering. General education and other required courses must be scheduled at reasonable times for the campus at large. Classes for majors and graduate students must provide some choices, be spread throughout the day and evening to avoid course conflicts, and be taught often enough to allow timely program completion. Faculty members at various stages in their careers require or demand particular assignments, such as classes scheduled on certain days or at particular times. Simply putting together this jigsaw puzzle is enough for many chairs; and it is no wonder that so much curricular change occurs by accretion and indirection. The department chair is central in helping faculty understand that shaping curriculum solely around faculty self-interest is no longer viable, whether in a public institution with performance mandates or in a private institution that is tuition dependent.

Given these pressures, curriculum management is an essential first step toward identifying areas that warrant review for efficiency. Faculty are quick to claim the essential nature of a course even if enrollments are persistently small. Faculty may resist any effort to increase class size; substitute less expensive labor, such as part-time work for tenure-track faculty; or offer courses less frequently. The more productive approach to efficiency looks not merely at reducing the inputs but rather at analyzing the outputs. For example, a decrease in the number of students failing or withdrawing from mathematics courses or general chemistry reduces the costs of reteaching the course in subsequent semesters to students who need it for graduation. An increase in overall retention dramatically increases resources from tuition and reduces the per-student cost of campus infrastructure, such as libraries, computer labs, and residence halls. Grade reports, enrollment patterns, and retention rates are just a few of the data that chairs can make available to faculty to support a realistic assessment of resource use and target areas for change.

Because the catalog and course schedule are the department's most visible representation of itself to others, chairs can also use catalog revision and course scheduling as opportunities for reflection. More than anything else, department chairs need accurate historical information on course offerings and curricular change if they are to lead effectively. Without it, there is little possibility of understanding the dynamics of the curriculum as it exists, much less where and how change might be appropriate. One of the most useful reports, often available from the registrar, is a five-year history of department course offerings and enrollments compared to enrollment limits. While faculty members may perceive only that enrollments in a formerly popular course have decreased, the enrollment report may show that a change in general education or major requirements several years before has shifted students from that course to another. The effect of offering two sections of a course rather than one may become clear. Courses that are being offered too often may be identified. In some departments, the report may assist in tracking student interests toward or away from particular topics and fields. In a department that is experiencing a decline in the major, the report may show which areas are most vulnerable to lost enrollments. All of these factors, and others, can be used by chairs to introduce curricular issues for discussion and to encourage faculty members to align their teaching requests with departmental resources.

Because of the chairs' responsibility in most institutions for the decisions that go into scheduling courses, chairs understand probably better than anyone else the true resource issues in the department. Given sufficient data and help with analysis from the institutional research office, they can be frontline allies in creating institutional efficiencies. Although scheduling is not entirely a zero-sum game, adding courses and sections when resources are finite inevitably requires trimming in other areas. Widespread discussion in the department can assist in bringing faculty into the design process and encouraging shifts from lower to higher priorities. Aligning programs and resources with changing institutional missions is a function that is best performed at the department level and best led by an informed and collegial chair who can lead the department to understand how its activities contribute to the institution's overall goals.

Although all institutions need to seek greater efficiency to contain costs, there are times when additional resources are essential to initiate a new program or achieve a strategic direction. Public institutions are often successful in gaining additional general-fund dollars for technology-related programs and allied health programs that are deemed in the public interest. Federal support has been available, for example, to initiate nurse practitioner programs, develop special education, strengthen science curricula, and internationalize business curricula—all initiatives that match social priorities. Private foundations have a long history of support for strengthening curricula. To offset shrinking institutional resources, department chairs must be sophisticated and intentional about reviewing possible external sources and engaging faculty in writing proposals that are both innovative and connected to external perceptions of educational improvement. This effort to align resources with both needs and opportunities can be guided by consideration of certain questions:

- What data can the chair access to provide better curriculum and resource management?
- What efficiencies can be achieved in use of faculty resources without sacrificing quality in instruction and the curriculum?
- If external resources are sought to support innovation and initiate curriculum development, how can resources be eventually reallocated to sustain these programs?

Meeting the Accountability Challenge

Traditionally, regional accreditation has been the primary vehicle for ensuring minimum standards of quality. Because the central focus of accreditation, however, is overall institutional performance and viability, it rarely includes close analysis of the curriculum. Specialized accreditation, focused on a particular program, such as computer science, chemistry, social work, or music, addresses the specifics of curriculum and instruction according to specified standards to be applied to all programs. Not all disciplines have such accreditation processes, however, and not all institutions are interested in or eligible for specialized accreditation.

Program evaluation has long been common in higher education, but recent budget constraints, new ideas about strategic planning, and increased external demands for accountability have contributed to more systematic review of academic programs at many institutions. By the mid-1980s many models of campus program review had been developed and the majority of states were involved in program approval and evaluation (Conrad and Wilson,

1985). Internal campus-based efforts to review program integrity and determine resource allocation are commonly grounded in the institution's own sense of its mission and goals.

Although program review is sometimes seen by faculty as a burden that yields few positive results, some chairs have used it as an opportunity to foster department discussion and renew faculty commitment to department priorities. Indeed, the chair's management of the program review process can shape the final product either positively or negatively. If the process results in a defense of all the department's programs and activities and a hortatory call for more resources, it has probably accomplished little more than confirming the faculty's belief that they are not well understood by the campus at large and could do more if they had a larger share of the pie. Successful program review self-study reports, conversely, usually reflect a department's collective decision making about what it does well, what needs strengthening, and sometimes what can be eliminated.

Ideally, the impetus for change should come out of the department's self-study, and it often does. Merely placing difficult curricular and resource issues on the table for analysis can lead to a stronger sense of departmental cohesion and mission, as long as the chair and others are truly open to better ways of accomplishing goals. Some program review processes have led departments to propose substantial revisions to or even termination of degree programs, frequently as a result of the department's realization that increased resources are not forthcoming. Others have led to fruitful departmental or interdisciplinary collaboration among programs that had previously had little incentive to cooperate.

Occasionally, however, a program review will lead to an institutional decision to terminate an ailing program against the recommendation of the department. It is in those cases that a department chair's skills are most necessary. Although the natural response to a recommendation of termination is defensive, unless the review has been less than thorough and the data without foundation, it is usually counterproductive for a chair to decide immediately to lead the charge against change. After a comprehensive review in which everyone has had a chance to review the data and make recommendations, few administrators (or even members of faculty curriculum committees) are likely to want to spend much time considering how to overturn the recommendation.

Although each circumstance is different and depends on the campus climate and the institution's history of collegial or contentious decision making, there are strategies that a chair can employ to ease the pain. If the recommendation has been reached without collaboration or is based on faulty data, a reasonable representation from the department that additional issues should be discussed may be appropriate. But if the decision is the result of full-campus review, the most effective and profitable approach is one that allows faculty members the freedom to express their unhappiness while trying to seize the opportunity to lead the department in a more productive direction. Energy and time that previously went into a small graduate program can be channeled into revitalizing general education courses or redesigning the undergraduate major. More important for many campuses, faculty resources can be directed toward interdisciplinary collaboration with allied units. Presiding over a program termination may be the trickiest feat a department chair will have to perform, but the same strategies of open discussion, considering the alternatives, listening to every voice, and communicating to all constituencies can see a chair through even this trial.

In many public institutions, faculty and chairs do not have the luxury of time for analysis, discussion, and determination of their own direction. Changes in state standards for determining program continuance can cause almost overnight institutional responses and leave the vice president for academic affairs as the bearer of bad news that a department will lose a major, a masters degree, or a doctoral degree. Close monitoring of state council discussions often gives institutions indications that productivity standards are under discussion and provides some lead time for institutional discussions. More important, department chairs should not wait for the inevitable to happen because the bitterness left in faculty who believe they were ambushed does not dissipate easily and can poison departmental comity for a long time. Using the institution's own internal program review processes can provide an orderly means of shifting resources from moribund programs to those areas that are growing. Discussion of curricular

LEADING CURRICULUM RENEWAL 271

integrity and quality can be guided by the following fundamental questions:

- What kinds of regular reports from the registrar and the office of institutional research should a chair expect to support ongoing program review?
- What are the true measures of program quality?

Creating a Self-Renewing Department

Even though the curriculum is constantly evolving, departments can lose their vitality over time and get stuck in a rut. When faculty are asked to undertake curriculum study, they often resist, arguing that they do not know enough to be useful or that they would rather spend their time on their own work. No project, however, can create more intellectual energy than a well-led study of curriculum reform, for debate, values, alternatives are essential features of the process. One of the most consistent observations about campuswide general education reform projects is their impact as a powerful form of faculty development. Forced to make or defend choices, faculty come to understand their own beliefs about knowledge and learning. Listening to other bright colleagues describe new content areas and methods in their disciplines is akin to a graduate seminar. Most important, out of this shared reflection and engagement comes deep commitment to the new curricula.

The assessment process can be just as powerful as the creation of curricula. Despite some resistance to evaluation, faculty are still intrigued by what students write on the end-of-the-semester course evaluation. Departments that hold focus groups with their majors are surprised and moved by their students' responses. Major field tests for seniors can reveal significant gaps in a program. One department chair insisted that all the faculty take the senior exam along with the graduating students and then demonstrated that the students were weak in exactly the same areas that the faculty were. Surveys of graduates three years out always provide both useful information and kudos to the faculty who are most remembered. All of these sources of data, especially if shared and discussed, create a sense of shared ownership in the curricula.

Increasingly, department chairs are experimenting with ways to create ownership beyond the department and have invited alumni, faculty from other campuses, and faculty from other departments to participate in curriculum review and curriculum planning. Interdisciplinary teams ensure a fresh perspective on what seems old to those in the field. Some states require, as part of new program development, assurance that members of the community and employers have participated in the needs assessment and course planning. All of these approaches bring fresh views, create a vital learning environment, and strengthen intellectual engagement of the faculty. As assessment becomes a regular part of continuous improvement on a campus, faculty come to appreciate the value of reviewing regular feedback on courses and programs, and thrive on external validation of their efforts.

Despite the possibility that a student returning to campus after a twenty-year absence can slip back into the same requirements taught by the same faculty led by the same chair, it is unlikely that any institution has been entirely unaffected by the past three decades of curricular change. Although the external apparatus of the curriculum—courses, requirements, majors, the catalog, the schedule—may obscure the vitality of the change and renewal that has been taking place on virtually every campus, faculty know that they are not teaching the same material in the same way. Department chairs are ideally situated to lead, shape, and facilitate ongoing change. Working with administrators, faculty members, students, and outside supporters and agencies, the chair who understands the institutional context, the external environment, faculty and students' needs, and how to foster open debate makes an essential contribution to sustaining intellectual, institutional, and educational values.

References

Adelman, C. *The New College Course Map and Transcript Files: Changes in Course-Taking and Achievement, 1972–1993*. Washington D.C.: Office of Educational Research and Improvement, U.S. Department of Education, 1995.

American Council on Education. *Campus Trends*. Washington, D.C.: American Council on Education, 1988.

Association of American Colleges. *Integrity in the College Curriculum: A Report to the Academic Community.* Washington, D.C.: Association of American Colleges, 1985.

Association of American Colleges. *The Challenge of Connecting Learning.* Washington D.C.: Association of American Colleges, 1991.

Astin, A. W. *What Matters in College? Four Critical Years Revisited.* San Francisco: Jossey-Bass, 1993.

Baxter-Magolda, M. B. *Knowing and Reasoning in College: Gender-Related Patterns in Students' Intellectual Development.* San Francisco: Jossey-Bass, 1992.

Belenky, M. F., Clinchy, B. M., Goldberger, N. R., and Tarule, J. M. *Women's Ways of Knowing: The Development of Self, Voice, and Mind.* New York: Basic Books, 1986.

Bennett, W. J. *To Reclaim a Legacy.* Washington, D.C.: National Endowment for the Humanities, 1984.

Bloom, A. *Closing of the American Mind.* New York: Simon & Schuster, 1987.

Brubacher, J. S., and Rudy, W. *Higher Education in Transition: A History of American Colleges and Universities.* (4th ed.) New Brunswick, N.J.: Transaction, 1997.

Conrad, C. F., and Wilson, R. F. *Academic Program Reviews: Institutional Approaches, Expectations, and Controversies.* ASHE-ERIC Higher Education Report no. 5. Washington, D.C.: Association for the Study of Higher Education, 1985.

D'Souza, D. *Illiberal Education: The Politics of Race and Sex on Campus.* New York: Free Press, 1991.

Erickson, B. L., and Strommer, D. W. *Teaching College Freshmen.* San Francisco: Jossey-Bass, 1991.

Gardiner, L. F. *Redesigning Higher Education: Producing Dramatic Gains in Student Learning.* ASHE-ERIC Higher Education Report, vol. 23, no. 7. Washington, D.C.: Graduate School of Education and Human Development, George Washington University, 1994.

Graff, G. *Professing Literature: An Institutional History.* Chicago: University of Chicago Press, 1988.

Hirsch, E. D. *Cultural Literacy: What Every American Needs to Know.* Boston: Houghton Mifflin, 1987.

Kanter, S. L., Gamzon, Z. F., and London, H. B. *Revitalizing General Education in a Time of Scarcity.* Needham Heights, Mass.: Allyn & Bacon, 1997.

Knefelkamp, L. "Seasons of Academic Life: Honoring Our Collective Autobiographies." *Liberal Education,* 1990, *76*(3), 4–11.

Levine, A. M., and Green, J. (eds.). *Opportunity in Adversity.* San Francisco, Jossey-Bass, 1985.

Lucas, A. F. *Strengthening Departmental Leadership: A Team-Building Guide for Chairs in Colleges and Universities.* San Francisco: Jossey-Bass, 1994.

Minnich, E. *Liberal Learning and the Arts of Connection for the New Academy.* Washington D.C.: Association of American Colleges and Universities, 1985.

National Institute of Education. *Involvement in Learning: Realizing the Potential of American Higher Education.* Washington, D.C.: National Institute of Education, 1984.

Pascarella, E. T., and Terenzini, P. T. *How College Affects Students: Findings and Insights from Twenty Years of Research.* San Francisco: Jossey-Bass, 1991.

Stark, J. S., and Lattuca, L. R. *Shaping the College Curriculum: Academic Plans in Action.* Needham Heights, Mass.: Allyn & Bacon, 1997.

Chapter Twelve

The Academy as Learning Community

Contradiction in Terms or Realizable Future?

Peter M. Senge

Whether we like it or not, colleges and universities place themselves in a position of leadership in society. They do so because they presume to provide an intellectual framework and moral foundation that will be valid into the future. "Local line pioneering" dean of engineering Gordon Brown used to say, "To be a teacher is to be a prophet—you are not preparing a student for the world of today but for a world twenty to fifty years into the future" (personal communication). No question is more germane to any institution of higher education than, "Are we preparing students for the future they will live in or the past we have lived through?"

Such a question was far easier to address in times past when the pace of change was slower and the future at least seemed more predictable. Academic fields evolved slowly, befitting the inherent conservatism of intellectual communities to slowly accumulate widely accepted notions into an ever broadening corpus of received knowledge. The expectations of society were relatively stable as to what a college graduate should know and be able to do. Economic growth provided steady increase in financial resources for education and research. There was little competition for higher education's niche as the sole source of college degrees.

Today, these features of the university's landscape seem decidedly foreign, distant memories of a time long past. The pace of advance in many academic fields has accelerated dramatically. The credibility of colleges and universities, along with all other major social institutions, has declined. There are few schools that are not under intense economic pressure. And a whole new set of competitors has emerged with today's electronic communications media. "What is to keep universities from going the way of banks?" asks Dee Hock, founding CEO of VISA International. "In 1970, if you wanted a loan you went to a bank. Today you use your credit card" (personal communication). What will keep the same disintermediation from occurring in higher education, once quality providers can make the best lecturers on any subject available through the Internet, complete with course materials, testing, and personalized feedback?

Yet despite these dramatic changes, the culture and practices of colleges and universities have by and large changed little. The focus is still on teaching rather than learning. The professor still controls the classroom. Individualism and competition still reign, from individual students pitted against one another to individual professors who likewise compete for status, power, and often money. "Technical rationality" still ranks as the prevailing epistemology, disconnecting theory from practice and sending young people into the world with heads full of ideas and "answers" but little experience in producing more effective action.

Perhaps most seriously of all, most of the members of the academy seem still to see little cause for concern and little reason for fundamental change. Most teachers cannot imagine a day when there will not be students cued up at their door waiting for their words of wisdom. Administrators struggle with financial stress by simply reducing headcount while often simultaneously boosting enrollments. Executives keep returning to alumni, or to state funders, for more money to keep the machine running.

Having lived in universities for the majority of my life, I believe that the problems run deep. In a nutshell, universities and colleges have become the preeminent *knowing institutions* in a world that increasingly favors *learning institutions*.

The Origins of the Learning Organization

The Learning Organization is a vision. It is not a model. It is a not a summary of best practices. There are no Learning Organizations in the sense of particular institutions that have arrived and should be emulated. In another sense, every organization that survives is continually learning: sensing changes in its environment and adapting.

The real issues that led to serious interest in organizational learning were twofold:

1. As the world becomes more dynamic, are institutions, especially traditionally successful organizations, able to accelerate their rate of learning? As retired Shell executive Arie de Geus (1997) put it, "The ability to learn faster than your competitor may be the only sustainable source of competitive advantage."
2. What is required to tap the imagination, commitment, and creativity of all members of an institution?

The work that I and my colleagues have been involved in for almost twenty years has suggested that these two questions are really two sides of the same question. Organizations can accelerate their capacities to adapt and continually reinvent themselves only by tapping the capacities of their people. There are no magic formulas or technical fixes for organizational learning. It is a deeply human activity that reflects human communities functioning at their best rather than their worst, which seems to happen so often in today's organizations.

Over many years, a cornerstone of our work has become the idea that there are certain *core learning capabilities* that determine the ability of teams and organizations to learn. The *five disciplines* framework, first introduced in *The Fifth Discipline* (Senge, 1990), presents tools, methods, and underlying theory for developing such learning capabilities, which fall into three broad areas:

• *Aspiration:* To what extent are people oriented toward creating what they truly care about, to addressing the largest and most important issues that concern them? Or is people's work only about solving immediate problems, reacting to crises, or pursuing goals set by someone else?

- *Reflective conversation:* How people talk with one another, especially about complex and conflictual issues, sets the tone for collective learning. To what extent do our conversations make us more aware of our own assumptions and ways of seeing? To what extent do they produce shared understanding, deeper meaning, and effective coordination of action? Or do we "talk at" one another, engaged in never-ending win-lose struggles, leading ultimately to disengagement, where the real issues are discussed in the ladies room or the ubiquitous hallway conversations.

- *Understanding complexity:* As the world becomes more interconnected and dynamic, our conditioned ways of thinking become more dysfunctional. To what extent can people see how their own actions and habitual ways of operating create their problems? To what extent can they see how their own "local solutions" might be the source of difficulties for people in other parts of the organization? Do we see the underlying interdependencies and "systemic structures" that are generating problems, or only the problem's symptoms?

It is important to stress that these are capabilities not ideologies. They involve particular skills and bodies of internalized knowledge that can be built only over time. Many people advocate taking a "systems perspective" on issues but have no ability to do that. They talk passionately about "needing to understand the system" but cannot begin to explain what they mean and what specific implications their entreaty suggests. The same is true for leaders who advocate listening and "dialogue" but find themselves unable to hear truly another's point of view that differs from theirs, or to raise difficult issues directly without invoking defensiveness in others, or to advocate their views forcefully while at the same time encouraging others to inquire into their own views. Genuine aspiration is more than just having a goal; it is living one's life in service of what matters most deeply, something that most adults have long lost track of.

Finally, these core learning capabilities themselves constitute a whole. This is the meaning of the "three-legged stool" in Figure 12.1. Take away any one of these capabilities and the stool collapses. Without aspiration, there is no real reason for learning, especially if the learning is difficult, such as when we must "unlearn" habits of thought and action which we have acquired over a lifetime. Without aspiration, what learning occurs happens only when there is a crisis, when we have no choice but to change. Without reflectiveness and the capacity for real conversation, there is no mutuality, there is no fiber that connects people changing together. Without conversation, there may be lots of visions but there will be no shared vision. Without a collective capability for conversation, even brilliant strategic insights will end up creating polarization as people try to impose their ideas on another. Without the capability to understand complexity, there is no insight into the deeper causes of problems, quick fix solutions dominate, and even powerful visions become connected to dangerously oversimplified views of reality.

From Theory to Practice

Each of the core learning capabilities has deep roots, in many cases in academic research. My own training was in the field of systems dynamics, understanding complex, nonlinear human systems. The roots of this field go back more than a hundred and fifty years in the engineering analysis of feedback systems, and almost as far in biology and the social sciences. The scientific roots behind the disciplines required to develop reflectiveness and more productive conversation are equally rich, in fields as diverse as philosophy of language, cognitive psychology, the psychology of groups, and the biology of cognition. The roots underlying aspiration are less in

Figure 12.1. Three-Legged Stool Diagram.

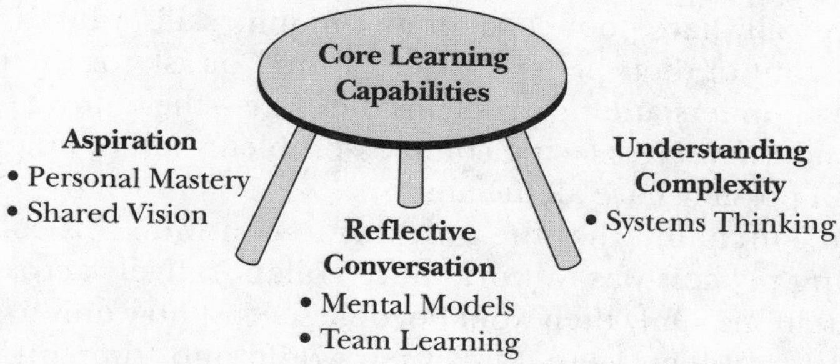

science and more in the arts and humanities, especially in the understanding of the creative process as passed on in all the creative arts.

The challenge that has engaged a great many people over the past twenty years has been how to get this broad range of ideas, tools, and processes into practice, how to have them gradually weave into the day-to-day activities of people working together in diverse settings. If they do constitute a potentially powerful foundation to accelerate and deepen organizational learning, the only way to discover what is required to realize that potential is through application. This incessant focus on application, especially in corporations, has led to continual evolution of theory, practical tools, and know-how. (A good introduction to these tools and practical insights can be found in *The Fifth Discipline Fieldbook,* Senge and others, 1994.) But it has also led to problems.

After more than ten years in training and consulting applications with individual firms, a group of us decided that we had learned enough to know that the way we were going about it was not adequate. We discovered again and again that the ways of thinking, interacting, and ultimately being that were nurtured through these principles and tools ran counter, often in profound ways, to the norms and practices of how most organizations, including quite successful ones, operated. We discovered that the culture of learning was very different from the culture of Industrial Age enterprises. What it means to be a manager in most organizations is to be in control; yet complex systems are not controllable in the ways managers seek. What it takes to rise up the hierarchy in most organizations is to be articulate, good at advocating your views and impressing people with your intelligence. This results in executives who typically have poor collaborative inquiry skills, who can never say in front of their peers, "I don't know," or ask for the help of others in understanding problems they face—the same executives who find themselves facing complex problems where no one person can possibly have all the answers.

We concluded that the only way to continue this collective learning process was to work more collaboratively across many organizations. Only then would people see just how universal their deepest problems were. Only then would one company's small steps be encouraging to others. Only then would the inevitable setbacks and crises that all organizations encounter not derail them—for they would be able to look at the progress that others were making and get themselves back on track. In a funny way we rediscovered a very old idea. In facing the challenges of profound change, there is no substitute for collaboration—people coming together out of common purpose and willing to support one another so that all can advance. Without actually intending it, we began to create a learning community.

In 1990, the MIT Organizational Learning Center (OLC) formed a consortium that grew to about twenty companies (mostly large, Fortune 100 companies). In 1997, the OLC became a self-governing society of companies, researchers, and consultants: the Society for Organizational Learning (SoL). Today SoL is rapidly becoming a global network of learning communities in different countries and regions around the world. (For more on SoL, see www.sol-ne-org.)

There have been many successes and many setbacks over the past ten years in developing the SoL community. Business units at companies like Ford, Intel, Hewlett-Packard, FedEx, AT&T, Harley Davidson, Lucent, British Petroleum, and DTE (formerly Detroit Edison) have achieved significant improvements in business results, sometimes surpassing past levels of success dramatically. Of course, it is never possible to definitively prove that any one set of activities caused any particular outcome in a complex organizational setting. Gradually, however, enough credibility has been developed to extend the learning ideas and approaches to be part of larger-scale undertakings—such as the "transformation" of U.S. Shell Oil (involving a radical new design and governance process and, over a five-year period, a dramatic surge of new entrepreneurial businesses) and the creation of Visteon, a wholly owned subsidiary of Ford, linking 85,000 people worldwide in all of Ford's components businesses. But for every dramatic success there have been failed starts and projects that continued but never produced significant business results, as you would expect for any significant new innovation. ("Learning histories" describing several of these long-term change efforts, written as part of SoL's research activities, can be accessed through the SoL Web site.) While disappointing, as much is learned from the shortfalls as from the successes.

The more salient learnings for academic institutions include the following:

1. Learning is not an "add on," to be done when we have some free time or at training sessions. Some of the most significant innovations have been in infrastructures and day-to-day practices, allowing teams and intact work groups to integrate working and learning.

2. The core learning capabilities provide a foundation, not a formula. Companies have continually innovated and extended their learning efforts, incorporating many tools and approaches not included in the original tools when we started SoL. (See, for example, the new fieldbook, *The Dance of Change,* Senge and others, 1999.)

3. There is no substitute for genuine commitment and commitment starts "at home." No one should be told to change their beliefs, or to adopt new values, or to change deeply habitual ways of doing things; efforts to employ coercive power to bring about deep change invariably backfire. Those who lead must be prepared to change themselves first, rather than focusing on how others must change.

4. The critical leaders of such changes occupy many positions and are not limited to those at the top. Surprisingly, there are several examples of companies who have sustained and extended significant change efforts over five to ten years with virtually no executive leadership. In other cases, where executive leadership has been important, change has been through leading by example and through supporting other leaders, not through speeches, official change programs, and grand strategies. Wherever significant change has been sustained it has always involved talented, committed "local line leaders" and resourceful "internal networkers." We believe that the role of executives in deep change is widely misunderstood, that these two additional types of leaders are greatly neglected, and that this is one reason so many change efforts fail.

Implications for Universities

Today there is growing interest in creating similar learning communities linking groups of universities. It is much too early to know if these collaborative arrangements will become successful, let alone whether or not they will show the way for broader change within the academy. But it is at least possible to frame some questions that might usefully guide the effort.

1. *Are we not all in the same boat?* The modern college is as much a part of the Industrial Age as is the modern corporation. "Our prevailing system of management has destroyed our people," said famous quality management pioneer W. Edwards Deming (personal communication). He was not talking about the system of management in corporations but about the system of management in all Industrial Age institutions. Indeed, he added, "The forces of destruction begin with the toddlers—a prize for the best Halloween costume, grades in school, gold stars—and on up through the university." This is a system of management we all have grown up with, based on bosses and subordinates rather than on teams. It is a system that emphasizes technical problem solving rather than deep inquiry into the systemic source of problems in our own behavior and in the design of our institutions. It is a system "based on fear" as Deming said, not based on aspiration, curiosity, dignity, and love.

If our educational system is as much an expression of the Industrial Age system of management as are corporations, and if there is evidence of significant progress in many corporations toward creating more learning-oriented cultures, then there should be hope for universities as well.

2. *Who are the local line leaders in universities and what is their role in the changes ahead?* The role of local line leaders in integrating new principles and tools into daily work practices has proven essential in the SoL member companies. While there have been many examples of corporations that have sustained progress for many years with little active executive leadership, there have been no examples of such progress without talented, imaginative, committed local line leaders. These are people with clear managerial accountabilities, such as product development team leaders, local sales managers, and manufacturing plant managers. Such frontline leaders are essential because without their efforts it is not possible to test whether or not potential innovations in fact add value. This requires people who are close to where value is being generated.

Teachers clearly operate at the heart of the value creation process in colleges and universities. So it stands to reason that they too would be the key to the innovation process.

Innovation in instruction must start with recognition of the simple fact that teachers teaching does not produce learning. Learning is ultimately produced only by learners. Learning is a process that leads to enhanced capacity of the learner. It does not occur simply because one is taught. What is conveyed between teacher and student must be internalized. But internalization is different than simply the ability to recall information. It involves new thinking and new acting. Moreover, learning occurs over time, and especially as learners engage in meaningful activities in their day-to-day life.

Much of the essence of all real learning is lost in conventional education due to the fragmentation of teaching from learning. In the Industrial Age assembly line model of education, teachers "do it" to students. Such an image probably would be rejected by most teachers, because it does not fit their espoused theory or self-image. But I would contend that it does fit the "theory in use," as evident in the practices of most college educators: lecturers conveying information that they decide (unilaterally) is pertinent, students expected to absorb that information and then proving that they have on tests judged solely by the inspectors on the assembly line—that is, the teachers.

To shift the Industrial Age model from teaching to learning, the role and responsibilities of the teacher need to shift. The teacher needs to become a designer of learning processes in which she or he participates along with the student. The teacher needs to operate more from a stance of *not knowing* rather than from *knowing*. The teacher needs to be willing to be a learner—perhaps a learner with greater experience in the area being explored than the student, but a learner nonetheless. And there needs to be mutual responsibility among learners and teachers for producing learning in both.

Such ideas are challenging for teachers whose identity is wrapped up with professing and being an expert. But being an expert is a short-lived advantage in today's world, and having "the answers" can actually be a disadvantage when what is really needed is the ability to inquire continually and make sense of what is emerging.

Such ideas about learner-centered learning are not new. Recently they have resurfaced, perhaps reflecting a broadening awareness of the need for such change. In a widely read article, Barr and Tagg (1995, p. 13) argue that "a paradigm shift is taking hold in American education . . . from teaching to learning." This is an encouraging development. But our experiences with learning in the corporate world have been sobering. Intellectual agreement is not enough. Everyone talking about learning is not enough. It is far easier to embrace the idealism of a learning paradigm than it is to transform traditional concentrations of power and authority in experts and managers, or than it is to sustain deep shifts in the values, capabilities, and unquestioned habits that made us all successful in the teaching paradigm.

3. *Can department chairs serve as catalysts and stewards of change?* Department chairs are the second crucial type of local line leader in higher education. Yet they are not bosses in the same sense as are traditional line managers in corporations. Typically they are teachers and professors themselves who are "on loan" as managers. In fact, the very term *manager* often feels misplaced to many faculty chairs. They serve for several years, then typically return full-time to their teaching and research activities. Although a few continue to move up in the administrative hierarchy, most have little aspirations in this direction. They are often recruited to the job and serve out of a sense of responsibility to the institution and to their peers and students.

Yet these differences are less significant to leading change than they might at first appear. In fact, in corporations that are becoming more networked and less hierarchical, local and middle-level managers are starting to look more like academic department chairs than traditional corporate bosses. Their authority depends on their credibility and persuasiveness rather than on their formal power. Their mandate is amorphous and continually in flux; in fact, one of their primary roles is to facilitate ongoing reflection and conversation to identify clear goals and establish agreed-upon strategies to move toward those goals. These strategic conversations link them vertically to those above them in the hierarchy, as well as to those below them. But they also link them horizontally, to partners in an ever-changing landscape of teams and alliances that form, unform, and reform to tackle particular tasks. Interestingly, this ongoing shift to managers as facilitators, coaches, and catalysts of change has brought renewed interest in recent years to philosophies of servant leadership and stewardship, in order to characterize attitudes and skills required to be effective. This is evident in the management literature in the writings of Robert Greenleaf (1977, 1998) on servant leadership, Peter Block (1993) on stewardship, and Joseph Jaworsky, in his book *Synchronicity* (1996).

One of the first things that department chairs need to do as servants of the larger change process is ask their member faculty what they see as significant challenges and opportunities for innovation. This does not mean that all faculty are just waiting to pursue radical innovations—unfortunately this is often not the case in many colleges and universities. It does mean that it is vital for any leader committed to significant changes to find out who their natural partners are. Very often you will find individuals who are deeply committed to innovation but who feel isolated and unsupported. Asking people with passion for creating something new how you can help is one of the most effective leadership strategies. Imaginative local leaders find countless ways to encourage ferment. They encourage networking among innovators in different departments. They organize field trips to different organizations that have succeeded in achieving breakthroughs. They introduce new tools, methods, and processes that help people develop better skills in collaborative learning (a particular short suit of many educators who have excelled throughout their lives as competitive, individual learners). They work to relieve specific constraints that hamper innovators, such as getting them more time, support, and relief from organizational pressures.

But beyond all these techniques, they take a stand for what is possible. Ironically, department chairs, and their counterparts in nonprofit organizations, are often seen as the ultimate bureaucrats. The willingness of people in such positions to commit themselves to fundamental change can send a powerful signal. But if there is one thing that has been shown again and again in our experiences of successful innovation, how they do it is the key. It is always tempting to tell others how *they* need to change. It is another, and far rarer, strategy to confront the changes needed in our own behaviors. Ironically, the greatest power of hierarchy in supporting fundamental change is not the power to direct but the symbolic power to *model,* to *be the change you are seeking to create.* Consider the following comments from members of a large product development team in an automobile manufacturer:

"I've known [the program manager] for 25 years. He was a typical senior program director when he came abroad—very autocratic and power-based, and always had been. But I've seen [the program manager] do a 180–degree turn in the last two years" [Roth and Kleiner, 1996, p. 25].

"We had been talking about open, honest communication around this company for as long as I've been here and I've been here for 29 years now. This was the first time I thought it might really work" [p. 15].

All shifts in culture start locally, because culture is the outgrowth of our day-to-day ways of doing things. People seeking to change cultures often get lost in abstract ideals and intellectual debates and forget that we re-create our culture in each meeting. As a long-time member of a university community, I have concluded that although there are many differences between colleges and corporations, internal politics and game playing is not one of them. As far as I can tell, the typical university is, if anything, a more highly politicized institution than the typical corporation. But I also find a hunger today among my university colleagues for genuine intellectual community. Many were drawn to their careers by the image of the academy as a setting for reflection and intellectual discourse. What they experience is often the antithesis of this ideal. Department chairs intent on creating an environment for innovation can start by asking themselves and their colleagues what they would have to change in their own ways of operating to move tangibly toward this ideal.

4. *What can university executives learn from other executives engaged in profound change in private industry?* First, that the "leader must drive change" mind-set is bankrupt. "Anyone who thinks the CEO can drive this kind of change is wrong," says Harley Davidson CEO Rich Teerlink (personal communication). "When I first came in as CEO," said Shell Oil CEO Phil Carroll, "everyone thought, 'Phil will tell us what to do.' But I didn't have a clue, and if I had, it would have been a disaster" (personal communication).

Somehow I think that many university presidents will find Teerlink's and Carroll's words comforting, because they are often acutely aware that the power structure of most universities and colleges makes the "leaders driving change" image virtually impossible anyway. Traditionally, universities have a much more distributed power structure than do businesses. Faculty with tenure are hard to "drive."

Unfortunately, far too many university executives conclude that this implies a kind of passive leadership, an almost caretaker mentality. On the contrary, the challenges of executive leadership in a learning environment are, if anything, more demanding than in the traditional image of executives as captains of the ship. These challenges require executives who are designers, not just speechmakers, and who work in genuine partnership with other leaders, especially the committed teachers and department chairs from whom many of the bold ideas needed for real change will come.

5. *Can the university redesign itself for the twenty-first century?* There exist major design issues that must engage university leaders at all levels. For example, many attempts at innovation tend to occur within the context of the classroom. But the classroom itself may be the fundamental limit in recreating higher education. The classroom reinforces a teacher-centered view of education. It easily becomes the stage for confusing teaching and learning. Moreover, it is a symbol of the overall isolation of the university from the larger world.

In order to rethink classroom-based education, we need to examine its underlying epistemology. Technical rationality, which dominates professional education and reflects the ethos of most university education, holds that students must first learn theory, then the methods based on that theory. It is "instrumental problem solving made rigorous by the application of scientific theory and technique," in the words of Donald Schön (1983, p. 21).

There are several problems with this view. First, from this perspective, knowledge flows "downhill," from universities, where it is discovered and codified, to practitioners, who put it to use. This positions the university and the university professor as *the* source of knowledge, creating a sort of institutional arrogance that views practitioners as inherently less important in the grand scheme of things. This arrogance then carries over into the educational process, where students are handed received wisdom, with little attention to how it integrates with their own knowledge from everyday life, or to how this wisdom is applied beyond classroom exercises. Finally, it tends to isolate professors within their respective scholarly communities and seal off these communities from the larger world—after all, there is little reason to do otherwise, because these scholarly communities see themselves as the source of new knowledge.

Where will we turn in looking for alternative models of the educational enterprise? One place to start is with the study that led to Schön's (1983) critique of technical rationality. This study involved trying to understand ongoing learning among diverse professionals. The professionals who continued to grow throughout their career, Schön concluded, engaged in "reflective practice." They developed the capacity to reflect continually on their actions in such a way that their acting became progressively more accomplished. They had learned how to learn. Schön's critique of most higher education was that by pursing the myth of technical rationality, it not only failed to lay a foundation for reflective practice, it also actively discouraged it. It reinforced a view that learning was all "in the head," that what it means to be smart is to have a lot of "right answers." This view in turn eventually leads to workplaces where people are continually trying to impress one another with how smart they are so that their ideas will prevail, rather than learning together.

I believe that this overintellectualized view of knowledge that divorces it from effective action and real-life contexts lies at the heart of the contemporary crisis of all Industrial Age educational institutions. We have fragmented the thinking aspects of learning from the doing aspects of learning and by so doing have undermined the educational enterprise more than we can realize.

To consider one radical alternative, SoL is organized as a partnership among researchers, consultants, and practitioners, involving both universities (MIT was the founding research institutional member) and corporations. SoL's organizational design follows from the simple notion that knowledge generation involves three critical dimensions: theory, tools and methods, and practical know-how.

Each aspect of knowledge is crucial. If any one dimension is neglected, the creation of new knowledge is severely compromised—resulting in abstract, nonactionable theory in academia and unquestioned and untested rules and norms in business—"ways we do things around here." In a healthy knowledge-generating process, the three aspects of knowledge creation are linked in unending spirals of interaction—most of which are severed in traditional education. Today, SoL's research, consultant, and corporate members are starting to work together to advance knowledge in diverse areas critical to the future of contemporary institutions, such as environmental sustainability, leadership, and large-scale change.

Viewed from the academic perspective, an especially important aspect of SoL's theory of knowledge creation is that practical know-how is not seen as some sort of lower-order knowledge. Rather, practical know-how is a necessary counterpart to theory and method, which both validates and generates new theory and method.

But academics are consistently discouraged from studying practical problems and how people in for-profit and nonprofit institutions wrestle with them. At my school, there was a young faculty member who was extremely knowledgeable about total quality management (TQM) when these ideas were first being taken seriously by American corporations in the early 1980s. But he was discouraged from pursuing this interest because it would jeopardize his chances for tenure. So, while he wrote papers on queuing theory, serious study of the tools, methods, and dilemmas for translating the quality management revolution from its Japanese incubator to western cultures was neglected. I think it is fair to say that this revolution was neglected by almost all of the "major" business schools. Few had serious research programs aimed at implementation of TQM methods, in part because most viewed the underlying statistical theory as well understood, and consequently not researchable. In making this judgment, they missed the point that the real issues were not technical but social—such as redistributing power and enabling frontline workers to assume more responsibility for improving work processes (Deming, 1982). Consequently, the quality management movement in America was mainly advanced by consulting firms, many of which sold standard programs rather than encouraging deep inquiry and serious testing of alternatives. It should come as no surprise that ten years later many viewed the TQM movement as a fad, and most ex post studies showed that most TQM programs had little significant impact— despite the fact that they had a major impact in a small number of firms and in many world-leading Japanese firms such as Toyota.

Finally, over the past twenty years, in our work in management and organizations, I have consistently found that some of the boldest, most important new theoretical constructs have come from practitioners—thoughtful people who wrestle with pressing issues in imaginative ways.

For example, my own interest in learning organizations did not stem from academic research; it was sparked by a study done by Royal-Dutch Shell in the early 1980s that focused on three inter-related questions: (1) What is the average life expectancy of large Fortune 500 corporations? (2) Why do so many die prematurely? That is, why is the average life expectancy, which turned out to be thirty to forty years, so much shorter than the potential life expectancy (many live more than two hundred years)? and (3) What seems to characterize those that live for hundreds of years? Eventually, the Shell executives concluded that the high corporate mortality rate was due to most organizations' inability to learn. In turn, eventually some linked this low learning ability to these companies' management seeing them as "machines for producing money rather than human communities" (de Geus, 1997). No academic had ever posed these questions, nor made the link between inability to learn and mechanistic thinking, as far as I know. Practitioners may lack the opportunity or the specific skills to codify and test their new ideas. But they are often less conservative in their thinking than their academic counterparts.

Building genuine partnerships in generating new knowledge between academics and practitioners will be very difficult for universities as long as academics do not value thinking and acting equally. Discounting practical know-how is a natural by-product of technical rationality and its worldview that prizes intellectual understanding over embodied capability. So too is discouraging action-oriented and other serious research aimed at studying the practical problems of achieving significant change.

Reconnecting thinking and acting and developing reflective practitioners represents a profound design challenge for postindustrial colleges and universities. It will require a willingness to rethink and reinvent the basic institution of higher education. To what extent should students spend their time at the university versus in the "real world"? How much of the educational process should be project based? How much should students work in teams, learning with and from one another, versus individually? How can we come to value practical knowledge on an equal footing with theoretical knowledge, and what types of research and educational processes are needed to enable the two to enrich one another? What types of relationships will have to develop between the university and the larger community of profit and nonprofit institutions to make this happen? What does all of this mean for the nature of a teacher's work in the future?

These are just illustrations of the types of questions that must be addressed in redesigning university education. But it is also important to realize that there are examples, both historical and contemporary, of the consequences of taking such questions seriously. One powerful illustration of integrating theory, method, and practice was the agricultural extension programs that developed in the later half of the nineteenth century. These programs, and the land grant universities that hosted them, had a substantial impact on the evolution of the practice of farming and the theory and methods taught to agriculture students. It is quite possible that America would never have developed into the bread basket of the world without this radical bridging of the academic and practical worlds. But we don't have to look just to history for examples of productive partnerships between the academic and practical worlds. In fact, much technological innovation today is being driven by just such partnerships between research universities and entrepreneurial businesses. Likewise, plenty of examples of fundamental educational innovation can be found—such as universities that have become strongly project-oriented and "universities without walls."

Yet such examples remain on the periphery—radical alternatives that have yet to penetrate the mainstream university establishment. Most education remains disconnected from practice. To the degree that some successful research connections have been forged between the academic and practical worlds in engineering and the physical sciences, these remain the exception that proves the rule of isolation between these two worlds, and little of this has carried over to the social and managerial sciences. If this is to change, leaders of all sorts will have to begin to engage with the types of basic design issues just posed.

6. *Where will the leadership for change come from?* It is easy to look at the depth and breath of these issues and conclude that only university presidents and boards have the power to bring about the types of changes needed. But if our experience over the past ten years within the SoL community is any guide, this would be exactly the wrong conclusion to come to. If one overarching lesson stands out from that experience, it is that leadership for profound change is too important, too multifaceted, and too demanding of day-to-day attention to be left to executives alone. Such leadership must come from many places, including some where no one is looking.

There *are* deep issues of purpose, identity, and strategy, and ultimately the concept of the institution and how it is organized, that must engage university executives and boards. But they must also engage the people who will actually build the new educational processes and programs. The limitations of executive leadership stem from the multiple constituencies that contemporary executives must satisfy and from their disconnection from the day-to-day operations of those institutions, where real change ultimately must take root. Creating fundamentally new institutions means embedding new ideas in new practices, and this requires leadership from those close to the front lines of the enterprise.

This is why I believe that the innovation processes needed within universities will center on clusters of faculty and, potentially, department chairs. The answers to basic design questions such as those posed earlier will differ from one discipline to another. Many cannot be answered in the abstract for the university as a whole. Rather, they must inform specific innovations in curriculum, degree requirements, hiring, and how faculty organize their time and work. The partnerships to be forged with those outside the university need to be anchored to specific educational and research undertakings. Key relationships will be built with individual faculty, students, and administrators. In all of these processes, university executives can help, but only if the real work is led by those closer to the action.

For example, department chairs committed to fundamental innovation are in unique positions to address the conflicting incentives facing individual faculty. The example presented earlier about the young faculty member who wanted to study TQM is typical of the type of issue with which department chairs should wrestle. There are many similar conflicts between relevance and traditional academic expectations. Many revolve around the tenure process and the way it can cramp explorations of new intellectual territory. Because it hinges on peer review, the tenure process can be equally discouraging of deviations from the substantive or methodological mainstream. Consequently, young faculty are often wary of venturing where there are not well-established peer communities. Yet the resulting conservatism robs the university and larger intellectual communities of some of their greatest potential innovators. Faculty chairs should be continually scanning the external world for important emerging issues, to which the university could make unique contributions. They could then counsel tenured and nontenured faculty alike in ways to approach these important but problematic areas.

Finally, if our experience in corporations is any guide, the radical changes that lie ahead will also require a type of leadership that is often virtually invisible given our traditional focus on hierarchies and formal positions of authority. Our research suggests that *internal networkers* or *community builders* play a critical role in shaping how organizations evolve. In businesses, these people can be human resources staff or internal consultants, engineers or salespeople. What is critical is their ability to cross boundaries, to connect innovative line leaders to one another, and to diffuse new ideas and practices within large organizations.

The reason that internal networkers are so important lies in the dynamics of how radical innovations spread. While formal hierarchies and official management actions (such as establishing requirements and formal standards) might aid in diffusing incremental innovations, basic innovations tend to spread through informal channels. This is analogous to the finding that in societies radical new technological innovations tend to be introduced into the marketplace by new firms rather than by existing firms, and that this tends to occur in waves of entrepreneurial activity such as we are experiencing today (Mensch, 1979). Formal authority and power based in management hierarchies is a poor vehicle to cause imagination, commitment, passion, patience, and perseverance—

the hallmarks of radical innovation that threaten the status quo. Rather, diffusion of radical practices tends to occur in ways that are unplanned and uncontrolled, through informal learning communities, or "communities of practice"—people who know one another, trust one another, and tell each other about exciting things they are involved with (Brown and Duguid, 1991; Wenger, 1998).

Who are the internal networkers in the university setting?

First, universities are quite different from businesses in the degree to which people can cross boundaries. It is typical for businesspeople in different functional areas, especially in large corporations, to be geographically dispersed, whereas those working in a university are more likely to be in closer proximity. Moreover, most faculty have personal and professional relationships with many counterparts in other universities, as part of extended intellectual communities—which is much rarer in business. However, these advantages notwithstanding, faculty are less likely to cross intellectual and department boundaries internally than to network with colleagues externally. Here the fragmentation of academic departments and disciplines is, if anything, more severe than in business. Most faculty tend to live relatively isolated lives, focused on their own teaching and immediate research activities, even though they have potential to connect with and learn from counterparts. Even those engaged in significant innovations tend to be a lot like entrepreneurs in the business community—passionate about their own innovations and blind to similar innovative efforts led by others.

Herein lies another area of potential leadership leverage for department chairs and innovative faculty members. Do they engage counterparts in other departments around the sort of design questions posed earlier? Do they create forums in which to share with others innovations developing within their own departments, and seek connections to like-minded faculty elsewhere? Within their own departments, do they make an effort to spend time with faculty eager to take risks and try new experiments? Do they help them meet their counterparts, even within their own departments as well as elsewhere? In our experiences, these are all critical leadership tasks because leadership is about building critical mass for change.

But my suspicion is that leverage will also lie in looking beyond the formal hierarchy and people such as faculty and department chairs in positions of authority. Paradoxically, what often makes internal networkers most effective is that they have little or no formal power or authority. This is what enables them to cross boundaries and quickly form new coalitions and partnerships, and makes them credible agents for spreading new ideas. It also makes them most open to new ideas, simply because they have less attachment to the status quo. Strategy expert Gary Hamel (1996, p. 76), exhorts business executives to engage the twenty-year-olds in thinking about the future: "When was the last time a generation-X employee in your company exchanged ideas with the executive committee? The bottleneck," says Hamel, "is at the top of the bottle."

Could this not be a critical leadership role that students might play in reinventing Industrial Age universities? Are not students those who are living more in the future than anyone else? Are not they the natural ambassadors of change? Are not they the ones who move about the system as a whole the most, and with the most ease? Do they not spread new ideas through telling other students about what is exciting and worthwhile? Are they not the critical allies of innovative teachers in reinventing the educational process?

"Students are the hidden resources for teaching," according to Barry Richmond, former Dartmouth College professor and founder of High Performance Systems. "Teachers everywhere are struggling to get the additional resources they feel they need to be effective in the classroom. What most don't recognize is that those resources are sitting right there in front of them" (personal communication). "A teacher is no longer a dispenser of knowledge addressed to students as passive receptors," says Jay Forrester (1992, p. 10). "Instead, where small teams of students explore and work together and help one another, a teacher becomes a colleague and participating learner. Teachers set directions and introduce opportunities. Teachers act as guides and resource persons, not as authoritarian figures dictating each step of the educational process." For the past ten years, Forrester has run an educational colloquium for MIT undergraduates in which the students develop new teaching materials, a practice Forrester started more than thirty years ago. The students learn the *system dynamics* methodology by applying it to help others learn. Similarly, I was involved this past year in a new graduate-level course at MIT aimed at helping students learn what it means personally to become more reflective about their own actions and assumptions (Orlikowski and Senge, 1999). In such an instructional setting, the teacher is not teaching in the traditional sense, because it is impossible to tell another what to reflect on. Teacher and student become colearners.

If making the students full partners in the educational process is an aim of fundamental innovations in instruction, might they not be the natural partners in reinventing the institutions of higher education as well? If learning is primary to teaching, students are not customers of the product that teachers sell. They are cocreators of the learning process. How can they be jointly responsible for the learning process and have no part in reinventing the institutions that might seek to enable that process? I suspect that they are already playing a big part in that reinvention. It is just that our hierarchical lens prevents most of us in universities from seeing that part.

Collaborating to Reinvent the Industrial Age University

My primary intent in sharing some of these ideas is to stimulate thinking. I apologize for laying out ideas that will inevitably be seen as impractical by some, because it is not clear how they are to be implemented, and old hat to others, because they are not new. Both reactions are correct, but they are also misplaced. In fact, they are the inevitable reactions of knowing organizations rather than learning organizations. The search for definitive answers is the bane of innovation. There are no answers for creating the new. New practical knowledge develops only from engaging in the hard work of translating concept into capability. Similarly, claiming that once an idea has been articulated it is no longer of interest is the retreat of the expert from the hard work of change. Experts have been developing theory and method for systems thinking for decades, yet most of our institutions, and most of our curriculum, remain as reductionistic as ever. Is this gap between theory and practice not where our attention should be focused? Finally, I believe that many academics will be inclined to reject these ideas because they are too closely tied to industry. I think this is an unfortunate defensive mechanism that keeps university people from learning from the world around them. In a world where creating and diffusing new knowledge is becoming the key to viability for all institutions, both business and university have a great deal to learn from one another.

In fact, this may be a key for both truly to innovate. The university has survived as an institutional form for a very long time, which suggests that it has strong capacities for adaptation. Indeed, a small number of universities are charter members of the "long-lived institutions" club. (I hesitate to add that this in no way justifies a belief that society will find it impossible to get along without the very large population of colleges and universities that now exists.) What features have allowed universities to adapt? Some argue that it is their decentralized governance system, which makes them more inherently able to innovate continually. An alternative view is that they simply have not had a competitor in their particular ecological niche, a condition that may no longer prevail, as I suggested in the introduction to this essay. On the other hand, businesses today do face the type of competition that universities are starting to encounter, and they are having to learn a great deal about how to think and operate institutionally in new ways in order to remain viable—something with which universities struggle.

Perhaps the most powerful lesson from the first ten years of developing SoL has been realizing the importance of SoL itself. I have come to believe that there is no substitute for building communities that cut across multiple institutions. There are no answers to questions like those posed in this chapter. Many of the most important questions are undoubtedly missing. There seems to be no substitute for enabling thoughtful and committed leaders of all types to work together to chart the territory. A small group of leading institutions, willing to innovate and share, becoming committed to their own and to one another's progress, and willing to be studied and serve as laboratories, could become leaders in learning how to learn as educational institutions.

Several years after starting SoL, a person attending his first meeting of people from the different companies told me, "I understand what this is. This is Alcoholics Anonymous for managers. We are all addicted to command and control, to looking for the right answers, to displaying our knowing rather than revealing our not knowing. And we all think someone else has the power to change things. The only way to shed the addiction is to come together."

I laughed but could not get his comment out of my mind. We probably are all addicted, more than we can see, to the "prevailing system of management," as Deming called it. And perhaps we can only see the addiction collectively.

To create a better way, we will need one another. A few daring university leaders are starting to move in this direction (Awbrey, Scott, and Senge, 1996). While the challenges are immense, are the risks any greater than pretending that the future will look like the past?

References

Awbrey, S., Scott, D., and Senge, P. *Learning to Change: A Proposal to Develop a Center for Integrative Universities*. Working Draft, Oct. 1996.

Barr, R. B., and Tagg, J. "From Teaching to Learning: A New Paradigm for Undergraduate Education." *Change*, 1995, *27*(6), 12–25.

Block, P. *Stewardship*. San Francisco: Berrett-Koehler, 1993.

Brown, J. S., and Duguid, P. "Organizational Learning and Communities of Practice: Toward a Unified View of Working, Learning, and Innovation." *Organization Science*, 1991, *2*, 40–57.

De Geus, A. P. *The Living Company*. Cambridge, Mass.: Harvard Business School Press, 1997.

Forrester, J. W. "System Dynamics and Learner-Centered Learning in Kindergarten through Twelfth Grade Education." In *Road Maps* (Chapter One), System Dynamics Group Education Project Working Paper (D–4337). Cambridge, Mass.: MIT Sloan School of Management, 1992.

Greenleaf, R. *Servant Leadership*. New York: Paulist Press, 1977.

Greenleaf, R. *The Power of Servant Leadership*. San Francisco: Berrett-Koehler, 1998.

Hamel, G. "Strategy as Revolution." *Harvard Business Review*, 1996, *74*, pp. 69–82.

Jaworsky, J. *Synchronicity*. San Francisco: Berrett-Koehler, 1996.

Mensch, G. *Stalemate in Technology*. New York: Ballinger, 1979.

Orlikowski, W., and Senge, P. "My Dad Is Getting Smarter Each Day: Creating a Practicum for Reflection Among Graduate Students." SoL Working Paper. Cambridge, Mass.: Society for Organizational Learning, 1999.

Roth, G., and Kleiner, A. *The Learning Initiative at the AutoCo Epsilon Program, 1991–1994*. Cambridge, Mass.: Society for Organizational Learning, 1996. (www.sol-ne.org)

Schön, D. A. *The Reflective Practitioner.* New York: Basic Books, 1983.

Senge, P. *The Fifth Discipline: The Art and Practice of the Learning Organization.* New York: Doubleday, 1990.

Senge, P., and others. *The Fifth Discipline Fieldbook: Strategies and Tools for Building a Learning Organization.* New York: Doubleday, 1994.

Senge, P., and others. *The Dance of Change: The Challenges to Sustaining Momentum in Learning Organizations.* New York: Doubleday, 1999.

Wenger, E. *Communities of Practice: Learning, Meaning, and Identity.* New York: Cambridge University Press, 1998.

Index

High Performance Systems, 296

Higher education: entrance of women into, 8; German scientific model of, 8; implications of Learning Organization for, 282–297; Industrial Age model of, 283, 284, 289, 296; making student learning focus of, 161; paradigm shift in, 78; planning/monitoring of, 168; post-W.W. II changes in, 8–10; redesigned for 21st century, 288–293; reinventing Industrial Age, 297–299; sources of potential leadership in, 293–297; technology teaching plan and environment of, 229–230; technology to reduce costs, 219–220. *See also* Academic departments; Curriculum

Hock, D., 276

Hocker, J. L., 26

How Colleges Affect Students: Findings and Insights from Twenty Years of Research (Pascarella and Terenzini), 190

Howery, C., 146, 147

HTML computer language, 223

Huber, M. T., 101

Hugo, V., 135

I

Idiolects, 83

Indiana University-Purdue University–Indianapolis, 107

Industrial Age model, 283, 284, 289, 296, 297–298

Institute for Academic Technology (University of North Carolina), 216

Instructional design quality, 237

Intel, 281

Internal networkers, 294–296. *See also* Leadership

International Association for Management Education, 255

Internet: assessment resources on the, 191; distributed learning over the, 216, 226–227; searching assessment literature on, 192. *See also* Web sites; World Wide Web

Interpersonal Conflict (Hocker), 26

Interpersonal level of resistance, 66

Intradepartmental level of resistance, 66–67

Intrapersonal level of resistance, 64–66

J

Jacobs, L. C., 191

Jaworsky, J., 286

Jensen, M., 26

Johns Hopkins University, 247

Johnson, D., 59

Johnson, F., 59

K

K–12 service-learning clearinghouse (University of Minnesota), 210–211

Kanter, R. M., 38

Katzenbach, J., 15

Kennedy, D., 110, 209

Key, M. K., 39

Knowledge: as scholarly work components, 101; social construction of, 77. *See also* Learning

Kotter, J. P., 4, 34, 36, 42, 43, 48, 52

L

Laissez-faire approach: to faculty development, 155; to student access to computers, 232–233

Leadership: change failure due to untrained, 46; during assessment process, 187; failure to communicate style of, 49–50; guidelines for chair, 12–28; sources of potential, 293–297; transformational, 199–201, 210, 287–288; using assessment to enable, 174, 186. *See also* Academic department chair

Leaming, D., 124

Learning: assessing educational processes of, 179–180; assessment to improve, 191; changing from teaching to, 284–285; core capabilities of, 277; curriculum and student, 262–264; distributed/flexible/networked, 216–217, 226–227; faculty vs. student patterns of, 209; incorporating technology into, 162, 220–226; research on student, 167–168; system dynamics methodology for, 296. *See also* Knowledge; Service learning

Learning communities, 79

Learning Organization: from theory to practice, 279–282; implications for universities of, 282–297; origins of, 277–279